It's all Sales

People buy from people

Original title: Verkopen doe je altijd, mensen kopen van mensen
Translation: Marieke Klaver for 'Good Luck English Language Productions, the Netherlands
Cover design: Robyright, The Netherlands
Layout design: Wizard Wise, The Netherlands
Publisher: Wizard Wise, The Netherlands
Distributor: Lulu.com
ISBN: 978-94-90520-01-4

www.itsallsales.com

It's all Sales

People buy from people

Dick Tol

Wim Bouman

Preface

Under the principle that you are only successful in life if you are able to sell yourself, Dick and Wim wrote this book. Dick committed his practical and life experience to paper in the shape of short stories and anecdotes interspersed with his learning moments.

Wim subsequently analysed and interpreted the real-life stories and anecdotes by applying his experience and theoretical knowledge.

The book contains a large number of stories and anecdotes that can be read in sequence or separately. It is, of course, possible to concentrate on the stories or just read the analyses. Still, a combination of the two could also prove worth your while.

This book is intended for those interested in Sales and who are also convinced that 'people buy from people'. It is also relevant to those interested in real-life experiences, for they will find stories they can relate to and may even benefit from in a business setting but also in their private lives.

Introduction

Many among us would like to write a book. I always wanted to write one myself but I never came round to doing it because I did not know what to write about and for whom.

Something was stirring in me, though, and when my friend Wim asked me to deliver a guest lecture with real-life sales stories, I all of a sudden had the point of departure I needed for my book.

Under the principle that "You are only successful in life if you are able to sell yourself, your work and your achievements" I wanted to write this book, since the above is what I strongly believe in.

Fortunately I found Wim willing and able to analyse my real-life stories and anecdotes by applying his experience and theoretical knowledge. The combination of experience and theory makes this an interesting book for students and others interested in testing their theoretical knowledge by practical experience.

Living in a world that focuses more and more on the individual and where intuition and feeling are dominated by rationalism and materialism, we continue to believe in the old selling principle "people buy from people" This should not be forgotten.

The book consists of a large number of stories and anecdotes that can be read in sequence or separately. They are private, business and market related stories and anecdotes. It is of course possible to concentrate on the stories or just the analyses. Still, a combination of the two could also prove worth your while.

Standard code of conduct for a salesperson

Some people say that they are born to sell. This is not necessarily true, because you can learn to sell. When it comes down to it, everyone is selling something to someone. Look at your own life and be aware that you learned to sell yourself as well. It already starts in infancy when you have fight for your position in the family. You do that by selling yourself and that continues in school, with your family, with friends, girl or boyfriend, the in-laws and at work with regard to your boss and colleagues. You are always selling.

Think about what you did as a salesperson with your hair, your clothes, the meeting etc. and assess your feelings. Were you nervous? Were you incoherent? Were you well prepared? Were you able to say everything you wanted? Did you listen properly? And did you reach your goal?

The above is a simple outline of the sales process. When you analyse the sales process, it all starts with good preparation, followed by the actual sales and finally the evaluation of the sales process. This process, in fact, comes naturally to people.

We can, however, learn about these sales processes from others. There are a number of rules we can learn which will always contribute to a successful and positive result. Perhaps you are already familiar with these rules but we will repeat them anyway.

1. Love people and enjoy dealing with them.
2. Be willing and able to communicate because no products were ever sold without communication.
3. Believe in the product or service that you offer. Speak realistically about the product or service you want to sell. Do not lie but there is no need to tell the whole truth.
4. Know your customer. There are many ways of gathering information and there is, of course, always the Internet.
5. Think positively.
6. Always be in a good mood, wear clean and decent clothes, keep your hair tidy and make sure there is no body odour. Also, dress for the occasion and the type of customer.
7. Make sure you possess some general knowledge of what is going on in the world and in particular in the customer's environment. The customer will appreciate it if you can talk to him about the latest developments. This knowledge may also be useful to break the ice.

8.   Always treat your customer with respect. Listen carefully to what he has to say. Anticipate on his story and adapt your sales pitch accordingly when possible.

9.   Try to make the occasional joke when dealing with a customer. Laughing is good for people's health; it makes people happy and puts them in a good mood. Cheerful and happy people are more likely to buy.

10.   Always evaluate the visit afterwards. Keep in mind, though, that it does not matter what *you* thought of the conversation but that the customer's feelings are far more important. Try to find out.

Remember: People buy from People!

We all know the principle that you have to look at your own behaviour to understand that of others. Look at what you do when you buy something. Sometimes you can buy an item everywhere but you still go to the one shop where you like the service. One bad experience and you will never return. Think about other examples of your own buying behaviour.

Remember that in sales it is always important to determine what is important to your (prospective) customer. The rules given above are important but are useless unless you and your customer are not on the same wavelength. Be genuinely interested in your customer because he will know if you are not sincere. He will never say so, but the result is that he will not buy from you. And you? You will never find out why the deal went wrong and you will continue making the same mistakes. When it comes to selling it is not the product that you sell, but what the product or service will do for your customer.

The youngest in the family needs to sell himself

I was born the youngest child in my family. The birth of another child had, in fact, been against the doctor's wishes, for he had forbidden my mother to bear more children after the difficult delivery of my brother. My brother had preceeded me by three years and my sister by four. They did not differ a lot in age and enjoyed playing together.

It was a rather old fashioned family, with my mother running the home and looking after the children and my father earning a living, working hard as a mason. Both contributed to the post-war reconstruction of the Netherlands. According to my sister I was a cry-baby and a bed-wetter and as a younger brother I felt a bit left out. Still, we were a warm and happy family.

We lived in the country in a small village of about fourteen hundred inhabitants. The village was divided into two religious groups[1]. On the one hand we had the Dutch Orthodox Reformed community with their own churches and schools and on the other hand the Dutch Liberal Reformed community and secular people with a public school. We lived in a terraced street with on one side of the street the entrance to the Orthodox School and on the other side the entrance to the Public school. Fortunately, we belonged to the Dutch Liberal Reformed community. However, even for us Sunday was the 'Day of the Lord' and we could not ride our bikes but were only alowed to go to church or go for a walk.

On Sunday afternoons we had to go to Sunday school for which we had to memorise a psalm. If you had memorised the psalm correctly and could recite it, you were awarded a number of points. For Christmas they always organised a big Christmas feast in our church and we were given a book and Christmas sweets. If you had amassed many points your book was larger. I was perfectly

---

[1] Dutch religion is not always easy to understand because the same word (reformed) is used for both Orthodox and Liberal Protestant communities. In the 16th century the Dutch fought a war of independence against Roman Catholic Spain. This war did not only lead to political liberty but also to religious liberty. Protestantism took over as the official religion and The Dutch adhered to the teachings of Calvin. Until the 19th century Roman Catholicism and other religions were either forbidden or tentatively allowed. In the 19th century a rift in the Dutch Protestant or Reformed Church became apparent. Some communities wanted to adhere to the orthodox teachings of Protestantism whereas others favoured a more liberal approach. From then on the Orthodox Reformed Church and the Liberal Reformed Church went their separate ways until the late 20th century. The above sounds simple enough if it was not for a number of separate protestant communities stemming from the two main ones, with different degrees of liberalism.

capable of memorising a psalm in a few hours time and then forgetting about it altogether.

At home we always had to pray and say grace for the food we were about to receive and in between the main course and dessert a text from the Bible was read. For us, the children, it was very difficult to concentrate and continue to listen seriously to the Biblical stories which we did not understand. This sometimes bwulp led to amusing incidents since it was difficult for us to keep a straight face. Fortunately, my parents were blessed with a good sense of humour.

As the youngest it was not easy because I always had to play the child when joining the games of my brother and sister. As I was not allowed to participate in any other way I was left to my own deviced whenever we had to stay indoors. I had to survive, but was also able to learn a lot from my brother and sister. Most of all I learned to appreciate what my parents tolerated from them, so that I could cleverly avoid making the same `mistakes`. I already understood quite well that if people like you, life was definitely easier.

Nevertheless, I did remain for the rest of my life the ´youngest´ who could say everything with humour and without beating about the bush.

I learned to earn my position within our family. In addition to that, I learned a lot about faith and the Bible. The ten commandments and the beautiful stories relating the miracles of Jezus served as a guideline to me.

Be aware of what your customers and prospective customers do. How they behave and how they react. Then, determine your strategy to approach them. The more you know, the more successful you will be. This also goes for continuing to learn from colleagues and keeping up with specialist literature. Continue to acquire knowledge and use it if and when appropriate. And most of all, be yourself; for in sales to imitate someone else simply does not work.

A very strong faith

I will always remember my grandfather on my father's side as a special person. He was the head of a family of seven, consisting of four daughters and three sons. When I got to know him as a child, he was no longer working and his health was deteriorating. He had a heart condition and was deaf. The result was that he had to stick to a salt-free diet. If you wanted to talk to him you had to make that known to him first. He would grab a copper ear trumpet and put this to his ear. You then had to shout into the ear trumpet. He usually communicated with us by means of his strongly developed body language. He was a dear old granddad and I loved him a lot and I felt that he loved me and his other grandchildren. And perhaps I was special to him since I was his namesake.

My granddad was the son of a farmer but had always worked as a farm hand. Entrepreneurial as he was, he had bought a piece of farmland on which he grew potatoes, vegetables and fruit for private use and for selling in the market.

My grandparents lived in a small house close to the embankment in a small village. Still living with them were two unmarried daughters and an unmarried son. The son was quite religious and was elected minister on the church council. The two aunts were rather frustrated for not having found husbands (one of them was even abandoned on her actual wedding day) and eventually both of them had become seamstresses. They both had very dominant personalities and always knew best. They considered themselves experts on how people should behave which they conveyed especially to my granddad and other family members.

This situation really bothered my mother but she was not strong enough to stand up to them. My grandmother, on the other hand, was a very forceful woman and ruled over the two aunts and two men in an unyielding manner. Those three women were definitely forerunners of women's liberation.

My aunts obviously also knew what was good for me and whenever I came to visit them I was always greeted with hot chocolate milk with a nice big fat skin on it. I hated the hot chocolate milk and spent quite some time on working out ways to ditch the hot chocolate in one of the flower boxes. This was not easy because the aunts always made me sit on my chair until I had finished the horrible concoction. Unfortunately, I could not expect any help from my parents.

In the orchard behind the little house, grandma and granddad also kept a pig. Granddad used to sit there on a stool in front of the pigsty watching us kids play around him with the grunting pig providing the background noises. The pig was fattened up and subsequently slaughtered. Unfortunately, we only ever got the offal turned into brawn for the meat was sold. I hated the brawn because we had to eat it very often.

Granddad enjoyed our play and sometimes he beckoned us towards him and gave us a sweet from a small box, which he carried in his pocket. The odd thing was that granddad never felt the need to use his ear trumpet whenever he was outside. I suspected granddad of being very clever and pretended to be deaf in order not having to listen to the dominant women in the house.

When we had all gathered around the table at meal times, we first had to say our prayers. Our religious uncle would embark on a lengthy prayer, as a church minister would. This always took such a long time that it was almost impossible for me to keep my eyes closed. I would then glance through my eyelids at granddad, who was invariably busy with exchanging his salt-free potatoes for salted potatoes from the main serving dish. He was quite skilful at that and when he caught me watching him, he winked at me and put his index finger in front of his mouth. I thought it was great, especially since my granddad and I now shared a secret and became even better friends.

My father had an enormous respect for his father and told me a number of remarkable stories about my granddad, who was a religious and spiritual person. Granddad did believe in God but not in a church.

At some point my father told me the story of his miraculous escape during the Second World War. One day my father was picked up by the Germans to be put to work in a factory somewhere in Germany. When they discovered what had happened, my mother and my little sister had gone straight to granddad's house. My parents lived in a neighbouring village and until then had managed to stay clear of the Germans. My mother lived in great fear of the Germans so when my father was picked up, the first thing she did was to go to my granddad for help and advice.

My granddad was in his usual spot in front of the pigsty and listened to my mother's account of what had happened. He held her hand and told her not to worry because my father would come home that night. And that is exactly what happened. My father never knew why he and five others were released. This was truly a miracle!

Towards the end of the Second World War it was dangerous to be out on the streets. Many Allied planes flew overhead and shot at anything in sight in order to chase away the Germans. People had been advised to stay indoors. Already a farmer from my granddad's village had been killed. The family had forbidden granddad to go outside to his farmland.

One day granddad got up and told the family that he had had a conversation with God that night and that he had asked God if he was to be killed by an Allied bullet. God had told him not to worry because he would die in bed. Granddad subsequently set out to work his land. And he was right because eventually he breathed his last at the age of 81 in his own box bed.

I thought it was truly amazing to have a granddad like that. We were friends and understood each other. Of course I also loved my grandma but that was different

What I learned was that, when it comes down to it, there are powers (a God) above us, that determine our lives and we know nothing about. Simply believe was the best I could do to become a good human being.

It is very important to believe in yourself. You have to do the things you do because you want to do them and not because others expect you to. You are responsible for the things you do. Make your own plans and try to realise them. The belief that your own truth makes you strong is the first step towards realising your plans. First of all, you need to make realistic plans with realistic goals. Determine, for your own use, your own position at this point in time. Ask yourself the question what you need in order to realise your goals. Which skills do you need in order to realise your goals. And finally, assess which problems you may encounter when realising your plans. Establish whether you can solve these problems or how you can turn the problems to your advantage. Once you have solved the problems the road ahead is clear to realise your goals. You will see that you will be successful. There is, however, one golden rule: You must believe in success!

Being good to others

My granddad and grandma on my mother's side were very special people. I knew them better than the grandparents on my father's side because the former lived in the same village we did. It was a very small farmer's village with no more than fourteen hundred inhabitants. When they were younger my grandparents ran a fruit and vegetable shop in the village.

In those days my grandma was responsible for the fruit and vegetable shop and my granddad, son of a gentleman farmer, turned trader. He had enough brothers to take over the farm. As a trader he, for instance, bought goods (even for farmer's wives) in the big city and then sold them for a profit to the farmers and their wives in the village and surroundings.

When I was a still a boy, my grandparents had already closed down the fruit and vegetable shop. My granddad only continued to work as a slaughter man of game (turkey, chickens, hare, pheasants, rabbits etc). During the hunting season he was always extremely busy since it was custom to have game for dinner at Cristmas.

Chicken in particular was considered a treat for Christmas dinner. My granddad knew which farmer looked after his chickens properly (good feed) and which farmer did not. He, therefore, was well informed on the quality of chickens and eggs. Granddad bought the chickens and eggs from the surrounding farmers and grandma sold the eggs at the front door to customers (families) in our village.

In this little village everybody knew each other quite well and my granddad played his own 'games'. Sometimes he said to a farmer, one he did not particularly like, that the hare he had brought in was not shot properly. (Containing too much shot) and that he had had to throw it out. My granddad then gave the hare (there was of course nothing wrong with it) to a poor family to have for their Christmas dinner. And sometimes he swapped good and fat chickens for underweight chickens thereby dividing the food evenly between the rich and poor. He was a good man who wore his heart in the right place. He was a real Robin Hood of the modern age.

My grandma did "charitable" work in her own way. Whenever children of large families came to buy eggs, she always asked how many brothers and sisters there were and gave them sweets with the eggs to take home. In doing so she gave away the profit but she was well loved in the village and everybody knew her as a warm and loving person.

Together with my grandparents lived an unmarried uncle. He was always arguing with his father, my granddad, especially about the weather. If granddad said the wind was blowing from the west, my uncle said the wind was blowing from the east. Both always wanted to be right which invariably led to heated arguments interspersed with humour. On some occasions my granddad also turned naughty. He would walk over to the window to look west and on walking past my uncle he let out a loud fart infuriating my uncle even more. They only stopped teasing and having a go at each other when my Grandma told them enough was enough and that they had to put a stop to their bickering. Grandma was very sweet, but also definitely in charge.

The lesson I learned from my grandparents was that it is good to be a decent and friendly person.

An important starting point for a salesperson should be the following: Be a good person and allow others to love you. If and when your customer loves you he will not go to the competition. How to achieve this? By being polite and honest and by being genuinely interested in a customer. Make him your business friend, know what your client does, what he is interested in, what his problems are etc. A good understanding of a customer is 75% of a successful business deal. If, in addition to that, you also turn out to be a good provider of information the customer will know that he is dealing with the best. In the end the customer buys from you and not from the company you represent.

Bad selling on my first day in school

At the age of six I had to go to Primary School. On that first day my mother took me to school. The school was situated in our street so it was only a two-minute walk from home to school and vice versa. For the girl who lived next door it was also her first day in school and because of her I did not feel quite so alone. She was a pretty girl with long blond curly hair. We had already been playing in our street for a long time.

The village we lived in was quite small. You could still play in the streets and there was, of course, informal social control. Everybody knew each other. It was something altogether different for us to go to school and we realised our carefree days were over. Fortunately, the girl from next door occupied the desk in front of me in the classroom.

The teacher was a middle-aged woman with hairy legs who behaved like a dragon. I really did not like her. She was insincere and the rich children and children of important parents were favoured above us, blue-collar worker's children. I had to put up with her for as long as three years. Luckily, my mother was on the board of school governors, which led to me having a preferential position. Therefore, 'dragon lady' had to be nice to me.

I was bored to tears that first day in school. The day seemed to last forever and being cooped up in a classroom for a very long time did not help. I discovered that behind a slide in my desk an inkwell was hidden, filled with beautiful blue ink. I played with it for quite a while because you could open and close the slide.

All of a sudden I had this brilliant idea. I asked the girlfriend sitting in front of me whether she had already discovered the inkwell. When she gave an affirmative answer I asked her to blow hard into the inkwell. She did, of course, exactly as I asked. She trusted me implicitly since I was her neighbour and playmate. The result was terrible, though. Her face and hair had turned completely blue and she started to cry incessantly. I thought she looked wonderful and my new, laughing schoolmates thought so too. I was their hero for as long as it lasted. Unfortunately, the teacher did not share their feelings.

First of all, the teacher sent the girl home and then strode towards me. She grabbed me by the scruff of my neck and positioned me in the corner of the room with my back turned to the class and my classmates. Standing in this position I had to wait until after school hours. It took forever and I felt the pain in my neck for three days.

After school, the teacher had gone to my mother straight away and had told her the story. When arrived home I received my punishment immediately, meaning

I was not allowed to go and play outside. My mother hastened to apologise to the neighbours with regard to my appalling behaviour in school earlier that day. Then she informed me that she would tell my dad as soon as he got home and there would be hell to pay. This did worry me a bit.

When my brother and sister got home my mother divulged the story immediately. I sensed that they showed me some more respect. They, however, also pointed out to me that there would be hell to pay as soon as my dad got home.

As soon as my dad entered the house my mother gave him all details of the day's events. I just sat there looking bashful, but I had the slight impression that he could hardly control his laughter.

Of course I could not have been more wrong. He gave me a piercing look and told me to behave better and if anything like this were to happen again, I would be in serious trouble. So, in a sense I got away with it.

'Dragon lady' taught the lowest three grades and the principal the highest three grades. The principle was a kind man but an alcoholic and drunk most of the time. When he was drunk there were no lessons but were we allowed to draw.

Because of this I missed many basic lessons. What was very special about the school, though, was that we had an annual school fete and were allowed to stage a play. For this play real costumes were hired. I truly loved being on stage and learning my part. Of course I usually landed an important part, my mum being on the board of school governors.

I learned that it was better to adapt my behaviour to that of others regarding their roles. Moreover, I learned to adapt to different roles through playing parts on stage.

Quite a story! It is of course important to maintain good relationships with your fellow students and those who are your 'betters'. In my opinion it is also better to stay friends with nice girls. If, on the other hand, you do have the nerve to play tricks like this, then you will undoubtedly have the nerve to approach new customers. It is difficult for a salesperson to go back to a customer. And it is also difficult to ask a customer for an order. You need guts in order to do that. Having guts makes the difference between getting an order and going away empty handed. It is, for that matter, also possible to circumvent the 'yes' and the 'no' when dealing with an order. Ask the customer "what quantity were you thinking of" "what colour would suit your company best?" "When would you like us to deliver?" Now it is no longer a matter of whether the customer will place the order, but what quantity, colour and when the customer wants the goods delivered.

Entrepreneur in a small village

My father was a mason and had been employed by different building contractors. He worked very hard to contribute to the post-war reconstruction of The Netherlands and was good at his trade. Connoisseurs could always tell by its structure whether my father had built a particular brick wall.

My mother used to have a good position when she was young. She worked as a housekeeper at the mayor's house in our small village. From the mayor she had learned that it is was very important for children to have a good education. Since her father had been an entrepreneur, she motivated my father to study and become a building constructor himself.

And that is exactly what happened. My father set up his own business as a building constructor. His first commission was to build a garage for the garage owner in our village. These were difficult times for us, since we had to live on a strict budget until my father would have his first completion and money would come in. These were terrible times for me because I had to wear one of my sister's underpants and I wore trousers that were darned. I was deeply embarrassed. My mother, though, never once complained and she stood right by my father and tried to run the house as frugally as possible.

For my father it was the right moment to start his own business. My mother still was in touch with the mayor and he had told her that it was good for competition to have another building constructor in the village. It fitted in with the mayor's and city council's policy.

This policy had a funny side effect. In our small farmer's village we had two grocers, two clothes shops, two bakers, two hairdressers and from then on also two building constructors. This meant that we, because of our business, had to switch bakers, grocers etc. every week. For in the end my father wanted everybody's custom.

The family received some preferential treatment and my mother also bought groceries from an uncle in the neighbouring village. This uncle used to visit every Monday to write down the required groceries in a booklet and delivered the groceries on Friday. He was very much aware of what my mother needed and when, for instance, she had ran out of coffee he reminded her of the fact.

There was one problem concerning the competition. The wife of my father's main competitor worked the switchboard at the post office and she had to put through many phone calls from and to my father from potential customers and suppliers. She could listen in to every conversation, which is exactly what she did. That is how the competition always knew a lot about my father's business.

It was a good thing that many deals were still concluded verbally and settled locally. My father's clientele expanded considerably since he was honest and supplied good quality for a reasonable price. He was truly capable of calculating the costs of a building to the very stone! No materials were lost and money was saved.

The lessons I learned from this formed the basis of the rest of my live. Key values were; hard work, entrepreneurship, honesty and being clever. These were passed on to me by my parents and grandparents.

Always be alert when it comes to your customer. Be aware of when he needs you. Keep in touch and make sure he knows you. What it comes down to is that the customer awards you the order and that he wants you to get it. Whenever you have the opportunity to do something for your customer, you will only make your relationship stronger. Give advice, or refer to an expert to deal with his particular problem.

Selling in High School

For Dutch middle class children it was customary to attend the local school for advanced elementary education or, if that was not feasible, girls would attend the school for domestic science and boys went to technical college. Only the children of the local dignitaries were allowed to go to High School. My sister had already finished the advanced elementary school and my brother was still attending. My only option was to go to the same school.

During his schooldays my brother had acquired quite a reputation for being mischievous and from the start I was allocated the front desk in the classroom. Since they knew my brother, they thought it better to keep a close eye on me. My brother truly was what you call mischievous. Later on he became a police officer and rightly so, for you know what they say, it takes a 'thief' to catch a 'thief'.

That first year I was an excellent student. I got high grades and it was all the more remarkable since my basic training had left a lot to be desired given the problems I had had with the alcoholic teacher. The only thing I had learned there was drawing.

The school's principle discussed my grades with my parents and advised them to let me sit the entrance exam for High School. I would lose one year but that could be compensated later on. This advice was exactly what my mother wanted to hear on account of her belief in a good education. So, I was allowed to go to High School.

Before I started school my parents discussed the matter with me at length. They told me this was a big opportunity for me and that they were enormously proud of me but that from then on I had to come up to the mark on my own. Their parents had not allowed them to study and my brother and sister had attended a different school, there was nobody qualified to help me.

I felt extremely grateful and I made up my mind to work really hard because I did not want to disappoint my parents. My parents were immensely proud, for I was the first middle class boy in the village to go to High School. My parents now belonged to the important families in the village and bought the family a pew in church underneath the pulpit close to the dignitaries. My parents supported me in any way they could and tried to create good studying conditions for me. They also loyally attended every single official parents evening and student performance.

When I started High School there were 244 pupils. It was a small community with the inevitable informal social control. I felt like a fish in water. We did have to go to school six days a week, of which the Wednesday and Saturday were half school days. Moreover, I had to cycle 14 kilometres (9 miles) back and forth come rain or shine from our small village to the larger village. It was all worth it.

I was an active pupil. During the breaks I organised a library together with the Dutch teacher. I was also the president of the school's sports club and organised tournaments in school holidays. Next to that, I was a member of the drama society and was vice-president of the board of the High School club. At the elections for the board I had received 242 votes out of a possible 244 votes. The principle complimented me personally upon this remarkable accomplishment, for according to him this was a first ever. I was, of course, proud of myself.

After the third year students had to choose between taking A subjects (languages) or B subjects (mathematics). My results were average and during one of the parents' evenings the principle had advised my parents it would be best for me, since I was a boy, to take B subjects. Fortunately, he also added that it might take an extra year, but that in the end it would be worth it. I was kept down in the fourth grade, but my parents accepted that because they knew I had worked really hard.

For the final exam it was possible to gain four math exemptions. Much to everyone's surprise (including my own I have to add) I gained three out of the four exemptions. I passed the exam and was overjoyed.

What I learned was that if you commit yourself to the school and put in extra effort the school will reward you for it by means of rounding up your grades.

It's all sales

Getting high grades is not enough. It is important that those who matter to you are aware of your high grades. Communicate, without being arrogant, how well you are doing. To do this requires strong personal skills. Another subject emerging from the story is, "doing the extra bit for your customer" putting in an extra effort. Thinking along with your customer instead of only fulfilling your obligations will lead to the customer holding you in higher esteem, which will result in a closer relationship.

Dress for success

Fortunately my parents had been prepared by the principle for the fact that I had to be kept down a class. For this reason I had new classmates who were about two years my junior. I did, however, feel more comfortable with my new classmates than I had with my former classmates. It was to be an easy year for me, which offered the opportunity to find out what else life had to offer.

The construction business, including my father's company was prosperous and there was enough money to go round. My parents had set out to build their own home in the same village my school was situated. My father built the house in his spare time and I had to help out on Saturday afternoons and sometimes during school holidays.

During every summer holiday I had worked on a farm. Being idle was unacceptable where I came from. I had gathered potatoes, picked beans and strawberries and peeled bulbs and had saved enough to buy my brother's moped. My brother had bought a real motorbike. My father paid for the petrol and now I went to school by moped.

In those days, as was common, I sported sideburns and a moustache and was rebellious. Moreover, I was a Beatle-fan and always listened to the Pirate (illegal) radio stations on my transistor radio. The inevitable teenage battle with my parents was a friendly battle and I was fortunate in the sense that my parents were willing to understand me. My mother borrowed my transistor radio to listen to listen to a famous Dutch song request show while doing the dishes.

Money was not a problem and "Op-art" and "Pop-art" were becoming all the rage. My mother gave me an "Op-art" shirt, a green jacket and a pair of checked trousers. No necktie but a bright red bow tie around my collar completed the whole. A very colourful outfit which was not exactly easy on the eye. The principle complimented me on my dress sense in front of the whole class and said I looked like a French troubadour. All this contributed to my popularity.

At the time there was a beautiful fair-haired girl in second grade and she fell madly in love with me and I with her. Soon we were 'dating' and before I knew what hit me the most beautiful girl in the entire school was sitting behind me on my moped with her arms wrapped around me. What else do you need as a man? It was our first love, but we were young and innocent. It was too good to last.

Not much was going on in our village and the surrounding area for young people. There were a few pubs, but we wanted to go out and dance to music by the Beatles, the Stones and other bands. Whenever one of the girls in my class celebrated her birthday a disco party was organised usually in the garage of her parental home. Luckily I usually got invited to those parties. When the parents were out of sight we used to put on slow music and in couples we could slow-dance closely together. As soon as the parents returned the couples broke up again and it was back to more acceptable forms of dancing. Those were fun and exciting times.

In those days I got to know 'women' and also that being well dressed is important. The sixties were a wonderful decade for us and we had the feeling we were really changing the world. I learned quite a number of dumb-blondes jokes because everybody felt inclined to share them with me.

When it comes to sales it is important to dress for the occasion. On the whole people expect sales people to dress in a fitting suit. It could also be that the target group derives certain ideas about a person from the way he is dressed. If this creates a positive image, then it works. If not, you are conveying the wrong message. If, for instance, you visit a youth centre in a three-piece suit this will definitely distract from the message. So, think in advance about whom you will be visiting and dress accordingly.

Selling your skills in a small village

The village council in our village was dominated by religious Orthodox Reformed members. For a long time our village did not have a sports club since according to the Orthodox Reformed church, wearing sports clothing equalled nudism and that was against God's wishes. Nudism was sinful.

When I turned sixteen, the village council (which by that time consisted of more liberal members) agreed to the formation of a soccer (European football) club. I enjoyed sports of all kinds and I took part in many sports when in High School. As kids we used to play soccer in the streets of our village, so I already knew how to play the game. Fortunately, my father allowed me to join the club.

One of the farmers in our village, also a keen soccer player, had made a piece of farmland available that was to serve as a soccer pitch. On weekdays sheep and cows were grazing away happily. On Saturday afternoons the animals were chased off, their droppings removed and the match could begin. On some occasions a herd of cows would cross the field during a match. And as I discovered first hand, nothing beats a cowpat when it comes to making the perfect sliding.

Two senior teams were formed and together with my friend and neighbour I joined the second team. I played in the inside right position whereas my friend played in the outside right position. We did not have a trainer and the team was selected every week by 'three wise men'. Every week it was exciting to check the line-up of the teams and to see whether you were selected. The line-up was displayed every Friday morning behind the shop window at the butcher's. We all gathered there to discuss and analyse the matches, line-up and opponents.

At some point the board of governors of the club had decided to take up a door-to-door collection to raise funds for the club. The members of the board themselves called upon people to donate money. They also came to our house and my father talked to them. I could not overhear what was being said because I was upstairs in my room studying.

Yet, when I went to check the line-up of our team at the butcher's the next Friday I could not find my own name on the list. I was shocked until the boy standing next to me pointed out that I had been put on the first team. I checked and yes, I could hardly believe it. My name was on the list of the first team. I beamed with pride. As soon as I got home I told my father what had happened. He simply said he had expected it and he smiled at me while giving me a wink. I thought the world of my father as you can imagine.

It was not just the money that mattered; I also played well and displayed clever tactics. In my first match I scored the winning goal. Great, wonderful, I was over the moon, but not everyone appreciated it. What I had not known was that the striker on the team was very dominant. Every player had to pass the ball on to him and he was the only one allowed to score goals. I obviously had not understood the team hierarchy. The striker was extremely angry and refused to say a single word to me after the match.

The next Monday the regional newspaper came out with all regional match accounts. Above the account of our match my name figured in bold print proclaiming me the winner of the match. I was ever so proud and quite a number of people including my classmates and teachers congratulated me on the victory. Now I was a real local hero. I continued to play well and scored many important and less important goals.

The lesson I learned was that I was well up to playing the part of local hero and how to adopt a successful attitude as a team member. If you score and are successful, your position is never under discussion.

Sales people should be free to do as they think fit, otherwise they will become playthings of their surroundings. A salesperson should have an extended knowledge of his product, the market and the competition. If the salesperson has a manager constantly telling him what to do, he will never be able to develop into a good salesperson. A salesperson needs to have a mind of his own. He needs to do things of his own accord because he feels it to be the right approach. If this is the case, he is a natural salesperson.

Selling your story to the police

As the proud owner of a moped I now belonged to the group of cool guys in the area. I was a gifted soccer player, popular at school and I was dating a blond beauty. Does life get any better for a 16 year-old a Beatle-fan? I was not short of money because sometimes my brother and sister slipped me some cash. I did have to work hard for school, though.

In the mean time my brother had trained as a policeman and had left home. My sister had trained as a nurse and rented rooms elsewhere. Earlier on I had bought my brother's moped. My brother had never been happy with the maximum speed of the moped, which is why he had its engine turned up. The moped could exceed the maximum speed of 40 kilometres (26 miles) per hour easily; it could do 65 kilometres (42 miles). Of course my parents did not know anything about this. My brother had asked a friend who was employed at the local garage to do the job. This happened to be the same garage my father frequented and the two had charged the costs to my father's account. I had one very clever brother.

In the meantime the police were after us. If you got caught with a turned up engine on your moped they would confiscate it and would return it to you the size of a regular parcel. Staying clear from the police was sports on a high level.

My brother came home during weekends and he used to tell me stories about his colleagues who worked as police officers in our village. He knew those who worked in our village quite well and he used to stop by and have a chat with them. It was a small world in those days. They could not befriend just anyone and they always had to be at their best behaviour because they were under close scrutiny. Even when off duty they were treated as police officers by their acquaintances. All this was part of the day's work.

Riding a turned up moped and not getting caught by the police required special skills. We always informed each other on possible road checks. One day I was out of luck. I was stopped for a check. I could not get away for I had spotted the 'trap' too late. Of course I told the police officer my moped's engine was not turned up. This statement was rewarded with a disbelieving look from the police officer. That really worried me and all of a sudden images of me cycling to school took shape in my mind.

I then decided to try the friendly approach. I told the police officer my brother was a fellow police officer and he had been the previous owner of the moped. That certainly got his attention and he asked me for my name. As soon as I told him he started laughing and told me he and my brother had attended the Police Academy together and had had a wonderful time at school. I implied that the moped of a police officer could not possibly have a turned up engine. I talked until I was blue in the face and with the desired effect. Naturally the police officer believed me, gave me a firm handshake and asked me to give his regards to my brother.

What I learned from this was that when under pressure I was able to be smart and creative to save myself from a difficult situation. Sometimes it is better not to tell the whole truth. In some cases telling the whole truth is not the wisest thing to do.

It's all sales

In the selling process and in other situations as well, it is better to tell the truth and not to lie. The truth and nothing but the truth. A salesperson discusses the matter in hand intelligently. He does tell the truth, but does not necessarily include everything. He only conveys what is important to a potential customer. Things you leave out are not exactly lies. A true sales person is smart and acts accordingly.

A horrible first job

After graduating from High School and the great party that was thrown afterwards, I did not have to think about the future yet. It was customary to go to University after having finished High School. In my case that was different, though. I had already lost two years when in High school and I had to fulfil military service obligations first, due to Dutch army conscription regulations[2]. I had already been passed for military service and was to train as a non-commissioned officer for one and a half-year. The only problem was that I did not know exactly when I was going to be drafted.

At that point in time I did not really know what to do with my life and I considered going to medical school after military service. The advice from school was to go to drama school, since I had been a successful performer in High School plays. I never shared this with my parents, the diligent workers, since I could imagine that having an ´artist´ in the family was not exactly what they had in mind.

I could not just sit back and relax until my draft papers arrived. No, I had to find a temporary job, which happened to be in the sugar factory in our village.

Working in the sugar factory was a seasonal job. I became a lab assistant and had to work in three shifts (including weekends) and had to determine by experiment whether the samples that I had to collect at different measuring points in the factory, contained sugar. In that way they could establish whether there were any leaks in the production process. One of the problems was that I felt like throwing up most of the time because of the horrible stench in the factory. I sincerely hated the job. Chemistry had never been of much interest to me but now that I had to work with it, its importance became clear.

I had to work all the time and no longer had much time to spend with my friends. The group of friends we had formed during our high school days was falling apart anyway. My former classmates had all gone to University and I felt very lonely in those days. The only good thing about the job was that I earned money and was able to pay my mother a contribution towards housekeeping.

I also decided to put my hard-earned money towards driving lessons. At least something useful would come out of it. My driving instructor was a young

---

[2] As of 1997 conscription in the Netherlands has been suspended. Until that point in time every healthy boy in the Netherlands over the age of 18 had to fulfill military service obligations of about one to one and a half year.

attractive woman and on some occasions we had to laugh so hard that it completely ruined her make-up. There was, however, a driving test I needed to pass. People expected me to pass first time around. This was not a problem as far as the theoretical part was concerned, but when it came to the actual driving test that was a completely different matter. During the first test my examiner had to intervene otherwise I would have 'kissed' another car. The second test ended up in me having an argument with 'that jerk' about whether I had or not crossed a line on the road. Next time I had learned my lesson and was friendly to my examiner. I did make a few mistakes but I passed.

The lesson I learned from this is that it is of the utmost importance to have a job that you enjoy doing and that if you need to depend on others, it is in your best interest to be friendly to them.

As a salesperson you always depend on someone. You depend on yourself and your potential customer. Without you a customer will not buy anything. This dependence is intrinsic to the selling process. You need to sell the customer something he needs (otherwise what is the point in contacting a customer). The only problem is that the customer must buy from you and not the competition. If you know the customer's needs, you have to link the qualities of your product to the customer's needs. Only then will the customer understand that your product is what he needs.

Selling a disco

During my final year in High School we had moved to the village where I went to school. My father had built his own home in his spare time and in doing so had made my mother's dream come true. She felt quite the lady and had reached her goal.

I now lived close to my school friends. We lived in the famous sixties and loved the music of that time. There was one problem, though. We wanted to go out dancing but there were no discotheques in the village. There were a few pubs but they were not my scene. We usually met on a Saturday night and walked along the embankment in the centre of our village.

That is why two friends and I had decided to start a disco for the youngsters in our village. Given my experience on committees in High school, I appointed a Board of Directors and together we compiled a plan to exploit a private disco. The father of one of my friends was a member of the village council. He arranged access to an abandoned house and we fitted it up as a private disco. That was not enough, for we had decided to start a public disco. We asked the mayor's son to become a member of the board. He attended the local High School and felt honoured by being asked to join the board. He was not what I would have called a real friend, but we needed him.

We obtained all required permits and licenses and gathered a large group of young people willing and able to renovate the premises by applying a fresh coat of paint, putting up disco lights etc. All this without funding just by re-using items people found in their attics. One of my friends was the DJ and brought along his stereo and played records, most of them special requests. We were very proud of what we had accomplished and called our club ´Fire´.

We had to submit to regular checks by the police. Every Saturday evening they came to close the place at eleven o clock. At a quarter to eleven we turned up the lights and started playing Rock and Roll music. The police also checked whether there was any alcohol on the premises since that was not allowed. ´Fire´ gained quite a reputation and eventually we had to turn away a number of visitors because the place was full.

I was there every Saturday night whilst working my first job and if I was not on duty, also during my military service. We felt free and were able to play our own music. And my army uniform impressed the ladies.

As directors of the disco we had organised a Christmas party on Boxing Day, including lunch and a dance party afterwards. And the idea was that the men were to invite a girl to be their partner at the lunch table. I had no idea about

32

who to invite even though there were some rather obvious attempts from a number of girls to get me to ask them. I ignored them.

And all of a sudden there she was…... I had seen her before with a friend, but there she was again; a beautiful, slim girl with abundant long hair. I had also seen her when I had worked for my father in construction during the summer holiday and she had passed the building site every day. Before I knew what hit me I asked her to be my date. Fortunately she accepted and on that Boxing Day we fell madly in love while dancing to music by the Beatles. (Oh Donna……)

I learned that sometimes it is important to choose the right people to reach a goal. You do not always have to like them. And I also learned what a wonderful feeling it is to be in love.

When it comes to sales it is important to assess your current situation. Sometimes it is smart to deploy so called 'testimonials'; these being people who are important to your target group and can convey a positive message about your product. This will affect the sales opportunity positively. If one of those people, somebody who for instance is important to the industry, can point out to your prospect the positive qualities of your product, the chance of a sell will increase.

Learning to sell in the army

My dream to become a doctor was soon forgotten once I joined the army. I trained as a non-commissioned officer. This took about six months and after that I was to put into practice for another year what I had learned. I could not complain because in those days every Dutch boy was subject to conscription and here was another opportunity for me to go for the highest attainable. I was to become a Sergeant with a storm troop and commanding officer of a tracked vehicle. I saw my training as an experiment towards becoming a manager later on.

At first I was highly motivated. I was proud of the fact that I was to become a sergeant. It was to be my first managerial position and I had this notion that it would be appreciated in business if I could enter a position as sergeant on my CV. I, therefore, started my training as a non-commissioned officer in high spirits.

The actual training contained a lot of theory but also practical exercises and every subject was concluded with a test. In order to become a sergeant you had to pass every test. The physical tests in particular were tough. As a sergeant you had to be in better shape than the regular soldiers since this would give you a natural authority. I got to know my body well and both my physical and mental resilience kept improving.

My emotional resilience was also tested. For us it was very important to be able to go home on Friday and spend the weekend at home. Before we were allowed to leave, the Lieutenant subjected us to an intensive inspection of our possessions, bed, locker and our equipment. It all had to be in tip-top shape otherwise you were not allowed to leave for the weekend. On a Friday afternoon everybody was completely stressed out.

On one particular Friday I had had a haircut at twelve in the afternoon and was, in my opinion, ready for inspection. The Lieutenant moved in front of me, gave me a hard stare and barked at me that my hair was too long and I needed to get it cut before I could leave. I was furious but was not allowed to respond. I had to put up with it and replied: "Yes Lieutenant my hair is too long"!

In the meanwhile all the others got on the bus to the train station and enjoyed their weekend. I had to walk three kilometres (2 miles) to the village (because the army hairdresser's had already closed) get my hair cut (again!) and walk the three kilometres back again and wait for inspection. The Lieutenant failed to show up and I had to walk another four kilometres (2.5 miles) to the station to catch a train that would take me home. This was what you call training your emotional resilience. I hated the army!

As a Sergeant you occasionally were appointed duty officer at the army barracks. The General would show up to inspect the guardroom and the prison, which was right behind it and as duty officer you were responsible.

When it was my turn to be duty officer it was a hot Saturday night. In order to protect us from flies we had sprayed insect repellent that should kill the horrid creatures. Everything was ready for the General's inspection, or so I thought. Everything looked 'spic and span' until a fly on the ceiling decided to die at the worst possible moment. And of course it dropped dead right in front of the General. For punishment I was once again appointed duty officer the next weekend. I hated the General and the dead fly!

On some occasions things did turn out right. One night when we had had a few drinks too many we noticed that a new group of recruits had arrived during our absence. They were all sound asleep. We quickly bought a case of beer and in order to wake them up we turned the fire hose on them and hosed them out of bed. Unfortunately, our new mates did not appreciate their rude awakening. We did, but it meant that we had to report to the general the next day.

We stood to attention in the General's office and feared the worst. He looked from one to the other and then all of a sudden started laughing. He could appreciate the joke and thought it a good idea to straighten out those 'wimps'. We were not punished but in stead allowed to go home for the weekend.

I learned many lessons when serving in the army and looked back favourably upon this forming and important period in my life. Living a disciplined life, dealing with difficult circumstances and also obtaining insight into human nature. And most of all, I learned how to survive.

A salesperson needs to be strong and perseverant. On many occasions you will get 'no for an answer' and may have to call nine or ten times in order to get an appointment. If this is the case you may think your product is not good enough. Getting negative response while you believe in your product. If you start developing negative thoughts toward your own product, consider your career over. Good salespeople can deal with this and they know they can sell anything to anyone. Most of the time you do not know what the person on the phone is thinking and what his feelings are the moment you phone. Sometimes it is just not the right moment. After all, he does not know you as a person. But you have to persevere, because next time round, things will work out.

Bad sales to spend Christmas at home

As a spoiled boy it was not always easy to hold one's ground in the army. There were many lessons I was forced to learn far away from home without parents to protect me. I, once again, had to survive and fend for myself. I learned all about discipline, how to fight and how to get by on insufficient food and drink and how to maintain my position amongst other aspiring sergeants.

All these lessons turned out to be very important for the rest of my life. I had to reach goals I did not really believe in. And I was there together with people (fellow soldiers) who had joined the army against their will and did not want to be in the army altogether. Despite our feelings we had to keep the lieutenant happy, if not punishment awaited us. I learned to walk the fine line between right and wrong.

At the same time it was not easy to motivate your subordinates. You had to be rude to one guy, kind to the next in order to get them to do what you wanted. But, take my word for it; I never achieved anything by handing out punishments.

In the Netherlands it was a commonly held belief that the army would make a man out of you. And I found out the hard way that this is true, for I learned to drink and even to drink myself stupid. I learned that being drunk does not always lead to success and that mostly there was a high price to pay.

Two weeks before Christmas my fellow Sergeants and I, after a day at the barracks, had gone to the non-commissioned officer's bar, had a party and had drunk way to much beer. We had forgotten all about time and by the time we had finished drinking the mess had closed. We decided to go into town and have a bite to eat at a Chinese restaurant. We were still wearing our regular uniforms because we did not feel like changing into the mandatory dress uniforms. All six of us climbed into a deux-cheveaux car owned by one of us and made for the village. The car rolled back and forth on the road. We simply opened the top and that solved the problem. On arrival we found that a large American car was parked in front of the restaurant with a Vauxhall car parked behind it. We desperately wanted to park our car in between the two cars and brought this about by pushing the American car forward with our bumper and the Vauxhall car backwards. Parking made easy, or was it.

We definitely displayed some obnoxious behaviour in the restaurant. One of the other guests came up to us and asked why we were not wearing our dress uniforms. We informed him in no uncertain terms that he had to mind his own business. The Chinese restaurant was situated next to the church and one of us could not stop himself and urinated against the church door. After all this we drove back to barracks, singing loudly all the way.

On our return the duty officer and his soldiers were waiting for us and after having parked the deux-cheveaux we were incarcerated immediately. We had to sleep it off first and when I woke up the next morning I feared the worst. All of a sudden it dawned upon me what we had done the night before and how stupid we had been.

The duty officer came to collect us and took us to the commander in chief, a General. When I set eyes upon him I recognised him immediately for he was the man who had addressed us at the Chinese restaurant and the owner of the American car. You did not have to be a genius to know that we were in deep, deep trouble. We were, of course, severely punished and were not allowed to go home for three weekends. We also had to stay at the barracks for Christmas and New Year. We accepted the punishment with style because we knew we had been wrong.

Then I realized that I had to tell my parents. Now how do you tell your parents who are so proud of their good, successful and sweet youngest son? I had to come up with an alternative and I realised that I still had to get a smallpox vaccination. After having had the shot you needed to remain under supervision of a doctor for three weeks. I went to see the army doctor and asked him whether he could give me the shot right there and then. He was a bit surprised since I wanted it right before the holidays, but he did comply with my request. Now I had an acceptable story to tell my parents and they felt really sorry for me because I missed out on the Christmas festivities.

I learned that it was a good thing to drink within limits and that I had to stick to the rules. But, that I managed to save my reputation by not telling the whole truth.

A salesperson enjoys a lot of personal freedom, which he needs to be able to handle. He should enjoy being a solo performer. There are, however, times when you might be led into temptation, start your day a little later, do other things during the day, or stop working a little earlier. If this gets out of hand, you will get onto a slippery slope. Your results will suffer as will your enthusiasm for the job, time spent on the job and the relationship with the company you work for. Working days will get shorter, which will lead to more pressure. Your results will decrease and people will start asking questions. Before you know what happens you spend more time and energy on making excuses than on your real goal: selling.

Selling in a team

After having finished my training I was appointed Sergeant with the storm troops. I was in charge of a Panzer Infantry Division of 12 soldiers. The guys on the team were not highly educated, physically strong and were raised in the ghettos of the large Dutch inner cities. And I, a spoiled and highly educated youngster, had to work with them. I always had the army hierarchy and discipline at my disposal, and when I first met them I made it absolutely clear to them that since we both did not like conscription we had to make the best of it while it lasted. We had no choice. They understood the message.

I was not easy holding my own ground with on the one hand the officers and on the other hand the conscripts. And with my fellow sergeants the situation was even more difficult. I have to say we had struck unlucky with our commanding officer. The Major who was in charge was really aiming for a career in the army and on every occasion he 'volunteered' our platoon for service. I trained my men well and one occasion we were proclaimed the best team. My fellow-Sergeants did not appreciate this and were jealous. They held it against me and branded me a show-off. There was nothing left for me to do but to curb our competitive spirit. Inconspicuous behaviour was better. As a manager of the platoon I learned a lot and became attached to the men and them to me.

The fanatical Major had planned a commando training for us of two weeks. We had to move from the centre of the country and infiltrate in the south of the country. This had to be done at night, on foot in full marching kit. During the day we had to remain invisible and find a place to sleep. They had appointed a 'real' enemy from which we had to liberate our food. We did not always succeed in doing this. I carried the map and fortunately we were all in good shape.

After a number of days of walking without proper food we were exhausted and the heavy machine guns and rifles posed problems. We only had water to live on. Every day they told us what food there was available but in the end it was not there. We were both physically and mentally completely worn out.

Irritation struck and if the men suspected they had to walk round if only for a mile they felt it. I had to pay close attention to the map and make sure to choose the shortest route.

In the end we were so tired that we were capable of sleeping standing up against a tree in full kit. Even our platoon's 'tough guy' I found one night crying in his sleeping bag. Both physically and mentally he was beat. I did not say a word to anyone. I had to continuously motivate the team and myself. And eventually events did lead to a competitive spirit. We all wanted to make it.

After six nights without food, they had given us the details of a location where food could be found. On our arrival there were a number of 'enemy' soldiers with living chickens, which they released as soon as they saw us. Next, a horrendous scene unfolded. Some of the men put their bayonets on their rifles and first chased off 'the enemy' and then started to hunt down the chickens. I do not know who ran faster the 'enemy' soldiers or the chickens. After having caught and slaughtered the chickens we had to light a fire and roast the chickens. This took too much time and we ate them raw. We behaved like animals.

They had promised we could rest in a cave over the weekend, but during our last night when everybody was highly motivated to reach our goal, I fell to pieces. I could no longer walk, my strength had left me and all I could do was stagger forward. At that point I as convinced I was not going to make it. My kit and rifle were scoring my back and I was completely spent. My mind wanted me to go on, but my body simply refused. But I was the leader of the platoon; I just had to go on!

And just when I thought it was the end for me our 'tough guy' came and walked next to me. Without a word he grabbed my kit and rifle and started carrying them and thanks to him I made it to the cave before the weekend. We hoped that there would be food for us in the cave but it turned out there were only a few biscuits.

That night in my sleeping bag I cried my eyes out which fortunately no one noticed. I was exhausted. The ensuing week we all made it back to the starting point. Our whole platoon reached the end goal and we were very proud. Out together, home together.

The lesson I learned is that shared misery is good for creating a team spirit and also that my mind and body can endure quite a bit of discomfort.

When in sales you are a soloist. You make your own plans, visiting schedules, you visit clients and potential clients, you can win and you can lose. Most of the time you will be left to your own devices. This is not a problem because this is part of the job you have chosen and this is what you like about the job. Still, people are not soloists by nature and therefore a salesperson is not either. A salesperson wants to be part of a team as well. His sales team, his sales manager, his colleagues are important in order to share successes and perhaps also failed deals. Even a salesperson wants other people to listen to him. And sales management of a company should create opportunities for salespeople to meet and talk to each other.

Selling work to people

Once my time in the army was up I did not really know what I wanted to do. Construction and in particular my father's company was not doing well. Construction workers made higher demands, which were not incorporated in my father's budgets. I, therefore, could not go to medical school because I was without a sponsor. I had to find a job, but what kind of job, I did not know.

In those days there were plenty of jobs for educated young people. Companies bent over backwards to recruit people. By mail I receive a job offer in the industry of the future, i.e. computer operator at a bank. The wording of the job offer appealed to me and I decided to apply for the job. The main office of this particular bank was situated in the only large city close to our village.

I got the job and I started off working in shifts. A two-week day shift followed by a two- week evening shift. The evening shift was only finished when all the work was done. I started to earn reasonably well and in particular the team bonuses and overtime made the difference. I was part of a team consisting of one shift leader and four computer operators.

The bank used two large mainframe computers (IBM 360-30) situated in a large computer room. The computers still worked with punch cards and paper tape. As a trainee operator I had to start work with dealing with the punch cards, data entry and the output of the computers. I had to operate different machines, preferably at the same time.

My job comprised sorting, punching holes in and joining together the punch cards. I also had to split and decarbonise the paper. It was hard work in this real production process. The machines, all working at the same time, produced an awful lot of noise. And if had to work the evening shifts I, occasionally, would not arrive home till four a.m. The extra money made it all worth it, though.

At the end of the month, quarter and year additional programmes had to be run on the computers and we had to work overtime in the weekends as well. The computer centre's manager would come up to us, look at us one at the time an say for instance, "I can tell by the look in your eyes that you can work extra on Saturday night". This is how he selected people to work extra, for which you were paid double. Computer time was expensive, so the computers had to be used to their full capacity.

My goal was to be allowed to use the main computers, but I had to wait for another trainee to be appointed so I could move up one step on the ladder. I had to learn on the job from others who were not eager, to put it mildly, to share their unique knowledge.

It was quite a challenge to run programmes on the computer simultaneously so that they would finish at the same time. In that case all the operators could go home at the same time. My shift leader was good at that. We had made a deal that we would always go home at the same time when the work for everyone was finished.

There were also computer programmes that needed a lot of time to run. One of them was called 'Mystery' and this programme took three hours to finish and had to run every night. The programmer of this programme was what you would call a real 'whiz-kid' and was well respected at the bank as the programmer of this complex programme.

The management had decided to change suppliers and move from IBM to Siemens. Our new computers were installed in a newly appointed calculus centre in a different building. Now we all had to take training courses to learn how to work with the new computers. I seized this opportunity and was no longer dependent on other operators so show me the tricks of the trade if they felt like it.

All existing programmes had to be reset for the new computers and as it turned out "Mystery' was so badly programmed that after the reset it took only one hour for the programme to finish. This meant that the programmer of 'Mystery' fell from his pedestal and decided to leave the bank.

In the meantime I learned to operate the main computers and became quite proficient. I enjoyed testing the new programmes and in doing so learned what these programmes could do. But in the long run it became more and more a routine.

Whenever we were running long programmes there was always time for a practical joke. Especially during the evening shift when we were the only ones in the building, we were tempted towards pranks. We used to walk through the building to deliver the computer output to the bank employees and learned exactly on which desk we could find cigarettes. We smoked for free.

Every night there was a night porter present and one of them had the annoying habit to sneak up on you silently when you were working and suddenly put his hand on your shoulder. In doing so he scared us out of our wits, our hair standing on end. We decided to teach him a lesson. He had to walk his rounds through the entire building several times a night. In every department he had to clock on which he did without ever turning the light on. On one particular night we had put on white shirts and hid under the desks in one department. As soon as he was in plain view we got from under the desks at the same time. We scared the living daylights out of him and he started to rant and rave. After that, as we could not help but notice, he always turned on the lights when he went on his rounds and he stayed away from the computer centre.

I learned to work in production and in a team with its own hierarchy. I also acquired a taste for working with computers and everything surrounding it, but my main 'drive' was to make a lot of money through hard work.

At the onset of your career there are many things that appeal to you. You do not really have an idea about what to do. That is the time in your life to explore job prospects. Not only by approaching your job seriously but also by taking the time to play jokes, you learn how to deal with clients and colleagues. That is also the time to discover your own style; by experimenting with ways to be successful.

Selling myself to my future father-in-law

We were young and in love and had been dating secretly for about three months. Secretly meant that I had not yet been introduced to the parents of my girlfriend and she had not met mine. Etiquette demanded that I had to meet her parents first, before she was to meet mine. She was the third daughter of a family of seven children (four boys and three girls) and she was the youngest but one. Her married brothers and sisters I had already met on a few occasions.

The impression I had of her parents was not favourable. Her family appeared to be old- fashioned with her father as the head of the family ruling over his offspring from the living room while her mother ruled from the kitchen. The boys were favoured above the girls. Her father was very religious and had been a member of one of the rather strict Orthodox religious communities.

When I got to know him he no longer went to church, but Sunday's rest was sacrosanct to him and the radio and television were to remain switched off. He had worked hard all his life dredging ditches. In his spare time he gave riding lessons because he had worked with horses during his time in the army with the cavalry. He gave these riding lessons to the 'rich kids' in the village and that was a part of his life he kept strictly separate from his family life. All the children were afraid of him and if you were not in his good books, that was the end of it for you. That was the impression I had of him.

His views were difficult for children to understand and that is why his orders were not always obeyed. The mother would protect the children and formed a buffer between her husband and her children. In that way she had carved out for herself a position of power with regard to her children. The night I was to visit her parents for the first time I was dead nervous. I had already walked around the block three times when I finally mustered up enough courage to ring the front door bell. Her mother opened the door and was very friendly while she led me towards the living room where I was to meet the father. I entered the living room and shook his hand. He said 'hello' and 'take a seat' and that was it.

He was watching a show about equestrian sports on television. He was watching intently and it struck me that even before the horse jumped he could predict whether it would fail or not. He really knew what he was talking about. He never said one word to me, though, and I felt rather uncomfortable. My girlfriend was still up in her room doing her hair so we could go out babysitting the son of her eldest brother.

All of a sudden the door opened and an elder sister entered all dressed up and ready to go out. Her father took one look at her make-up and said quite rudely:

Go upstairs immediately and remove that muck from your face, you look like a clown. She left the room crying and obeyed his order because without his permission she was not allowed to go out.

After a while he turned his attention to me and said: "My daughter is still young and you need to have a lot of patience with her" I nodded that I had understood. That was the entire conversation I had with my father-in-law that night. Fortunately, he did approve of my girlfriend's make up and we left her house to go babysitting. My girlfriend remarked that my father probably liked me. I did not understand this because I had not said anything at all. I felt relieved, though.

Two months later it turned out that her father was seriously ill. At the hospital they had diagnosed him with lung cancer. He had been smoking too much for many years. From that moment on he had to go to hospital in the big city once a week to receive radiation treatment. Since I worked in shifts I was often at home during the day and I used to drive him to hospital on many occasions. During that period our relationship improved and I realised that deep down inside he had a warm heart and was a kind and good human being. The rudeness just being a façade he hid behind.

My girlfriend used to work in a garden centre as a sales assistant and doing jobs around the place. She liked the work. All of a sudden her father wanted her to give up this job. One of his 'rich' horse friends needed a housekeeper and he had promised to send his daughter to help out. She hated the idea because all she wanted was to become a hairdresser. After a few months I dared to raise the issue with my father-in-law. My girlfriend had been offered a job in a hair salon and could go to hairdressing school on Mondays. I managed to convince my father-in-law that it was a wonderful opportunity for his daughter, my girlfriend. I promised to foot the bill for the hairdressing school, and that is exactly what happened.

After radiation therapy his health improved somewhat and he was allowed to work part-time at a children's farm. He loved both animals and children, which made his treatment of his own children, seem all the more odd. Most of his children were afraid of him and did not dare to stand up to him. My girlfriend also had a bad relationship with her father because they were hardly able to communicate with each other. This situation was reinforced by the fact that he favoured her elder sister. He also favoured her over the other children, which caused friction among the children. I was aware of the fact that something out of the ordinary was going because the elder sister also sat on his lap quite often, which was rather strange I thought.

Her elder sister had been dating a farmer's son for about two months when she ended up pregnant. Her father was in tears when she told him. He was all cut up about it. Later that day he told my girlfriend that the pregnant sister and her boyfriend were to come and live in the parental home and due to a lack of space my girlfriend had to go and live with her elder brother. My girlfriend felt abandoned and this arrangement did nothing to improve their relationship. I never said anything about the matter for it was his house and he was master of it.

A year later and three months before we were to be married my father-in-law's health turned for the worst. The cancer cells had spread throughout his body. He was admitted to hospital, but nothing could be done to cure him. Something extraordinary happened while he was in hospital. He was facing death but at the same time he bore witness to God's goodness. He made remarks about God and the Bible, which unfortunately, I could not understand. Given the seriousness of his illness he should have been in a lot of pain, but he was not suffering. Even the doctors treating him were impressed and they decided he could spend his final days at home and not at the hospital.

At home we had to compile a care and night watch schedule for all the children and their partners. He received many visitors in those days and he radiated faith and peace. It was a true miracle. The nights I was alone with him I noticed that he was awake and spent his time looking outside the window towards the sky. He was waiting for God to call him to him and made a number of very sound remarks. I only wished I could understand his words, but I was too young for that.

Right before he died he asked all his children and their partners to come to his deathbed one at the time and said his good-byes with a personal proverb and piece of advice. Finally, he called his wife to his side and thanked her for all she had done for him. Then he waved at us and died. Many people his family did not know existed attended his funeral. They were his friends, rich and poor, who had come to say goodbye. I regretted that I had not had the opportunity to get to know him longer and better!

I learned to adjust to life in another family but most of all it became clear to me that there was something (a God) above us, who could still perform miracles. It gave me something to think about. My carefree youth was over.

It is difficult for a salesperson to determine your starting point when you meet a customer for the first time, and especially if you are aware of any internal friction. The best approach is to observe and not be judgmental. You can always ask if you can come back when the time is right. This will definitely be appreciated by your client and will put your client in a good mood during a next visit.

Selling without a result

Working with computers at a bank did me a world of good. There was so much to be learned. The computer age was still in its infancy. My choice to start my career in this industry proved to be a good one, even though I had to start from scratch when I started as a computer operator.

Working shifts allowed me a lot of freedom during the day, which I put to good use by driving my father-in-law back and forth to the hospital. Later on, when we were allocated a house by the city council I used my time off to prepare it for residence.

Our team consisted of five men. Three operators and colleagues had an Indonesian background. Working in such a small team in which people had to rely on each other day and night could only work if you were friends. If the computers were running their time consuming programmes it was time for fun and games. I learned among other to play chess and checkers. Playing games together strengthened our friendship and we were always willing to help out with good advice. One of my colleagues went on holiday to Spain for the first time. We led him to believe that in Spain only goat's milk and goat's cheese were available and that there were no groceries for sale. So he left for Spain with a car loaded up with groceries. On his arrival he discovered that next to the Camp Site a huge supermarket was located that sold everything he could wish for. He was not amused, to say the least.

The same colleague enjoyed calling random phone numbers in the middle of the night and as soon as somebody picked up the phone he just said "sorry, wrong number." He loved it when the person on the other end of the line got angry. We did not particularly like this hobby of his and on one occasion I did the same thing to his mother, handed him the receiver and winked at him. He took the receiver from me and listened to what his mother had to say. That was the end of his nocturnal telephone escapades.

Around that time something else happened that made a lasting impression on me. The programming manager was a nice guy and he talked often about his wife and children. He kept a picture of them on his desk. I realised I had to be nice to him because I wanted to become a programmer one day as a next step on the ladder and in order to do so I needed him.

Through the grapevine I heard the story about him and his secretary. They were having an affair and as soon as senior management found out, they were both fired on the spot. I was truly amazed because as far as I was concerned this was unacceptable behaviour for someone with a wife and children. I decided never to have an affair at work.

I learned more every day and slowly matured. We now worked in another building and opposite the building was a hotel. We discovered that many guests never bothered to close their curtains and lots of interesting stuff went on in those rooms. If we were on the evening and night shift our shift leader would keep an eye on the hotel windows and check if someone turned on the light. He then went to a dark floor in our building and while sitting in the dark, he would assess whether something worth watching was going on. It was an unusual way to get sex education.

A number of inhabitants of one of the former Dutch colonies lived temporarily in the Netherlands and dreamt of the day they could go back home and establish their own free state. This community was not too happy with the (lack of) efforts by the Dutch government towards their goal and in order to enforce their arguments they high-jacked a train. The Dutch nation was shocked by this event and it led to the police carrying out extra checks in order to prevent a situation like that from happening again. Especially 'coloured' people were kept under close surveillance.

One night we had forgotten to close the blinds on the windows and hotel staff across the street saw our three Indonesian colleagues at work in the computer room. They notified the police immediately and when we left the computer room unsuspectingly we did notice that the security man downstairs was rather nervous. We still had no clue when we left the building at 5 a.m.

All of a sudden we were caught in the blinding light of a floodlight and confronted with a large number of heavy armed policemen. We were handcuffed and carried off to the police station straight way. We were locked up in separate cells and after an hour they interrogated me. I explained quietly that it all had been a mistake and that we had only been doing our job. We did not have access to the phone number of one of the bank managers. The thought had never occurred to us. And why should it.

Eventually they managed to contact one of the bank managers who, oddly enough, was not even aware of the fact that people were at work during the night. We had to wait until the Manager of the Computer centre came in for work at nine a.m. He hurried to the police station and made sure we were released immediately. It did not feel good having been treated as a criminal and it left quite an impression on me.

The lesson I learned from this is, that sometimes you have to prove your innocence to people who do not wish to believe the truth. I also learned not to start an affair at work because it might have a negative effect on your career.

The basic approach of a salesperson should really always be the same. He needs to be open and above board. He needs to attract people. Only with people around you who are genuinely interested you are able to tell your story. They can become you buyers but they can also become your ambassadors. In actual fact this is what networking is all about; surround yourself with people who will in turn surround themselves with people. In the end any situation you may find yourself in can serve a purpose, if only that of a good story to tell.

Selling a marriage

After my time in the army I returned to live with my family once more. My brother, the police officer, had already left home and only came back weekends. Shortly after I had returned I had a serious fight with my mother. She still wanted to treat me as a child and I felt like an adult male after my time in the army. This caused friction and we even stopped speaking to each other until my father put an end to that and convinced my mother to treat me differently. I did no longer feel comfortable living at home.

Another problem I had to tackle was my drinking habit. In the army I had made a habit out of drinking heavily and I could no longer keep that up at home. I soon managed to control my drinking. Out of my salary I bought a car and I felt more independent.

My girlfriend also did not feel happy at home. She had a bad relationship with her parents and with her sister who was favoured by both her parents. As soon as she got home from work she immediately had to set about doing chores and hardly had any time to herself. When she was not at work I picked her up and we practically lived in my car. Sometimes, when her mother was cross with her there was no food provided for her and we went out for snacks.

In our village there were special parking spaces where couples could drive to in their cars and make out. We spend a lot of time there because we felt at ease. We spent much time discussing her problems and it seemed the only solution was for us to get married. My girlfriend also had a difficult time when her father fell ill and we knew he was going to die. My girlfriend did not want to accept that and I could not make her face up to the inevitable. We had been on holiday together with my brother and his wife because that was the only way people who were not married could stay somewhere. During that holiday we had become engaged and on our return there were no presents from her family. She felt disappointed and it made her sad. We both felt hurt. There was not much love lost between her and her family.

Those were the days of the sexual revolution and it happened often that a young couple was forced into marriage because the girl got pregnant. My mother had advised my girlfriend to take the contraceptive pill. This pill had not been available long on the Dutch market. My girlfriend had to obtain them secretly from her doctor because her father was strongly against the use of contraceptives. In the meantime I paid a visit to city hall and applied for a rental house.

Because of all the implications of my father-in-law's illness and in particular the spiritual and religious side of the matter, we started going to church again.

Through my sister we got acquainted with a separate branch of the Dutch Reformed Church. The minister of this church was a special person. He had been confined to a Japanese concentration camp during the Second World War and he applied the bible to modern times. It was fascinating to sit and listen to him. The church was always filled with mostly young people. Together with my girlfriend I attended the confirmation of faith classes.

We wanted to take our wedding vows in church and for this my girlfriend had to be baptised. The minister became very special to us and he taught me many things about religion. He was aware of the religious and spiritual insights of my father-in-law and helped us trying to understand it all.

Three months before my father-in-law passed away were allocated a house by the city council. It was a cheap terraced house and given the low rent we could not turn down the offer. There was hardly any money to fit up the place and our parents could not sponsor us.

We did manage to furnish the house with a number of indispensable items because I had gone bargain hunting. I had to make most arrangements on my own because my girlfriend had to work and was too distressed on account of her father's illness. She was in no mood to enjoy anything at that point in time. She was often ill and suffered from bilious attacks. Living together was out of the question and we decided to set a date for our wedding. Our parents granted us permission. My father-in-law expressed the desire to live long enough to see it happen. Unfortunately, it was not meant to be.

Two months after my father-in-law died we got married. It was a sober occasion out of respect to my father-in-law. What should have been the best day in our lives was all about my father in law's passing. I was very tense that day and I hoped my girlfriend was not to suffer from one of her attacks. Everybody was sad and unhappy on our wedding day. Our own minister did hold a special and beautifully worded sermon and he gave us all heart. It was time for us to get some rest in our own home.

I learned to believe in God (my God) again. Not because I was forced to, but because I wanted to and had seen His wonders. The most important lesson in my entire life.

Having faith is important in sales. It does not matter whether you faith in God, the church or yourself. The fact that you feel supported in what you do and think makes the difference. It is a spiritual strength you develop and will help you further ahead and provides the ability to perform well. It is he ability to exceed yourself. Do not underestimate this force. Sales people, who make a deal with their first customer, will score above average the rest of the day (scientifically proven). What sort of force is that? The least you can do is to start your day with a customer or prospect where you are likely to be successful. This will help you the rest of the day.

Good job, bad sales

The two-shift schedule had now been changed into a three-shift schedule. The computers were used more and more and given the high costs involved they had to be used around the clock. Working shifts was putting a strain on me and I could not go to evening classes. I needed the extra money that came with the late shifts, though, to furnish our home.

After a few years working as computer operator I had become quite accomplished. This eventually led to my appointment as second in control. I was in charge when the shift leader was ill or on holiday. I experienced this as a big responsibility.

Still, one of my colleagues, who was not as skilled as I was, had been promoted to the position of programmer. This made no sense to me and when I confronted my manager he told me that I was good at my job and that I just had to be patient.

This annoyed me since I wanted the position of programmer and I wanted it badly. I soon understood they were taking me for a ride. The computer centre was to move to another city in the centre of the country. We had not been informed and management had already made an inventory of who was to move with the company and who was not. I was a good operator and they decided that I would be willing to move. Of others they had estimated that they would quit their job. They had to keep a sufficient number of operators in order to get the work done.

That is why they did not offer me the opportunity to become a programmer. It was not in their best interest to promote me to the position of programmer. As it turned out there was no form of financial compensation for people to relocate. I would have had to move from a cheap rental house to a more expensive rental house. I felt badly treated and decided to look for another job.

Most banks had their main office in the capital. There was only one bank based in the city I lived close to. That bank was interested in me and my skills and they hired me as a shift leader with on the condition that I could train to be a programmer. In the end I did get my promotion after all and even a pay rise. At their computer centre I learned to operate two NCR100 computers followed by a NCR200 computer.

I learned a hard lesson. I had not been paying attention and had trusted my managers. They served their own interests and mine were of minor importance to them. I also learned to assert myself.

As a salesperson you always have to deal with the situation of the client. If what is on offer, the price, service and quality are in keeping with what the customer wants, then it makes sense for him to buy from you. What you cannot perceive, though, is the client's personal situation. He could have a bad relationship with his boss, his boss could have a good relationship with a competitor, he could have problems with his wife etc. These are all reasons for a customer to postpone or cancel his decision. The reasons behind this are often invisible to the salesperson. Different interests play a part that often do not have any bearing upon the sales situation. If this happens, ask yourself whether you have done everything in your power to get the order. If that is the case, then do not doubt yourself. Many salespeople do this, which leads to a lack of self-confidence. A salesperson lacking confidence is doomed to fail.

Selling my skills versus loyalty

The bank I now worked for as a shift leader was a midsize bank with about 80 branches all over the country. About 300 people worked at the main office. The computer department consisted of a manager, two senior programmers and two junior programmers. I worked at the department with five other operators, divided into two shifts. The punch card division was also a part of the computer department and during the day five young women (the so called 'punching ladies') were responsible for transposing all computer input into punch cards.

The Manager of the Computer Department decided together with two senior programmers which programmes had to be developed for the two computers (NCR 100 and later two NCR 200 computers). They both had a background in finance and (thought) they knew what the bank would benefit from. We had nicknamed one of the senior programmers "John the Patch". He wrote computer programmes that nobody understood and if the programme would crash at night he would arrive at the office straight from the pub (sometimes drunk) and patch the programme up so we could continue. He never told anyone exactly what it was he did. Compared to my position with my previous employer, the automation process of this bank was lagging behind. They paid me well, though, and I needed the money for my family.

Sometimes we had to punch the cards ourselves in order to restore data entries into the computer. It was not easy to enter the domain of the 'punching ladies' and try to get hold of a punching apparatus. The women could be really horrid and if they did not like you, you did not stand a chance and they would be very rude to you. I tried to remain on friendly terms with them because I needed their services.

I definitely stuck my neck out when I gave some advice to one of the ladies. This particular girl was still single and had a serious squint. It was a miracle that she could punch cards at all. She confided in me and told me she would have her eyes operated on as soon as she had found herself a date. I directly advised her to do things the other way around. Tricky, because she looked at me intently (at least I think she did) but when I gave her a heartfelt smile, she accepted my advice.

Later on some of the 'punching ladies' got into a serious argument over an apple. They actually fought each other and three of the ladies were fired on the spot. The whole affair made quite an impression on me.

Without informing our managers the management of the bank, after having received direct instructions from the National bank, had decided to bring in an external accountant to restructure the Automation Department. They had called in an external consultant's agency and running parallel to the existing Automation Department they were forming a new one. My manager, who had been working for the bank for years and was emotionally involved in the day to day running of the bank, was furious and genuinely upset. He had already spoken to the Managing Directors and had left the boardroom crying like a child. He had always carried out the job very efficiently and effectively without overspending. And now a new manager was hired who was allowed to spend loads of money. It just was not fair and he did not understand. He refused flatly to cooperate with the new manager and his team.

This left my colleague and me in the lurch. What about all the promises concerning our career? After a couple of months we found a job advert asking for programmers for our bank in a trade journal. These programmers would receive an excellent training programme of three months. And from the advert it became clear to us what their intentions were.

A whole new automation department was to be formed that would link all branches on-line to the main office, an ambitious undertaking in those days. I was excited about the whole plan because I wanted to be part of it.

By now my colleague and I were rather frustrated because they had forgotten all about us. We did muster up enough courage to approach our emotional Manager. He understood our predicament and agreed that we deserved a chance. And so we were considered for the position but we had to take a test first. Fortunately we passed the test and we were transferred to the new computer department run by the 'enemy'. I had the idea that now my career had really started and this pleased me immensely.

I learned from all this that it is sensible to keep business and private separate and not to get too emotionally involved with the company you work for. In addition, on the whole it is not a good idea to put together a team consisting of only women. I was, nevertheless, proud of myself because I had managed to become master of my fate.

It's all sales

The world around you changes constantly. Stay abreast of all these changes. Opportunities will arise but you have to notice them. The same goes for the customer, remain involved. Notice it when a client's behaviour changes. What is going on? Go and check it out. Take action and be an entrepreneur.

Selling a lower pay status

After our wedding we were happy with our council house. Even though the house was situated in the 'impoverished' area of the village, we felt like a million dollars. My wife worked five days a week including Saturdays in a hair-dressing salon while I still worked in shifts and also weekends. Because of my schedule I spent a lot of time at home during the day. We spent our money on the basics required for setting up home together. We had started off without a washing machine but now we could slowly but surely buy new things. Especially the extra money I earned by working shifts and overtime definitely made a difference.

On weekdays I ran the home and did the cooking. On Saturdays I played soccer, in a lower ranked team this time because I did not have the time to attend training sessions. On Saturday nights we usually had people over at our place or we went out to visit friends. On Sundays we went to church and were more or less obliged to visit the family. That is how we lived our lives in those days.

And now things were going to change. I was offered the opportunity to become a programmer and that was to be the real start of my career. I also went back to evening school to take the only course available to become an automation expert. This course (AMBI) would take five years and I had to go school two nights a week in a different town.

My wife did not understand what my work involved but the financial implications were considerable since I would no longer get the shift and overtime bonus payouts. One night we talked about the financial consequences and our future together. There was no way she could ever make as much money as a hairdresser as I could in automation which is why we chose to invest in my career.

We also talked about having children and decided it would be best to start a family as early as possible. Our lives would change dramatically. My wife would stay home and run the home thereby enabling me to work and study. I asked her to make do with a smaller housekeeping allowance and I decided to sell our car. I was surprised by the reactions of our friends and family. They simply could not understand our decision.

I did manage to explain to my parents that this was only temporary and that things would improve later on. Of course I reminded them of the days my father had started up in business. In those days we also had to make do with less. However, my wife's family and some of our friends took delight in our (temporary) lower pay status and did not understand.

Soon after, my wife got pregnant and with all kinds of pleasure we started decorating a nursery. In those days we also had a tiny dog, a miniature Pekinese. The most beautiful moment in my life was when my daughter was born. It was such a special moment and I felt so grateful for this miracle. She was born on a Monday morning at exactly 12 a.m.

Our little dog was barking with pleasure and I could hear the alarm signal tests[3] in the village. This precious little girl, this miracle was to change my life.

I got up for her at night when she cried, let her blackmail me because she enjoyed it when daddy came to her when she cried. But sometimes I had to be strict and that still hurts to this very day.

I used to play with her and took her to visit my parents, family and friends. Together we listened to Abba songs whilst she was bouncing to the sound of the music. She absolutely loved it all. I was one of the first men in our village who dared walking through the village with a pram.

My wife went back to work on Saturdays in a hairdressing salon and I would take care of our daughter. I gave up playing soccer and took my daughter shopping instead. We became very close. Next to that, I studied hard because I now felt more than ever the need to get ahead in life. I would do anything for my daughter!

I had now experienced God's miracle of creating new life myself. It made me feel humble and full of awe towards Him.

---

[3] In the Netherlands every first Monday of the month the national alarm systems are tested at exactly 12 a.m.

Good things that happen can serve a purpose throughout your life. You probably know the feeling that when something good has happened you feel as if you are walking on air. That feeling does not have to end. When you have to undertake a difficult task and you feel insecure, think back of that special moment and let that fantastic feeling get a hold of you once more. You will notice that it will generate so much positive energy that you will feel much better equipped to succeed.

Selling a 'benchmark'

In order to become a programmer I had to take a programming course, apart from the AMBI course mentioned earlier. The programming course was based on individual coaching. It took about three months and halfway through the course there was an assessment. If it turned out that you were not suited to be a programmer you had to leave the course. I studied very hard and the most important thing I learned was to think more logically.

During the course we had to write a number of programmes and write them as effectively and efficiently as possible. Afterwards, your personal coach would check your work and if the work was up to standards, you would receive the detailed method and techniques. If your work was not good enough your programme was torn up and you had to start all over again.

We were really put through it and sometimes I thought I was back in the army. This training course to become a programmer was reputed to be the best in The Netherlands and it cost the bank a fortune. It goes almost without saying that I was very proud when I completed the course successfully with the much-coveted diploma.

We ended up with four fellow-programmers in one room. The Automation Master Plan for the bank had not been finished at that point in time and we had to work on some minor and temporary applications. There was not much for us to do as yet because the system analysts who had to provide the work for us were not up to speed yet. So, there was some time left for fun and games.

One of my fellow-programmers had been to University and had learned a number of tricks while he was there. At the time I was writing a programme for a special computer for a department with a rather stressed-out manager. On the slightest provocation he would lose his temper and most certainly when there was something wrong with his computer. He would then grab the phone and command me to his department to solve the problem.

The 'funny guy' in my department had unscrewed the microphone from my telephone and when the stressed-out manager phoned me, he could not hear my voice. He almost exploded and violently threw back the receiver. His response scared me out of my wits because I thought something was wrong with my programme.

What made matters worse in my mind was the fact that our programming department was considered quite costly and once again our reputation was under discussion. Of course the 'funny guy' had informed my manager and he had decided to play along. When I found out what they had been doing I felt awful because they had really made a fool out of me. In the end I did get my own back but only after a while.

In order to execute the Automation Master Plan it was also necessary to purchase new computers and also computers for all offices which would communicate 'online and real time' with the computers at the main office. Part of the deal with the hardware suppliers was that a benchmark programme was to be written in order to determine whether the suggested hardware was suitable for all our offices. It was a rush job and since I had a reputation for working hard and fast, I was selected to write the benchmark programme.

On receipt of the programme specifications I started the actual programming and of course also the testing on our possible new office computers. Our quiet days were definitely over. I received a lot of attention from people I had never seen before, who came to visit me in what we called our hut. They were extremely nice to me; laughed (too loudly) at my (sometimes feeble) jokes, got me coffee and offered me cigarettes. They even seemed genuinely interested in my wife and little girl. I was Mr popular. In the meantime they did ask me casually about the programme and the test status.

I enjoyed all the attention, though I did realise who these people were and what they were after. When all was said and done it was after all a six-million-dollar contract we were putting out. Then there were of course the senior manager of the computer centre, my own manager and the salespeople and their suppliers who were interested in me. There were, however, also others, employed by the bank that showed an interest, which I did not quite understand. The bank paid them, so what was it to them or did the hardware suppliers also pay them bribes? I discovered that everybody was looking after his or her own interests.

Once I had completed the benchmark programme successfully and the contract was awarded it became quiet again in our little 'hut'. People were no longer interested in me and to make matters worse I had to get my own coffee once more. The game was up.

I learned from this that some people are only nice to you when they need you. Salespeople fight for their bonuses and in doing so they sometimes forget the 'human aspect' behind the money.

Of course it is true that when people need you they show more of an interest than when they do not. Whether it is getting something done or looking for company, in one way or the other, people want something from you. Look at your own actions, and you will know this is true. For a good salesperson it is therefore essential to create a situation that others always need you. Success guaranteed!

Losing out because of opposition

I thoroughly enjoyed being a programmer. Every time I had finished a programme and it was tested on a computer I felt victorious, especially if it was good and ready for production. My first real programming job was to write a programme for the bank's Arbitrage of Exchange Department, based on the system analysis carried out by a system analyst.

The programme had to written in LCOBOL (a computer language) for a very special computer, a Burroughs B90. After compilation the programme had to be put on paper tape at the Head Office and then tested on the bank's own computer. My programme had to be as effective and efficient as possible to avoid unnecessary travel between the bank and Head Office. I also had to be extremely careful not to tread on the paper tape whilst feeding it into the computer. This first large job meant a huge challenge and commanded respect from my colleagues.

External consultants were busy compiling a new design for a Master Plan. Automation for the entire bank would be completely renewed. There was, however, growing resentment against the external consultants from the bank's senior management. As far as they were concerned this costly project would not lead to improvement and the old, internal automation managers supported their negative attitude. In the mean time us programmers were kept busy with what we referred to as interim-systems and reported directly to a new, young manager.

The Head of the external consultants was a special and dynamic person. He was the author and manager of this mega transformation process and he was direct and honest in his approach. He wanted to change the bank's operations and turn it in to a modern bank by means of automation. He was good at his job, highly intelligent and we respected him because we were aware of the battles he had to fight against those opposing the changes. Whenever you made mistake or were sloppy your name would disappear from the planning schedule which meant it was time for you to go and look for another job. He was tough, but his main aim was to win for the bank's sake.

Finally, the overall Master Plan for the automation was finished and approved of by senior management. This induced the external consultants and the head of their department to organise a huge party at a farm, in a village close to the one I lived in. My young manager had promised to come and pick me up by car to go to the party together.

At the time we had a small dog around the house, a miniature Pekinese that was in the habit of barking ferociously at anything that moved. I had told my manager to beware of the dog but I had not told him what breed of dog it was. As soon as he rang the front door bell he was greeted by what sounded to him like a huge animal. When I opened the front door I was surprised to find my manager at the end of the garden path looking somewhat frightened at the front door. Once he had had a good look at our 'ferocious' pet and had made sure it was actually a dog of some sorts and not a cat, he burst into uncontrollable laughter.

It was a great party and probably as a result of releasing all pent up frustrations and resistance he had experienced at the bank, the head of the external consultants got totally and completely drunk. For us the party led to fraternisation and we were now more than ever determined to change the bank's system because we felt it was of the utmost importance for the survival of the bank.

Now that the Master Plan had been approved it had to be divided into sub plans and later on into sub projects. One of the external developers, who was responsible for the development of the most important plan, the Basic System of the bank, worked on his plan around the clock under enormous pressure, together with our new, young manager. The stress and pressure eventually got the better of him and he fell seriously ill combined with a burnout. This made a tremendous impression on me because for the first time I had witnessed first hand what fighting opposition, work pressure and stress could do to a person.

My career was now skyrocketing. I studied in the evening to prepare for my AMBI diploma. In order to do so I had to go to evening classes twice a week and I had to take a test about eleven modules. All this went well and in my first year I passed the test for the five basic modules, but after that it got more complicated and maths in particular was difficult and taught at University level.

I learned in theory all about the automation process including programming, system analysis, system design, information analysis and project management. What I enjoyed most was to learn about the theoretical aspects and then being able to put it into practice at the bank.

I was promoted to system analyst after six months as a programmer and my new job involved compiling a system analysis for an interim system. I thoroughly enjoyed working together with the end users, the people at the bank, to put together a system analysis for a system they wanted to use.

The system ran smoothly and the end-users were satisfied, with as an immediate result that I was promoted once more. I became system designer and together with the end users I had to compile a system design for the 'letter of credit' process. This was a complicated internal process that involved almost every other process at the bank. The manager in charge of the departments supporting this process fortunately knew what he was doing and together we

designed a wonderful system to computerise the whole process. The manager
was an immensely sympathetic man and soon we became the best of friends.
Once the design was finished I was very proud of my work and I immediately
sent the design to the Board of Directors for approval.

We now worked in an open-plan office. One of my fellow-designers was from
Belgium[4] and his was not an easy life because he had to listen to a large number
of Belgian jokes. Sometimes he got fed up with it and he would throw a full
ashtray at my colleague and me to shut us up. This made us laugh even louder
because he never managed to actually hit us. Our young manager noticed what
was going on. He called us to account and forbade us to tell Belgian jokes
whenever our Belgian colleague was near.

So we gave it up. After about two months our Belgian colleague came up to us
and asked us why we disliked him and why we did not speak to him anymore.
He wanted to know what he had done wrong. We told him our manager had
forbidden us to tell Belgian jokes. Our Belgian colleague went to see the
manager immediately and talked things over with him. A little later we were
summoned into his office where he told us what he had decided. We were
allowed to crack Belgian jokes again, but our Belgian colleague would be
entitled to throw an EMPTY ashtray at us whenever he was fed up with it. A
true judgement of Salomon.

The Board of Directors never approved my sub design for the 'letters of credit'
programme. Our interim-manager and the head of the external consultants and
the consultants were fired on the spot. The enormous internal opposition
against the transformation process and ignorance regarding automation had
finished them off. We, young and eager enthusiasts were left in the lurch.

Nevertheless, the transformation process had to go on and a new interim-
manager was appointed who had to finish the process. He became the new
Organisation and Automation Manager.

*Business wise this was an enormous learning process for me. It made me see that you can only
implement a large transformation process with full and unconditional support from a bank's*

---

[4] Belgium borders on The Netherlands in the South. In one part of Belgium (the Walloon
provinces of Belgium) French is spoken whereas in the other half (Flanders) Dutch (Flemish) is
spoken. As long as people can remember there has been this (mostly) good-natured rivalry
between the Dutch and Flemish. This often results in the Dutch telling jokes about Belgians
usually implying that they are not the sharpest tools in the box. What most Dutch people do not
realise is that the Belgians tell more or less the same jokes featuring the Dutch.

It's all sales

In sales it is very important to find a balance between the different activities. An invariable problem is the balance between sales to customers and acquisition of new customers. You may not know which way to turn. Keeping existing customers is the cheapest option since the acquisition of new customers can be costly. The acquisition/prospect phase and the trial phase of the new customer can cost you more than it avails. In order for your business to grow new customers are important. Existing customers are of course also important and when it comes to them "up selling" en "cross-selling" are a must. When looking at the story above it also becomes clear that a balance between private and business is essential.

Selling a career that is taking off

My personal life was pretty regular. Our daughter mainly determined our lives now. We stayed at home usually and were not able to go out often. Going to bed late was not an option since our daughter was in the habit of rising bright and early. We no longer had a car and my wife stayed at home on weekdays and ran the home, looked after the garden, did the shopping and made sure that I could work, study and play the occasional game of soccer.

It is safe to say I was very busy and sometimes I had to work late. I always made sure, though, that we could have our dinner together and after dinner I played with my daughter and watched 'Sesame Street' on television with her. Afterwards I would put her to bed and return to the office to do some more work, or go upstairs and study.

To me it was important to spend my time wisely and the thing I really hated was the never-ending family birthdays. My wife had a rather large family and the family members all expected us to visit on their birthdays. In addition, our parents expected us to visit on Sundays. For me those family gatherings were boring and I felt there were better ways to spend my time. Now that I had taken up studying again I thought I could convince the families that I did not have time for these visits but that I loved them all the same. I tried, but it led to friction and a lack of understanding.

In order to unwind I played soccer again in a lower ranked team on Saturdays. We lived close to the playing fields and people used to phone me on weekdays to ask me to join in if they were a player short. Soccer was a wonderful way to relax because during a match I could not think about problems or business issues. After the game I never wanted to talk about work because I knew that I would end up solving business problems in my spare time as well. To me sports meant total relaxation. And much to my surprise I was proclaimed player of the year, because of my willingness to play whenever I could. I was proud of this achievement.

Since my career had really taken off now, our income had increased considerably and we could afford once more to buy a car. I bought an orange deux-cheveaux and since the car resembled a duck my daughter called it "Wak-Wak" after the sound a duck makes.

Not long afterwards I was offered the opportunity to buy the house of a soccer mate. His boss had offered him a house to buy but he was not interested and was wondering whether we would be interested. I was interested in buying the property and so we more or less changed houses, because they moved into our rental house in the same street. All this led to me working from dusk to dawn, which put a strain on our marriage. I continued developing myself but she did not. We grew apart. I hardly ever talked about my work at home because she would not understand and was too preoccupied with her mother and her family. This I could not understand or consider important.

We decided to go on a holiday to talk things over. During our talks my wife decided to go back to school and study for a secondary education diploma. We also decided to talk about the day's events for an hour or so every day before we went to sleep.

By now I had become very adept at taking tests and for every verbal exam I managed to broach a subject I knew a lot about. Examiners would then ask me detailed questions about that particular subject. My favourite subject was project organisation. In that way I succeeded in obtaining my full AMBI diploma. I belonged to a select group of people in my country of people who had obtained the diploma. I had passed the tests for eleven modules in five years, which was a remarkable accomplishment and in addition to that, I was the first person at the bank with an AMBI diploma. I was happy and proud but I had to acknowledge the fact that nobody in my family or any of my friends understood the significance of this diploma. Automation and everything associated with it was not known to them. I had to deal with and celebrate my joy on my own.

The lesson I learned was that it was important to find a balance between work, hobbies and private life. My sky-rocketing career had done wonders for my bank account, but had been disastrous when it came to my marriage.

It's all sales

When you sell capital goods and also fast moving consumer goods it is important to give attention to all those involved with a customer. Where capital goods are concerned we are dealing with a purchaser but also with the end user, the decision maker (for example board of directors) or technical services. They all play a part in the sales process. They all have their own interests at heart when it comes to making a decision. Many companies work with a CRM (Customer Relationship Management) system. This system can process a lot of information on all those who are involved in the buying process. Moreover, it will not do any harm if there is some opposition involved in the buying process. When it comes to opposition, the customer will share information about issues you were not aware of, but that were relevant to the customer.

Selling a project

The new internal management of the Organisation and Automation department was busy converting the Master Plan into a feasible automation process that was acceptable to the bank. The plan was to computerise all bank-related processes and have the different branches carry out online transactions which were processed centrally and real-time on mainframe computers the same day.

After the dismissal of the external consultants some employees had become disappointed. To motivate us we were all allowed to attend a seminar by James Martin, the automation guru, in Copenhagen. This was my very first time on an airplane, which resulted in me being deaf the entire day we spent in Copenhagen.

The Master Plan for the automation of all bank processes was based on a number of solid starting points and was revolutionary in its approach. In those days no other bank had a system like the one planned. As part of the Master Plan a Basic System had to be developed. All administrative basic processes were part of this Basic System. Customer and account details, interest calculation methods, financial reporting, bank statements production etc. etc. had to be developed as part of the Basic System. In addition to that, a number of projects were defined of which the automated processes had to be linked up to the Basic System.

In the meantime I had once more been promoted and this time to Project Leader. In this capacity I was responsible for the realisation of two projects. My projects ran smoothly and we had already finished the design phase and the analysis. The Basic System Project had not been finished yet, so we had to wait until that was finished. Meanwhile, more than a hundred internal and external organisation and automation experts were employed at the Organisation and Automation department.

The pressure on those responsible for the Basic System was enormous and my young manager had already called in sick and had been diagnosed with a burn out. This was the second victim of the realisation of the Master Plan. Everybody involved was completely stressed out and slowly a general sense of defeatism was spreading.

The waiting also had its effect on me. I did have some negative thoughts about a possible successful outcome even though I still believed in the merits of the Master Plan. Another manager was appointed and he was only concerned with looking towards the future and was not interested in the day to day running of the business. We also had the feeling he was of no use to us since he refused to solve our problems. I did not like him and the dislike was mutual.

72

I was not at all happy given the present working conditions and I decided to apply for another job outside the bank. It was not too difficult to find a new job with my diplomas and experience and after only a short while a large insurance company hired me. On a Friday morning at nine a.m. I had a meeting with my Manager. I handed in my resignation and told him in no uncertain terms what I thought of him. He accepted my resignation and called the Senior Manager to inform him of my resignation. I felt quite relieved.

The same day at 11 a.m. I received a phone call from the secretary to the Senior Manager who asked me to meet the Senior Manager later that day at 2 p.m. This surprised me for these proceedings were highly unusual. My Team Supervisor and good friend smiled secretively when I told him. I had hardly met the Senior Manager because he had been too busy structuring the Master Plan. At 2 p.m. sharp the secretary let me into his office. The Senior Manager was not alone for the HR Manager was also present. My initial sense of relief was soon replaced by worry. Was there something wrong with my contract? Did I have to refund money for the training courses I had taken? It made me feel rather nervous.

The Senior Manager started off by saying that he had been informed of my resignation. He added immediately that he did not want me to leave and that he appreciated all the work I had done for the bank. I still did not see where he was heading. He then told me that there was hardly any progress regarding the Basic System. I could not agree more because I had had many conversations with my colleagues on the subject and I had also indicated what could be done to get things started again. Before I knew what hit me the Senior Manager offered me the position of Project Manager for the basic system. "You are the only one capable of turning this project into a success as a Project Manager and what is more, I will give you the same financial reward as your prospective employer". He ordered the H&R manager to draw up a proposition.

"But you have already appointed a project manager" I said! "Well," the senior manager responded, "this will come as a surprise to him but we are going to dismiss him". I continued by telling what my parting words to my manager had been. The Senior Manager looked me straight in the eye and told me he was convinced that I was the only one who could save the bank. He ended our conversation by asking me to reconsider and inform him of my decision on Monday morning 9 a.m. I left the office totally upset.

On my return from the Senior Manager's office my colleagues who were dying to find out what was going on surrounded me. My Team Supervisor was smiling because he was the one behind it all. I managed to say as little as possible because I had to get used to the idea myself first. I had one whole weekend to make up my mind.

I had been used to the fact that I could not discuss work related affairs at home. I kept business and private strictly separate and for outsiders it was hard to understand the significance of what was going on. I decided to unwind and on that Saturday and I played soccer as if out of this world. I scored twice, one of my goals being the winning goal. During the 'third half' of the match I got seriously drunk en ended up asleep on the couch that Saturday evening. I woke up at midnight, went to bed and tried to get some sleep. That Sunday morning I caught myself planning how to proceed with the Basic System project. Had I already decided?

The senior manager's faith in me had released something inside me. I loved the bank, the colleagues and I had always felt at home there. And without pride and thinking pragmatically, I became more and more convinced that I was the right man for the job. My promotion was good for the bank and the realisation of the Master Plan. I strongly believed in this and I was convinced of it.

That Sunday afternoon I went to my study and asked God for His blessing. It suddenly went all quiet and I decided to take the job. Next day I informed the senior manager, who was genuinely pleased with my decision. From that day on we became friends and he supported me all the way. His support turned out to be essential for a successful outcome of the project.

Once again I learned that when there are serious problems, I thoroughly enjoyed solving them. Winning was my main concern and I was capable of motivating myself and convince those around me to join my winning team. The importance of an important assignment with regard to the survival of a business motivated tremendously. I had to be supported though; otherwise I could not be successful.

One of the success factors of a sales person is mental resilience. It can be the difference between 'just' doing your job or the desire to win. The power inside you that you can develop by focusing on winning is of the utmost importance. You can accomplish much more and you will accomplish much more. You will also inspire others with this approach, which will lead to an increased effect. By this I do not mean the opportunism that so many people display nowadays, but real involvement in everything you do.

Selling as a project manager

In my new position as Project Manager of the Basic System project I started off by interviewing all those involved in the project. In this way I was put into the picture and I got a number of ideas to jump-start the project. The first thing I did was adapting the project organization and I put people in strategic positions that I could trust to do the job properly. I also removed unmotivated workers that I could not use from the project. For some this was a painful experience for others it was a challenge.

Next, I compiled a detailed project plan in cooperation with all those involved, so that everybody knew what was expected of him or her and nobody could hide behind others. I continued to hunt down problems until every problem that was on the critical path was solved. As a Project Manager I turned into a real 'hunter'. And if a problem could not be solved during the day it would have to be done in the evening or at night or during the weekend. I made a point of always being there myself and I was always available in case of problems. And eventually I did it! We managed to stop the leak and (albeit slowly) our 'boat' was capable of leaving port.

At the time there were many problems concerning this enormous project that had to be solved. One of them was that it took a long time until the compilation of the database was completed. Unfortunately there was only one person available that could perform this task and I kept motivating him to work extra. It was impossible to have more than one person on this job. In addition to that, the manager of the calculus centre refused to take on the extra work required for the development and testing of the new system. As a result I had to put together as part of the project, a team of workers for the new calculus centre.

On occasion I knew new lengthy test runs had been started and I would go at night to the calculus centre (back and forth) to reset the test runs if necessary. The hardware supplier had told us that it was better to develop smaller programmes but as it turned out this approach was bad for the computers' performance. We had to import 'cheap labour' from India to convert the small programmes into large programmes. In short, for every problem there was a solution and before long the ship sailed on its own, full speed ahead.

The next step was for management to gain confidence in the sailing ship. There were times when only the Senior Manager and I believed in a successful outcome of the project. This because the project was going over budget and took more time than expected. Fortunately the Senior Manager was an excellent sales person when it came to convincing his superiors. And since he was quite influential within the bank, due to my association with him I also became more influential.

We had appointed one single user to run the tests. He would implement large test runs based on new specifications and new procedures. Since he always wore a green shirt to work we called him "Test Hulk" after the huge, green cartoon and television hero. One morning I received a phone call from the (over) excited senior manager and I was summoned to his office.

The "Test Hulk" was already in the senior manager's office and both did not look too pleased. The Senior Manager told me without much ado that I had been telling him all went well concerning the project but that Mr "Test Hulk" had just told him when he ran in to him this morning that things were not running smoothly at all. I kept quiet and let the "Test Hulk" tell his side of events. As it turned out all of that night's results of the test run had failed. After analysis it turned out that the "Test Hulk" had made a mistake in interpreting the procedure and had forgotten to fill in a compulsory field. Small wonder all the test runs had failed. In order to redirect attacks like this I started work at 7 a.m. every morning and reported to the senior manager at 8.30 a.m.

In order to speed up the testing and the project it was also necessary to work weekends. To motivate the workers we had established care facilities for our children since we all had children of a similar age who were allowed to 'play office' with each other. My daughter enjoyed this and loved going with me to the office.

One Saturday night we had all been invited to the Senior Manager's house for drinks and afterward we would go to dinner in a restaurant. Arrangements had been made for my wife and me to join the senior manager at his table. Quite an honour. I did notice that at first my wife found it difficult to keep track of the conversation but the senior manager's wife was very kind to her. I sensed what was going on and decided to provide some general entertainment by telling funny anecdotes.

This was a very tiring project and I was always working and that was expected of me. The captain always needs to be on deck. The whole project took four years of frustration, overtime, tiredness and motivation. Fortunately my Senior Manager still supported me in all my decisions and took my advice. I was, therefore, able to reward people with nice extras for the wife and kids, a trip or a dinner all free of charge. Rewards like this had a motivating effect on the team.

By now everybody had noticed my influence with the Senior Manager and tried to make use of it. When the project eventually finished and the Basic System was implemented I was immensely proud. It had definitely given me grey hairs but victory was mine. Champagne never tasted so good. The ship could sail without problems in excellent conditions.

What I learned was that my belief in the importance of the project for the bank and the support of my senior manager had been very important in order to win. But that it was also important to keep a hands-on mentality. The team needs that and wants that. The extras were also a motivating factor.

If you are not convinced of your own ability to succeed, how can you expect other to do so? In order to be successful it is essential that you believe in your own success. And you will notice that when you start doubting yourself, results will decrease. This will become apparent in everything you do and will be noticed not in the least by those you have to manage.

If encountered by doubt, check whether your doubts are justified. If the latter is the case change the set-up into something you do believe in. The same thing goes for plans and issues contributed by others. Never go against the current but raise the issue with those involved. What is a successful approach for someone could be disastrous for another. Think about it and then do something about it.

Selling too much

Whenever we were working weekends we always ordered ready-made sandwiches from a cafeteria around the corner. The owner usually delivered our order to our building. We brought good custom.

Everybody loved his ready-made sandwiches, because of the high quality and extra filling. We appreciated that and kept ordering from him.

On one occasion when he made a delivery he conveyed to me that his business was a dream come true for him and his wife. They had wanted to start a cafeteria in the city centre for a long time and now it had finally come to pass. Both worked day and night to make a success of it.

Six months later when he came to make another delivery I noticed a sad look in his eyes. I asked him what the matter was. He told me this was his final delivery. Their business was bankrupt. I could not believe this, so I asked him what had happened.

He then told me that the inspector from the Inland Revenue (tax collector) had paid him a visit and he had according to the purchasing receipts (according to Dutch standard tax regulations) calculated how many ready-made sandwiches had been sold and how many cups of coffee according to the amount of sugar bags that had been sold etc. Only reality was different because the owner had put extra filling on his sandwiches to please his customers. As a result of this he had sold fewer sandwiches with less revenue than expected by the Inland Revenue. The owner had not been able to convince the tax people of the discrepancy in the revenue and the purchasing receipts. Subsequently he could not pay his taxes any more. Their dream was shattered!

I learned from this that sometimes you can be punished for being too good to your customers. I was genuinely upset and I wished I could have helped those people. We easily could have afforded to pay more for his services.

This story goes to show that a high level of service can also backfire. When in sales you need to build up your service level gradually. Too much service will put things in a wrong perspective. Service is an extra service added to the product. Service is intended to improve the functioning of the product. The first slice of cake tastes good; the tenth tends to be disappointing.

Earning more money can backfire

Because of my promotion to the position of Project Manager and the hard work and paid overtime we were now able to spend more money. I bought a bigger second-hand car (Citroen GS) and we added a new kitchen and a fireplace to our home. My father had designed the fireplace and had bricked it into our living room. All this building activity meant that we had to live upstairs for a while and it also meant that in addition to all the work I did at the bank I also did some of the renovating myself. Because of my evening classes my wife had been waiting for a renovation for ages and now the time had come to live up to my promises.

Our financial situation was improving which was not always a blessing. We lived in a working-class neighbourhood. Hard working honest people but not highly educated. When we were first married and still 'poor' we felt at ease among these people. Now that our situation was improving people became jealous and started to behave differently towards us. This became evident through negative remarks like "so now you don't want to have anything to do with us anymore" etc. etc. Not only people in our neighbourhood but also the family started behaving differently towards us.

We could now afford to buy more expensive clothes for our daughter. One day she arrived back home in tears and asked her mother if she could wear different clothes. It turned out the teacher had made a positive remark about her clothes, which had led to her being teased by her jealous 'friends'. They had even tried to tear apart her clothes.

In the evening I did some work at my daughter's school by serving on the Board of Governors implementing a new Dutch education law. Given my position at the school, people kept a closer eye on my daughter and she received more attention. I was also better informed on my daughter's progress.

In my spare time I wrote articles for our soccer club's monthly magazine along the lines of "people in and around the club". A couple of friends and I made up the editorial staff. Editorial meetings were great meetings full of jokes and fun and without any sense of structure. Usually five minutes before the meeting closed we put together a new magazine. Those evenings were a good remedy against stress.

My favourite church minister had retired. The new minister was a completely different person and a few dignitaries from the village were now in charge. I no longer felt at home with the church. I truly belied that my God is good and what I saw was that people were making a mess of things. I believe that there is something stronger and better than mankind and this something I call my God.

I no longer believed in the church as an institution. I still said my prayers every night before going to sleep and I never forgot. The content of my prayers changed to gratitude for everything I am allowed to do for others within my own limited means. God always came up with an answer albeit not always an easy one. Sometimes God opened my eyes in a very special way by showing me the other side of the coin first.

I tried to combine my busy working and social life as best as I could with my family life. I was almost always at home at dinnertime and would devote my full attention to my daughter. Later at night, before turning in my wife and I would discuss the day's events whilst enjoying a nightcap.

As times passed by it turned out that our marriage was troubled. My wife had given up on evening school and we inevitably grew apart. She no longer accompanied me to the business dinners and parties that were an important part of my job. She never felt at ease in 'my surroundings' because she could not take part in the conversation and felt lonely most of the time. On the one hand she wanted to be de the lady of the house, but she did not feel like making an effort.

Our conversations always evolved around her problems with her family and friends. We never discussed my problems at work and the like. It almost seemed as if she was not at all interested which is why I stopped talking about my work altogether. It took a lot of energy and I got nothing in return. The balance in our relationship was disturbed and us being together no longer had any added value. I blamed myself because to me it had been so important to have a career and education. My wife had helped me in achieving my goals by giving up her career as a hairdresser and running the home and raising our daughter instead. For this she deserved my full respect.

In those days I still played soccer in a lower ranked team consisting of friends. The older we got, the more important the 'third half' became. After the match we raised hell by having three beers to start with and then sing Dutch traditional songs at the top of our voices. Our singing set the pace of events and we had a great time.

All the men on the team had become fathers and our children were always present. Our matches meant party time to them. There were always chips, soda and sweets to be had and my daughter enjoyed coming with me to the soccer matches. On those occasions I never talked about my work, which was something most appreciated. I was able to help out some of them with sound advice. However, also some of my soccer mates could not hide their jealousy. I hated that because as far as I was concerned my behaviour had not changed in any way.

I learned that a fast career and increasing salary drove a wedge between my wife, family, the friends and me. I could not and would not stop it because this was the path I had chosen.

If you want to achieve something you have to make an effort. The best approach is in harmony with your surroundings. If that is not possible and you still want to reach your goal, you always have to persevere even if it has an effect on the choices you made earlier. People will always respond from their own perspective. Everyone has his own set of values.

Selling as a real manager

The big Basic Project had been completed successfully, which put an end to the dynamic life and unhealthy duress inherent in the position of project manager. I now fell into a sort of limbo. A reorganisation of the Organisation and Automation department had been announced and the department would now focus on the maintenance of operating, recently implemented systems.

My Senior Manager, responsible for the Organisation and Automation department had been promoted to the Board of Directors because of the success of the implementation of the Basic Project. He was very grateful for the work I had done as a Project Manager and promoted me to head of the Development and Maintenance Department (The Project bureau). I was now line manager of about eighty internal and about thirty external workers.

This was an enormous step up the ladder because I now became the manager of my own manager and manager of colleagues I had worked with up till then. I structured the department and appointed managers to the best of my ability and in such a way that we could perform as a team. It was interesting to note that everybody seemed to grant me my promotion. People thought I deserved the promotion for all the hard work I had done. As a manager I automatically joined the bank's Automation Steering Committee.

This new position was a whole different ball game. Until then I had only been responsible for the realisation of projects, but now I was responsible for the whole line and had to deal with H&R procedures, costs, budgets, investments, contacts with suppliers etc. etc. Not an easy job and I was running from one appointment to the other from early morning till late in the evening.

Fortunately I also had two secretaries at my disposal, who relieved me of many menial tasks. I learned much in a short time span and I had to learn to read and understand things fast. Also on the plus side was the fact that I had come from within the organisation and had completed an important project, so many subjects were known to me.

On many occasions I had to prepare for meetings and draw up responses and proposals at home. I had my affairs well organised which meant that many colleagues came to see me to consult documents and to ask for updates on upcoming decisions in the steering committee.

Because of my extended knowledge of the organisation and systems, my position in the Steering Committee was an important one. Yet, the work was now much more focused on maintenance of the systems than devising new ones.

My major problem was to keep staff motivated and keep them at the company. In those days many automation experts were lured away by software companies with fancy lease cars and big financial rewards. The main challenge was to make sure that people enjoyed their work and to accomplish this I always had to be available, even when they were working weekends. I had to solve both their business and private problems and motivate them with my presence, but even more by paying attention to them. At some point I felt more like a minister, preacher, imam, father, brother and good friend than their senior manager. This was not always easy I have to say.

My new Senior Manager had gained his experience by working for many years for our hardware supplier. So now he was a Senior Manager but my colleagues and I could not help wondering how he could afford the car he was driving on his pay. We had our doubts about who was footing his bills. He, however, did not know the first thing about software development and depended heavily on my input.

When I had first been appointed and had in turn proposed my managers for appointment, he had told me that the Head of the Programming Division was not up to his task. I totally agreed with him. He then asked me to dismiss the Head of the Programming Division. I went to discuss the matter with the Head of the Programming Division and he told me that two months earlier he had had a positive assessment from the Senior Manager. He was quite surprised to find that things were different now. And rightly so.

I was dumbfounded and confronted my manager with the recent events. He beat about the bush and I suggested giving the Head of Programming three months to get his act together. I would compile a list of points of improvement and we would go through the list together and evaluate progress in three months time. The way my manager had failed to confront the Head of the Programming Division was not the correct way to treat people. In this way I learned a thing or two about my manager.

A truly brilliant programmer showed up late for work every morning. He did fill in his time sheet correctly, but was never on time. One day he asked me for an interview. During our conversation he asked me for a rise. He had talked to some friends who had a lease car and higher salary from the company they worked for. I pointed out to him the differences between working at a bank and working for a software company and also that if he tried hard; he had a brilliant career ahead of him and could continue to learn.

I did comment upon his habit of turning up late for work. He did get my point but wanted to cut a deal anyway. He proposed that I should give him a rise if he showed up on time for work. He was in the wrong and still wanted to cut a deal.

Nevertheless, I looked at him and promised to give him a rise if he managed to show up at work on time for a month and that is what happened.

I had also appointed manager one of my colleagues who had taken the AMBI test with me and had been employed at the bank for a long time. We had never been on friendly terms and he actually thought he could do the job I did and indicated that he was after my position. I did appoint him manager so I could keep an eye on him. Many of his subordinates complained about him. He was incapable of delegating and still interfered with details.

I decided to have a conversation with him and discuss his performance. One day before this conversation was to take place, though, something really tragic happened to his family. Their new-born daughter died of cot death. A horrible and tragic event. You do not want this to happen to anyone. It distressed me deeply and when I attended the funeral and saw the little white coffin I decided to postpone the interview till next year. Other options had to be investigated and I did not feel like kicking someone who was already down.

I learned that it was very important as a line manager to be well informed and have experience of life. The most important thing is to love people and respect them, no matter what they do. For me it was impossible to be a hard-boiled manager.

It's all sales

A starting sales person wants to start off at the top. He is single-minded and wants to show everyone he is the best. A sales person needs to grow, though, and learn through experience. By means of ups and downs he will find his own way to proceed. Take your time. A good sales manager will be aware of the hidden qualities of his sales staff. And if you possess those qualities you will get the chance to show them. First of all you need to acquire as much general knowledge, business related knowledge and experience of life as possible. Make sure that you know everything there is to know about your line of business and the market. Read the trade journals and keep abreast of current affairs.

Reaching an agreement with the neighbours

We now lived in the third of six terraced houses. We were not free in our movements because whenever we were sitting in our garden the neighbours were there as well and we felt more or less obliged to talk to them. In addition to that, you could overhear other people's conversations literally. Nothing could be done about this because this was inherent in the type of house we lived in. For our daughter this situation proved to be a blessing because she could play with the children next door and there was always someone around to keep an eye on them.

My daughter was best friends with a girl from the same neighbourhood. They always played together and it was fun watching them. On occasion the friend used to stay for dinner. But before accepting the invitation to dinner she would always ask what was on the menu. When we told her, her standard reply would be" I don't care for that". I had already nicknamed her 'Lizzy doesn't care for that'. We always made sure we had a jar of applesauce in the house since that was about the only thing she did care for.

On our left lived a family of five. They belonged to the orthodox reformed church and on Sundays they went to church twice or even three times a day. He was a teacher at a school for orthodox reformed children. We were not close and on Sundays their children were not allowed to go out and had to stay indoors.

Once on a Saturday evening we had spur-of-the-moment party with my soccer mates on account of us winning the championships. We played sing-a-long music and sang along at the top of our voices. At twelve a.m. sharp there was a loud banging on the wall. This was our neighbour's way of telling us we had to stop partying because now the day of the Lord had started. We saw no other way but to put a stop to our party since having the police on your doorstep was not an option. I hated the whole situation and I could not help but feel that others were telling me what I could and could not do. That was definitely not the way I wanted to live my life.

Two weeks later on a hot Sunday morning I went outside to read the paper. I noticed that the woman next door and her children were sitting outside huddled closely together and whispering lest others would notice they were out of doors on a Sunday. Her husband had already gone to church. This was a moment I had been waiting for and I shouted "Good morning neighbours, lovely weather for the time of year isn't it?" That startled her and in two minutes flat she and her children had disappeared inside the house waiting for the husband to return. Living in a neighbourhood where people are envious and anxious that you do what others expect of you went against my grain. It went against my sense of personal freedom and the principle of 'live and let live'.

I learned that my educational background, which had resulted in a better position and more spending money had an effect on my family and our surroundings. It made me start thinking about the future for my family.

Also in sales you will encounter people with a different outlook on life. It is important to accept these people for what they are. If, however, they say or do things that go against your beliefs and convictions then it is allowed to confront them. But if you do so, always keep your own interests in mind. Winning an argument can lead to the end of a relationship.

Selling a project to the Inland Revenue

Because of forces in the market my job as manager of a large developing and controlling department meant I had more to do with H&R issues than working on projects as a project manager. Somehow I had the feeling that I was near the end of my career in automation. I had never been involved in strategic studies or had defined policy regarding automation issues. I experienced this as a missing piece of the jigsaw puzzle. Apart from the above, I also acted as super controller of the systems that were already running.

When a reorganisation was announced with regard to the implementation of the SDM[5] method and my large department was to be split up in a smaller sub division with project leaders and information analysts and a larger sub division that was to build systems, it was clear for me which way to turn. My friend, the Organisation and Automation Director asked me because of all the good work I had done as a manager to become Head of the System Building Department. I told him that I would rather be considered for the position of Head of the smaller Project Managers and Information Analysts division. My decision surprised him but he respected and accepted it.

In my position of Project Manager I became responsible for the development and construction of a Personnel Information System. This system was to be developed in collaboration with a supplier who would be allowed to put the system on the market once it had been implemented at the bank. The bank would receive a percentage of each system sold as return on its investment. I also became Project Manager of a new system for the execution of foreign money transfer. The faxes containing foreign payments from the different offices sent to the main office had to be converted into digital transactions and forwarded to the international system (used by all banks) to be processed. It was also possible to send a message through the system to all faxes at the different offices. This project had reached the test phase and the deadline was set at the following weekend 12 a.m. After that point in time the international system would no longer accept faxed transactions. The final product acceptance tests were planned on the Saturday prior to the deadline on Sunday.

On the Friday afternoon preceding the deadline I was at the head office preparing for the product acceptance test the following day. And on that day something terrible and unforgettable happened. At 4 p.m. the bank was raided

---

[5] System Development Method

by the police and Inland Revenue (tax) Inspectors, followed closely by a television crew. They were after 'money laundering activities' at the bank.

All employees were treated as criminals and nobody was to leave the department. I saw colleagues who had been working for the good of the bank to the best of their ability crying at their desks. The tax inspectors confiscated the entire financial administration of the bank. Through this raid the Inland Revenue Inspectors were to prove their point to financial institutions that they were serious about the clamp down on the 'money laundering circuit'

The whole situation left me with a serious problem because I had a test run to perform on the next day, otherwise we might as well close the bank altogether that following Monday. I managed to speak to the district attorney. I explained the importance of the test run to the bank and that we had to meet the deadline. He understood more or less the importance of the test run and accompanied me to the office of the responsible Managing Director.

At the directors' gallery I saw the signs with the names of the different directors on the doors. There had to be a leak, somebody from on the inside must have passed on information to the Inland Revenue inspectors. It had to be. When we entered the room a couple of policemen were clearing out the desk of the Managing Director and the content was put in boxes. The Managing Director was standing there, burning with rage. The district attorney managed to calm him down and let me explain the matter in hand. The managing director thanked me for taking the initiative and made arrangements for us to carry out the test run and start production with the new system.

The raid on the bank had made it to the news headlines on television. I arrived home later that night and whilst parking my car in front of the house I noticed some of our neighbours opening their curtains and staring at me. They knew the bank they had seen on the news employed me and they probably suspected I had already been arrested. The whole situation made me feel bad.

The next day we worked at the bank amidst policemen who looked after us and provided us with coffee and sandwiches. On the Sunday the District Attorney and the Director-general of the bank paid us a visit. They asked whether we had been able to get the system up and running successfully. Fortunately we could tell them we had succeeded to do just that. Next, they asked us to send a message through the new system to all fax machines at the different offices to inform them that all offices should open their doors to customers on Monday. Who would have thought that this would be the first message to be sent through the new system!

That particular Monday the newspaper featured a photo of my colleague and me while we were testing the computer system on Sunday. The newspaper had added the heading to the photo that people had been working very hard over the weekend to make sure certain information would not fall into the hands of the Inland Revenue inspectors. Complete rubbish of course. I was so upset I immediately cancelled my subscription to the newspaper.

I did learn a few valuable lessons from this. Through external events your life can be turned upside down and because you have no control, it can make you feel powerless. It is, however, also important to keep a clear head under difficult circumstances and keep doing what needs to be done, something I had learned whilst in the army. In addition I would never trust a journalist again. They created news.

Throughout your entire live you will have to deal with other people. What they think of you or say about you is something beyond your control. How you deal with it and to what extent you let it get to you is up to you. Your thoughts are your own and your own thoughts are what you make of them. In Sales you will often come across this situation because you will be influenced by people from within your own organisation and your customers. It is up to you to decide whether you let these people influence you or not. Consider the pros and cons on a daily basis.

Selling a move

I felt I had run into a deep personal crisis. I had the feeling I was no longer in charge of my own life. Everybody wanted me to play the part they had assigned me. At work I was the super system Comptroller and they expected from me a sense of humour, motivation and extended knowledge about the existing computer systems. My private life was determined by my surroundings, in-laws and my own family. My daughter's school determined when I could go on holiday, how we celebrated Christmas etc. On the soccer pitch they expected beer, jokes, motivation and advice from me. My neighbours envied my position and I also had to be careful not to talk about my work and my career.

My marriage was also at a low. My wife lived her own life with her mother who lived in the next street. She did run the home but refused to learn anything new. The feeling dawned upon me that all I did was give but got nothing in return. She did not understand the first thing about my work and its importance. She just was not interested and needed all her energy for herself and our daughter. That is why I thought it best if we would refrain from having more children. She simply could not have handled having more children. I was growing while her development had come to a complete standstill.

Sometimes I felt I could have a better conversation with my secretaries than with my own wife. I did respect her, though, for all she had done to enable me to study and get ahead in life.

I was happy with my daughter, though. We were good fiends and loved each other very much. I tried to spend as much time with her as possible.

I was suffering and I could not talk to anyone about it. Nobody was aware of how I felt because I only discussed my problems with my big friend, my God. I prayed to him on many occasions and thanked him for everything he had given me. I also told him that I felt miserable and at the same time ungrateful. Every time I had had one these heart to heart talks with my God, I would wake up the next morning with answers to my questions.

My God told me that I was not making any more progress. My life had become a drag and everything I did was based on what I already new. Others were dictating my life and because of that I had lost my true self. I had to regain my strength and had to learn more about myself and learn to say 'NO' if necessary. I had to take control again and not be led by others and try to please others all the time. Not everybody had to love me. My God gave me strength to see it through.

One of those nights I had the strangest of dreams. I dreamt that I was walking with two men behind the central station in our capital. Whilst talking we entered a restaurant. I had never seen the two men before in my life and at that time I did not recognise the train station or the city.

Later one night the phone rang. I was being approached by a head-hunter. He asked me whether I would be interested in working for one of the top five banks in the country. As it turned out he knew quite a lot about me and the job I had done and he offered me a 40% pay rise. This was a great opportunity because I knew exactly which bank he meant and that bank had the reputation for being an automation paradise. It was quite an honour to be asked to come and work for that bank. Of course I started negotiations with the head-hunter straight away.

The smile was back on my face once more and I knew that the recent turn of events would have quite a few consequences for my family and me. We would have to move to a small town close to the capital. I felt I did not have a choice, not if a wanted to get ahead.

I discussed the proposition with my wife and daughter. For my wife this move would mean that she would live far away from her mother and family. Much to my surprise she said she would enjoy moving for she would be able to spend more money and buy new furniture for our new house. I guess that at that point in time she did not understand how her life would change. My daughter also liked the idea of moving.

The lesson I kept learning again and again was that whenever I was in trouble, my God would always see me through the worst.

Religion is an important issue. Believing is in actual fact believing in you. The form you choose is not that important. It is all about wanting to achieve something. Call it praying, meditating, trance it is all about being able to communicate with yourself. By being in touch with yourself a second force will arise, a force that will show itself every time you decide to communicate with yourself. It will give confidence, inspiration, hope and creativity. It may seem a strange thing to do but try to overcome your hesitation and experience the revelation of a new inner strength.

Not everybody can be bought

My friend the Managing Director of the Organisation and Automation Department and I were very different people. He was already rich because of his father's company and in comparison I was a poor man. When he talked about cutting costs he meant asking the girl who did the ironing to come less often. I had to renovate my own house and mow my own lawn. We lived in completely different worlds but that was also what held the attraction. If he believed in you, you could always count on him. This was exactly what I needed to reach my goals but also his goals with regard to the bank. I, therefore, enjoyed working for him.

On many occasions we also discussed personal matters. I remember having an argument with him once in which he stated that anything could be bought with the right amount of money. I had my doubts about that and when he sensed this he became slightly angry and stressed his opinion that anything could be bought with money. I could not believe it and it was not an argument I would easily forget.

I was excited about the new job prospects with another bank because of the head-hunter that had approached me. And what was more; the manager of that particular bank was also interested in hiring me. They had made me a splendid offer, even including removal and furnishing costs. I felt proud because the bank was interested in me. I decided to accept the offer and embrace the new challenge.

I made an appointment with the Managing Director of the Organisation and Automation Department and told him I had found and accepted a position elsewhere. He responded by immediately offering me a new position within the bank and to match the salary of my prospective employer. He once again asked me to think about it over the weekend.

This time I did not get drunk. He had offered me a position as a direct advisor to him and other members of the board of directors. This was not what I wanted. As an advisor I would still be the super Comptroller of the computer system and advice could be ignored. I was too young for a position like that. I needed a challenge. Moreover, I had not planned to stay on at the bank. Nothing at the bank could motivate me anymore.

The following Monday I told the Managing Director that I would not accept his proposition and would leave the bank. For the first time ever I could tell by the look on his face that he was genuinely upset. He had not expected this to happen because he was used to winning and could not accept defeat. I looked at him and reminded him of our argument about whether people could be bought.

I could not resist telling him that I, for one, could not be bought. He looked at me, astonishment clearly showing on his face, smiled and shook his head.

After more than 12 years I was to leave the bank and my secretary and colleagues had organised a wonderful farewell party with plenty of special presents and profound speeches. And then it occurred to me that I was the first Automation employee to leave the bank out of my own free will and not because of illness or dismissal.

The Managing Director also came to say a few words and promised that I would always be welcome to return to the bank. His words made me feel appreciated and also made me feel small. I finally realised how important this man had been to me. This sign of appreciation was what I had worked for all these years. And now that I finally received it felt good. When I left with all the presents I felt empty, but free at the same time.

The lesson that I learned was that it is important to go your own way no matter what. Nobody owns you and you cannot be bought! Never look back!

In your career there will always be people who have an influence on you in one way or the other. The lesson that can be learned from the above is, always be aware of the goals you want to reach. Plan carefully and check regularly whether you are still on the right track. Do not let anyone persuade you to change track. Consider every suggestion others may offer but the decision is yours. Too often we try to comply with other people's wishes and lose sight of our own plans.

There is no such thing as a free lunch

And so I started my new job and a new challenge with one of the largest banks in The Netherlands. My new position was Automation Account Manager for the Payment Division. I had to take over the job from another Account Manager, who was to move to another division in a similar position.

When I first started out I was quite disappointed. I was to work in an open plan office without my own secretary and amidst other Automation colleagues. Only managers had their own offices in this division. I soon realised that I had to start all over again for nobody knew anything about me. All I had brought were my knowledge and my winner's mentality. I had to sell myself once more. The high financial reward was the only thing that could motivate me when I first started there.

My colleague helped me to sell myself to the bank. And believe me, his approach was quite something else. To start with, this colleague never showed up on time, in fact he never arrived at work before 11 a.m. If you informed after his whereabouts nobody knew exactly where he was. Management did not check his comings and goings. From his colleagues I heard a number of not altogether positive stories about him.

One day this colleague asked me which bathroom I used. I told him I always used the one on the left-hand side. "And that's where you go wrong" he said. "You should use the one on the right-hand side because that's where all the senior managers go. In there it will be much easier to get in touch with them." Another piece of advice he gave me concerned lunch. "If a supplier wants to meet you, always make an appointment around lunchtime because they will take you out to lunch and foot the bill."

On top of that he was also an expert at attending meetings that were important to him and frequented by important managers. He always positioned himself in the front row and made himself heard. And if the meeting was about an important project, he always made sure everyone knew he was involved in it. I hated his approach because I still had this principle that end-users and not Automation experts practised company politics. He was not well liked by his end-users and only the management of the Automation Division seemed to be blind to his ways. To me his approach was unacceptable and I did not intend to copy it. I would have to find my own way.

Given his approach to work it was by no means difficult to take over his tasks because he hardly did any work at all and kept himself busy by playing at being project manager. It was easy for me to do a better job and provide better service to the end-users, my customers.

There was one new and interesting aspect to my new job. In The Netherlands consumer payments were free of charge. In order to control the costs the banks had developed a combined infrastructure and had created systems for efficient and effective payment services. A central organisation set up by the combined banks supervised all this.

I had been appointed representative for our bank and I served on many different Committees, project and working groups of the combined banks. In addition to that, I was, of course, also responsible for the implementation of those projects with my own bank. All this I enjoyed and my projects received much attention because my bank wanted to keep up with the other banks. For me this proved to be an ideal way to meet many people working for different banks and to create networking opportunities.

There was a certain hierarchy involved whenever the combined banks convened. The largest bank and the largest shareholder were to do most of the talking and since I represented the number-five-bank in The Netherlands I was allowed to contribute to these talks as number five and certainly no more. I had to know my place. It was good that I figured out how this system worked from the start because it had an enormous influence on the decision-making process.

When I first started in my new job with this large bank I was sent on an internship with one of the local branches of the bank. Whilst talking to the branch manager I understood that there was quite a discrepancy between the way people thought in the local branch offices and those employed at Head Office. He told me and provided proof to back up his claims that there was lots of money up for grabs. Only procedures and lack of understanding prevented him from actually grabbing the money. I meant to do something about that.

What I learned was that some people are self-serving and do not care about their customers. This approach went against the grain with me and I did not want to operate like that myself.

When a company expands, internal systems develop that do not always benefit co-operation. As a result of that, it happens often that informal systems are created that can damage continuity. Especially when these informal systems are used to do damage. The colleague mentioned in the story above is very well capable of connecting with people, unfortunately he does not use his talents for the good of the company he works for. A salesperson benefits from having lots of different contacts, so he will have to do his utmost to connect with people. The more contacts he has the more opportunity to get his story across. Also internal contacts are vital, so also be creative when it comes to meeting new people.

Selling projects in a large organisation

The transference of running projects from the previous Account Manager of the Payment Division to me had been completed. I had to prove my worth to the organisation of end-users and show them what I could do for them. The opportunity to do so arose sooner than expected.

The Dutch Consumer Watchdog had discovered that our bank was the only bank that did not print the currency date on bank statements. The bank was accused of stealing currency days from consumers, meaning that it was not clear what consumers had to pay for services rendered by the bank. The Board of Directors had decided during emergency consultations that the currency dates had to be printed on bank statements as soon as possible. A high priority project and since I was the Payment Division Project Manager, I was put in charge of it.

This was not an easy job because a number of running systems had to be adapted. These systems were operated by a number of senior operators who really hated the idea that they had to adjust their existing applications. They had designed the systems in the past and were reluctant to adjust them because of possible fallout.

Those two senior operators, who we had nicknamed Laurel and Hardy after the two famous comedians, were difficult to approach. They wielded a certain amount of power in the organisation because of their knowledge of the old system and they were not averse to abusing their authority on occasion. They were not into solving problems but were good at adding new problems to the already existing ones.

I was fortunate in the sense that they had assigned a very clever external programmer to my division. He was a Medical School graduate and also held a degree in Highway Engineering, yet for some strange reason he had chosen to work as a programmer for a software developer. I had explained my problems to him and he immediately set to work. When we finally had arranged a meeting with 'Laurel and Hardy' both gentlemen started to throw obstacles in our way and bent over backwards to tell us that the adjustments were impossible. My clever programmer then opened his bag and presented them with a number of listings for one of the programmes and pointed out the adjustments to 'Laurel and Hardy'. They were completely baffled to say the least, and could not do anything else but accept the adjustments and implement them.

However, when the adjusted programmes were tested one of the many programmes contained an error. The programmer had forgotten to put a dot after a Cobol Statement. In situations like this 'Murphy's law' always applies because from that point on, anything that could go wrong, did go wrong. The Senior Manager of the Development Division was furious and demanded that the programmer would be fired on the spot. This Senior Manager did not know the first thing about Automation and had only been appointed because of his title and ability to go through the motions of being a manager. Fortunately I managed to explain to him the principles of 'Murphy's law' and the whole affair ended with a compliment for the clever programmer.

Our bank was known for its innovative and progressive approach and this became obvious on numerous occasions. Since I was responsible for inter-banking projects I could always count on the support of the Board of Directors. My bank always wanted to finish its projects first and show other banks that they were ahead of the game.

One of those inter-banking projects was the realisation of Rush Payment Processing (Rush Payment Service) between banks. I had taken over this project from my predecessor. In order to complete the project, a system had been set up in the central combined organisation all banks had to log on to. This did mean, however, that by just pushing one single button a large amount of money could be transferred to another bank.

I was worried about the security aspects surrounding these transfers. I was used to having the Internal Accountant Services or an Audit Committee involved in systems like these and they would impose strict safety measures on the system and its operators. Not one single safety regulator was involved in this important project and that really surprised me. I contacted the Secretary to the Manager Internal Accountant Services, told her it concerned an urgent matter and arranged a meeting. Afterwards I was told getting an appointment with this manager was quite an achievement.

Fortunately he did take the time to listen to my assessment of possible risks the bank was facing. I also gave my opinion on how the Internal Accountant Services or an Audit Committee should be involved in projects like this. He asked me to put together a presentation and present the project to all those employed by his division. (Twenty chartered accountants).

I informed my technical designer of the upcoming presentation. He was an accomplished cartoonist and immediately designed a huge octopus for me and to every tentacle he assigned a department and division that was part of the huge, complex octopus, the octopus being the project. In the right-hand corner he then drew a small octopus and put the name of the Internal Accountant Services in it.

I decided to include the octopus design in my presentation. The Octopus design said it all. I now had three slides, two about the project and the Octopus design. When I had to perform in front of the chartered accountants and showed them the Octopus design, you could have heard a pin drop. There was no further need to explain things and I could count on all the support I needed to complete the project.

Some of the project manager had noticed my approach as a Project Manager and awarded me the honorary title 'no-nonsense Project Manager'. And for the first time I did not have to work overtime to complete projects, for at this bank working overtime was not allowed.

I once again learned to sell myself at a new bank, using the knowledge and experience I had gained over the years. I learned to rely on my knowledge and experience and I went my own way. My eagerness to win and achieve my goals was my motivation.

It's all sales

Every move a salesperson makes is a new start. Every time he will be put to the test. This requires concentration on everything he undertakes. One good monthly or weekly result does not mean your work is done, because there is always a next week or month. Never lean back, no, every day is a new one in which you have to prove yourself. Who ever said selling was easy?

Buying and selling a house

As a result of one of the conditions that were part of my new job I had to move to a house within a 20 mile (30 kilometres) distance of the Head Office within the year. The bank would pay for the removal and part of the furnishing costs. I had collected all council brochures of towns close to the capital in order to select a house.

We did not want to live in the capital itself because we wanted our daughter to grow up in a smaller town with a bit more social control. So I started devising itineraries and selecting houses we could check out. Every weekend we went 'house hunting'.

This whole 'house hunting' business was not easy and at some point we got fed up with it. Our daughter no longer wanted to accompany us, which definitely ruined some of the fun. At some point we did get a useful hint from a real estate broker who told us that a house had become available for a price that would fit into our budget.

A divorced doctor's wife owned the house. Her dog, a black Bouvier des Flandres, followed us while we walked through the house. My daughter clearly liked the dog and as soon as we left she said, "Daddy, we should buy this house, I want to live here! And I want a dog like that as well". We bought the house and at weekends we were busy renovating the house. Once again my father was of great help.

Now that we had found ourselves a new home, we could sell our own house. There were already quite a few bids. Behind our house a few garages were located and one of them came with our house. One of my neighbours wanted to buy the garage 'cash in hand'. The real estate broker and solicitor saw no objections and we sold the garage separately.

These were hard and emotional times for me. I left home every morning at 7 a.m. by car and would not return until 7 or 8 p.m. unless there were any traffic jams or other problems en route. In addition to that, owning two houses and the sales process of one of them and the necessity to prove myself in a new job was wearing me out. Driving to and from work for three to four hours every single day was having its effect on my stamina and energy level.

My friends from the soccer team had organised a farewell match between my current team and the team I had started out with all those years ago. It was a highly emotional and fun event. And as usual the 'third half 'of the match that took place in the canteen was the highlight of the match. I decided to give up playing soccer altogether.

During the summer holidays we moved into our new home so my daughter could start at a new school after the holidays. We also bought her a beautiful fair Bouvier dog even though we had to wait for another six weeks until the dog could join the family. My daughter called the dog 'Bobo'.

The lesson I had learned was that I had to devote a lot of time and energy to my family, our new home and new surroundings. I spent a lot of time to create a desirable social environment for my family. It was definitely a blessing that I no longer had to work overtime and could reduce my time commuting.

All changes people go through, also the changes your customers go through need to be prepared. Changes involving for example packaging, construction, quantity, redevelopment of a product, delivery time, day of delivery, visiting days, they all matter. Do not take up the matter lightly because you never now how something which seems insignificant to you can be of the utmost importance to a customer. To trivialise these matters could have big consequences. People need to get used to changes. This has something to do with the fact that people are creatures of habit. Sudden changes can pose a threat and you could encounter resistance. Tread carefully when dealing with changes.

Selling 'plastic currency' in The Netherlands

In the entrance hall of our Head Office two cash points from different suppliers had been placed for test purposes. The Head Office employees had all been given plastic cards and could withdraw money from these cash points[6]. As Project Manager for the Payments Division I was responsible for this test project.

I tried to gain more in-depth knowledge about the cash point system by reading marketing reports from which I could conclude that the use of cash points by Dutch consumers would not be successful. That is what my bank thought. Consumers would not be able to deal with a plastic card with access code and would rather withdraw money from their local branch office. In addition to that, the operating costs of these cash points would be so high, that in order to make the machines profitable bank branch offices would have to be closed.

The combined banks started to get worried. The Dutch 'Postbank' (the number one bank in The Netherlands) was their main competitor and those involved were afraid the 'Postbank' would install cash points. The combined banks decided to install cash points without the 'Postbank'. To keep down costs the combined banks then decided to allow customers of other banks to use their cash points (guest use). Less cash points would have to be installed and the machines would be profitable faster. The banks would settle transfer costs and guest use among themselves. In order to realise all this, a system had to be constructed at the central organisation of the combined banks.

Already a project had been started at the central bank organisation, and in study groups people were already discussing the magnetic tape strip on the bankcard. One of the main topics of discussion was the security aspect concerning the card, access code and cash points. Most of those present were technical experts delegated by the banks.

Because of threats from the competition the project now received all possible attention from the combined banks. The banks delegated an increasing number of different experts to the work and study groups. Project managers, information analysts and banking professionals, replaced the technical experts who had been very knowledgeable with regard to security and the magnetic tape strip. I was delegated by my bank with the mission to complete the project in a way that would do justice to the bank's innovative reputation.

---

[6] A cash point is known as an ATM in American English

It was quite funny because the technical experts knew all there was to know about the magnetic tape strip and the access code but had forgotten all this was part of a larger scheme, the central system. Also, the larger banks wishing to install cash points, had to buy or build their own system in order to operate the cash points.

On an internal level the project went like clockwork. I was supported all the way by Management and in a short period of time we selected a computer (non-stop) and a standard system for the settlement of cash point transfers. This was an interesting process because when two other major banks discovered that we had already selected a computer they, without even so much as investigating the matter, bought the same hardware and software system. Yes, competition was rife, although we did co-operate.

Slowly but surely I realised how important security surrounding these systems was. It was a costly business to produce bankcards with access codes. If and when fraud was committed it could mean the end of the bank. Much was at stake and the pressure to realise the required safety measures was mounting.

Once the project had been completed successfully the Combined Banks Organisation organised an information meeting for the smaller banks. I was invited to address the meeting and I had to tell the banks that to install the cash points would prove too expensive for them. However, they could provide their customers with bankcards and access codes so their customers could withdraw their money from cash points owned by the larger banks. Of course at a 'guest use' rate.

The combined banks and the Postbank (with a completely different system) carefully started installing cash points in The Netherlands. And a miracle happened because consumers all over the country wanted to use the cash points and no longer went to the local branch offices. They would rather queue for half an hour than pay a visit to their local branch just around the corner. This led to a race between the combined banks and the Postbank to install cash points.

What I had to learn all over again is how misleading market research can be because what the customer says is not always what the customer does. The ease and anonymity with which people could now make cash withdrawals 24 hours a day made the customer embrace the cash point. I felt proud to have contributed to this.

Although properly carried out market research does not guarantee success, discarding the process can prove to be precarious. Take for example feasibility studies. If you are too much engrossed in your own product idea you might perceive your ideas as the truth. Or you do not carry out market research at all, or your tunnel vision is that strong that you view the outcome of research in your own light. It remains important that before you introduce a product in the market you carry out proper feasibility research. What remains is that you need to keep an open mind with regard to the results of market research and whether the results fit in with what you had in mind.

The market and the personal Computer (PC)

Completely out of the blue it was there. The Personal Computer. In my life in Automation the PC represented a true miracle. IBM had responded to its competitors Commodore and Apple by introducing PCs and setting-up a whole new division to produce these PCs.

It was almost impossible to grasp. I now had a computer on my desk with the same memory capacity as the computer I used to operate and which had taken up an entire room. A technological tour de force.

The trade journals had devoted a lot of attention to the PC but nobody really knew what to do with a PC. Most companies worked with a mainframe computer, which was linked up to terminals on employees' desks. Of course only on desks of those responsible for the computer input. True mainframe adepts were against PCs and did not like the idea one bit. PCs? Only suitable for playing games.

The first PC applications were for word processing, spread sheets and presentations. But the PC became an overnight success and the PC changed the entire workplace. Everyone wanted a PC on his desk, which made the PC the best tool to sell Information Technology (IT) to a company. Sponsored Private PC projects were established to help people own a PC and be able to operate it.

At my innovative bank I was introduced to the PC in a special way. One day on arrival at the office I was surprised to find an IBM Personal Computer on a table in the corner of our room.

We knew nothing about it and had not been informed beforehand. We were instructed to 'fool around' and at the same time find out to what use we could put it at the bank. An unlimited assignment! My curiosity and enthusiasm turned me into a genuine PC adept.

It is undoubtedly a wonderful development that has led to the fact that most people now own a PC and can reach out to the whole world through the Internet. Nobody could have predicted this.

Unfortunately IBM had forgotten to produce a good operating system to accompany their computers. Another smart manufacturer filled this gap rather quickly.

I learned that I found the fast developments in Automation fascinating and it motivated me to such an extent that I wanted to be ahead of all the others when it came to applying new computer technology. I kept learning by attending seminars and reading trade journals. Innovation was in my blood.

If people were not curious, development would come to a standstill. In sales you always have to be curious. Always gathering information about your customers, competitors, developments in the market, and developments in your sales area. By being curious you will discover new things, that you can develop yourself, so that this can lead to another subject for someone else.

Selling family life in a new village

We had now moved to a small village not too far from the capital city of The Netherlands. We lived in a semi-detached house in the more recent part of the village but at a walking distance from the sports centre, the playing fields and the school my daughter attended. Feeling the atmosphere in this village was a wonderful experience.

In the village we used to live in, it was normal for people to interfere in other people's personal life. People were judgmental and someone who displayed what was judged 'inappropriate' behaviour was no longer part of the community. People almost constantly talking about you behind your back and others tried to determine how you should live your life.

In my new village freedom was the rule. You could do whatever you wanted as long as you did not bother anyone else. People appreciated it if you were different and did not judge you. If there were anything they did not like they would confront you immediately and sort things out. I thrived in an atmosphere like this.

Because of my new job I had more time available to become a part of this new community. So I set about making our home cosy, visit new shopping centres, getting to know our neighbours and introducing my wife and daughter in the new community. We actually lived in what they called in the village the 'Posh Area' ,which meant that we had to adjust.

Our next-door neighbour was a kind woman who took my wife to the tennis club and told her not to spend so much time on running the home, but behave more like a lady of leisure. My wife accepted this new approach and after a while took tennis lessons, made friends of her own. That is how she became a part of the village community.

For my daughter things were a bit more difficult. She was enrolled in a school with kids that had known each other for years. Instead of taking a back seat and see how things would develop she aimed at confrontation and wanted to prove herself. One of the girls in the class was the natural leader and of course my daughter challenged her authority in the classroom. Whenever something unjust happened my daughter would be the first to challenge that. Her teacher could not deal with it and did not understand why my daughter always had to be so passionate in her response.

That year our village's was to celebrate its 900 anniversary and many festivities had been planned among which a junior imitation competition. My daughter was a huge Madonna fan and at home always danced to her songs and enjoyed doing so.

My daughter wanted to enter the junior imitation competition and I advised her to team up with the leader girl in the class, who also happened to be a Madonna fan. This worked out well and the two girls practised a lot together and eventually won the junior imitation show in our village. My parents were present during the show and were ever so proud of their granddaughter. Now everyone in the village knew my daughter and that is how she carved out her own place in the village.

One Saturday afternoon I was at work in the garden and heard loud cheering coming from the soccer pitch. I decided to go and have a look and my daughter came along as well. On the field I saw a mix of men, women and also a few children. An all female match was going on and it turned out that the ladies team in the village played at the highest level. This certainly contributed to a very pleasant atmosphere at the club and people were certainly kindly disposed towards women playing soccer.

Within minutes of our arrival my daughter ran in to a friend and the two of them took off to play elsewhere. I decided to go for a beer at the canteen. I just stood there on my own enjoying my pint when the Chairman of the soccer club approached me. Before long he asked me whether I had played soccer and I told him about my old club and he talked about his club. For political and technical reasons I did not want disclose immediately that my most recent contributions to the noble sport of soccer had been drinking a considerable amount of beer.

The Chairman said that given my past experience I could try out for the third team but that would mean I would have to attend soccer practice twice a week. I had always detested attending practice sessions but I also knew that given my current state of physical fitness it would not do me any harm to get into shape again.

I started playing soccer again and I attended the training sessions. A couple of old friends from the old village also played for the third team. They did not want to associate themselves with what they called those from the Posh Neighbourhood, which included me. During the first game nobody passed me the ball and they completely ignored me. I never said anything and pretended not to notice. In the second half I did manage to score a magnificent goal completely out of the blue and it also turned out to be the winning goal.

After the match I bought drinks all round and talked to all of them but I did not mention their unfair behaviour during the match. The next match there were no more problems, which meant that I had been accepted by the team. And through training hard and enjoying the game with a younger generation of players I had my new start in the village.

And then there was also our latest addition to the family, Bobo the fair Bouvier dog. It was a splendid, funny and self-willed animal. My daughter and Bobo had a special bond and as a part of that had also developed a special language. If there was not a friend around to play with, Bobo was the playmate of choice. He sometimes had to endure being dressed up in a sheet to play Bride. Not easy for a dog with a mind of its own. I thoroughly enjoyed watching dog and girl play together.

Early every morning I took Bobo for a walk in the park before leaving for work. These early morning walks were a great way to get a breath of fresh air and see nature awaken at the same time. I derived a lot of energy from this.

The lesson I learned was that it is not easy to move and integrate in a new community. It takes its toll.

It's all sales

The familiar problem when it comes to meeting new people is that people need to get a feel for the other. In order to establish good contacts you need a lot of information. As long as relevant information is lacking, people will fill in the blanks themselves by means of ideas, impressions, thoughts etc. As time passes by, the information will improve and people will adopt a suitable attitude. People get to know each other better. It does help if and when you are new to the game you do something for someone else, to show one's good side. In sales this is business as usual; meeting new people, getting to know people, assessing others, asking questions, obtaining information, giving information starting to like one another. This often but it could also take a few visits. Indispensable for a good relationship with customers.

Only selling to get a promotion.

Due to a reorganisation I had been transferred from the Central Automation Division to the Payments Business Unit. The Business Units had become responsible for their own projects, the Automation budget and initial phase and the functional design. I had only been employed at this bank for a year and was fortunate that the Payments Business Unit wanted me on board. I had hardly been able to lobby for a position with this division. If a Business Unit was not interested in offering you a position, you could start looking for a new job. Fortunately I was a 'desired object'.

As a consequence I now had to report to a different Manager. This Manager had been with the bank for a long time. It had been difficult to understand the rather complex organisation of the bank. I kept far from 'internal political games' and tried to prove my worth by doing my job well, or in other words, completing projects successfully. I had already scored by means of my direct and goal-oriented approach.

My new Manager was friendly to me and told me he had personally selected me to join his Business Unit. This surprised me for I had never met him or exchanged one single word with him. He had selected me, but not the other way around. I still had to get to know him.

As project Manager of one of my projects I became aware of a major problem in the group. The Chairman and the Deputy Chairman did not see eye to eye at all. If the Chairman supported something you could make a bet on it that the deputy Chairman would oppose it and vice versa. They were obviously involved in a power struggle.

This kind of behaviour was detrimental to the project and led to delays. I told my Manager what was going on and asked him to ask the Steering Committee to change the composition of the project group. My Manager was a member of this Steering Group and could solve the problem without involving me. I, for one, had to get on with the project and it would be better to keep out of the line of fire because I had to work with those involved on other projects.

My Manager's response to my plan surprised me, to say the least. He told me there was nothing he could do for me because at this point in time he was placed on salary scale 12 and intended to work his way op to scale 13. If he were to raise the subject during a meeting, his chances on promotion would decline. I was dumbfounded en decided to go to the Chairman of the Steering Committee straight away without informing my Manager and ask him to do something about the problem. The Chairman of the Steering Committee understood the problem and solved it without much ado. I did not tell him about the response of my Manager.

Some months later I had finished a course on a very important topic that was part of the payment process. I had passed the report I had written on to my Manager and had asked him to read it. He was very enthusiastic and asked me if he could have a digital copy of the report so he could add a letter of recommendation for the Automation Steering Committee. All this so they could include it in the decision-making process.

After a number of weeks I still had not heard anything about the decision-making process so I asked the Steering Committee secretary for an update. She did not recall ever having seen a document with my name on it. When I reminded her of the title she did remember the document but then said it had been registered under my Manager's name. She showed me the document and my name had completely vanished from the document. My name had been replaced by that of my Manager. This was apparently the right way to get to be placed in salary scale 13! My trust in my Manager had been reduced to an absolute minimum.

One day I was approached informally by one of the Managers of the Automation Division. They wanted to sound out whether I would be interested in becoming Project Manager for their new 'Core Banking' project. I had already successfully completed a similar project (The Basic System) for my previous employer. I immediately inquired after the conditions under which this project would have to be completed. It turned out that they were to put together a Business Unit for this very important project and not have it supervised directly by the Board of Directors. To me these conditions seemed unacceptable given the enormity of the project so I turned down their offer unless they were to change the conditions. I never heard anything about it anymore.

In the meanwhile the Board of Directors had decided, according to my manager, that we were to take a back seat in the meetings with the combined banks. He was to take over a number of my tasks because he had developed a taste for these meetings.

I could no longer bear the attitude of my manager. He was a very bad manager and had his secretary do nothing all day and then made her work overtime to finish his documents. No, hardly anyone enjoyed working for him. I decided to go and look for another job.

I learned that for some people their goals are not the goals of the company. To me it was always clear that you can only be successful in a company if your personal goals fit in with those of the company you work for. My mistake was that I had refused to get acquainted with the informal structures of the organisation.

On the surface of it, this story does not seem to have any bearing on sales techniques. The opposite is true, though. As a salesperson you certainly have to deal with situations like the one described in the story. Most salespeople do not recognise stories like these. Still, imagine you have quoted a customer and that the manager of the department involved has problems with his colleagues. Nothing will come of it, which leaves you wondering what went wrong. Your relationship with a customer needs to be good so they will pass on relevant information to you and you can establish what happened to your quotation. If you know the ins-and-outs of the sales process you can adapt your sales strategy accordingly. Knowledge = Power. Also try to help the customer with his problems. He will definitely appreciate that. A salesperson needs to keep an open mind towards a customer's problems.

Being available for a new position

I had run in to an ex colleague when presenting a mini seminar for banks about cash points. He had been employed as a database administrator and free-lancer with my previous employer. We had more or less lost touch but still exchanged Christmas cards. I had my doubts about him. He never looked you straight in the eye when sitting opposite you. Still, after the seminar we made an appointment to meet for dinner.

Over dinner he told me that the he was now employed as Director-general and hands-on Manager of a small software company. This company employed five professional consultants of which three were also partner in the Software Company. My host was also deployed as Interim Automation Manager with a mid-sized financial company.

He told me that this financial establishment had instigated the recruitment process to fill the vacancy of Automation Manager. He added that he wanted the position of Automation Manager but could not do both. He would have to give up his position as Director-general of his own software company and even sell the company.

He asked me to consider the situation and invited me to another dinner that would include his business partners. I did not ask him for more details but I the whole situation did not feel right.

One month later, during dinner with the business partners I could not help but notice that my ex colleague was rather domineering. Finally he showed his true colours. He wanted me to take the Software Company of his hands so he could take up the position of Automation Manager. I had not seen that one coming at all and the whole situation required quick thinking.

My gut feeling told me that I was not at all interested in becoming Director-general of a small software company as hands-on Manager. This was not what I had dreamed of. So I suggested to him in return that I would apply for the position of Automation Manager with the financial establishment and he could continue to run the Software Company.

This is exactly what happened. I was one of three candidates considered for the position of Automation Manager and I had many conversations with the senior H&R manager and the Director-general of the financial establishment. I was definitely interested in the position and regarded it as a great challenge.

At the same time a head-hunter had approached me for a position as Automation Manager with one of the major banks. During the interviews I had to explain at length why earlier on in my career I had decided to head a smaller department instead of going for the larger department. To the Director-general it seemed much more natural to opt for the larger department since that would have been more beneficial to my career. Because of my choice he had serious doubts about my managerial skills.

Fortunately I was able to convince that him I was qualified for the job and after a medical check-up they sent the employment contract to my home address. Somehow it did not feel right though, and I sensed this was not what I really wanted. I could not bring myself to signing the employment contract.

One day later the H&R manager of the financial establishment called me and told me that they preferred one of the other candidates for the position. As far as he was concerned I was the right man for the position but the Director-general had decided otherwise. They would start negotiations with another candidate straight away. I was disappointed and was happy to have another job option. Still, I could not bring myself to signing the employment contract.

The day before I was to sign the employment contract the H&R manager of the financial establishment called me once more. He asked me whether I was still available for the position because their preferred candidate had made unacceptable financial demands. His current employer had dismissed the other candidate on charges of fraud. Good news and it made me happy. I told him he had to make up his mind quickly and we made an appointment for the following day to finalise proceedings.

What a great challenge it was for me to become responsible for the overall Automation of the entire company. This would include setting up a professional Automation organisation and I would report directly to the Director-general.

I resigned and my manager told me he was not pleased. It was of no use to me to confront my manager with his poor managerial skills so I let it pass. As soon as he heard I was leaving one of the other managers raised the issue during a management meeting, implying that the bank was not capable of keeping good people. I was happy to leave. A big bank turned out too big for my taste!

Fortunately I had learned to take decisions intuitively and sometimes exercise patience. Letting time pass solves some problems. I also realised that a large company and the inherent company internal politics were not my cup of tea.

In sales intuition is an indispensable aid. Be aware, though, that not everybody's intuition is well developed. There are many different types of salespeople. The 'impulsives' (act now think later) 'listeners' (who base their entire decision on what they have heard), the intuitives (base their decision on gut feeling without details), thinkers (want to have everything worked out into detail). For managers this subdivision is important. Every different type needs a different approach. Especially when it comes to sales, the wrong approach can be a source of misunderstanding and irritation.

Selling in spite of opposition

I started afresh in my new position as Automation Manager. On my first day in the office the H&R Manager introduced me to my new colleagues, managers and senior management of the different departments. In the afternoon I was introduced to the six people working in the Automation Department and their Interim Manager.

The Interim Automation Manager told me he had been rather surprised by my appointment because no one had informed him about the recruitment procedure and that a new Automation Manager had been appointed to whom he was supposed to report. He made it clear that he strongly disliked the ex colleague who had introduced me to the company.

It was obvious that I had to choose my words carefully and not express an opinion because I could tell the six employees were listening in to our conversation and they apparently adored the Interim Manager. I set a date for us to meet to discuss matters in hand and get better acquainted. I also noticed that the Interim Manager was not too happy with the H&R manager, there was undoubtedly some tension between them.

The following day I had the first meeting with the Director-general. I reported directly to him and he received me cordially albeit formally. He assigned me to write an Information and Automation Plan. His personal advisors (the external accountant and the Director- friend of a software company) had advised this approach. I was given three months to complete the plan. He also told me, in answer to my questions, that there was no Board of Directors meeting or an Automation Steering Committee in the company.

He preferred bilateral meetings and set a biweekly appointment for this bilateral meeting. I also asked him for the company strategy and the company policy plan. Both were to serve as basis for the Information and Automation Plan, but had not been written.

It dawned upon me that I would have to write both missing plans combined with the Information and Automation Plan. An incredible challenge because I had never done anything like it before. I wisely refrained from sharing this information with the Director-general.

At home I consulted every piece of specialist literature I could lay my hands on, searching for methods and approaches for compiling an Information and Automation Plans. This seemed to be a unique enterprise because I could not find anything useful in print. I contacted some friends and ex colleagues in my network but they could not help me out either.

There was nothing for it but to get started and compile a plan that would be a cross between a strategy cum policy plan and an Information and Automation Plan. In any case it had to be a plan that was approved by all members of the Board of Directors and that would provide structure when it came to implementing the Automation Plan. I started off by interviewing all fellow managers and in doing so learned a lot about the company and the products it sold.

What I learned was that this company was unique in The Netherlands. 200 people worked at the Head Office while another 750 people were employed at the branch offices. The main products were exchanging foreign currencies and exchanging cheques and credit cards for money. Also a number of by-products were sold like phone cards, maps, travel insurances etc.

In addition to that, a number of bank-products were on offer and in order to provide this service the company had acquired a small bank. This small bank sold its products straight through the Head Office, but also tried to bring in more branch offices to sell its products. My new company was therefore a combination of a finance shop and a bank. Branch offices could be found on central train stations and at border stations between The Netherlands and the neighbouring countries.

As a side effect I also learned a lot about the frustrations and resentment of the managers and Board of Directors. The interviews put me up to speed. The Comptrollers, one of the two Deputy Director-generals, tested me by presenting me with a difficult technical problem and had me solve it. In his previous position he had been responsible for the Automation Division. He told me to attune my plans with him first because he was the most important man in the company. He detested the Interim Automation Manager and arranged his own Automation equipment. He for one had a very expensive printer on his desk that could print in red and black. He also made a number of unfriendly comments about the Director-general.

Then there was the H&R manager who was so frustrated with regard to the Director-general and the Comptroller that every time we got together I had to spend at least half an hour listening to him unloading his frustration.

The other vice Director-general, who was responsible for Marketing and Sales, was a man who kept an innumerable amount of stacks of paper in his office. During an interview he would receive a call and start rummaging around in the stacks of paper. He was Chairman of the Shareholders Meeting and considered himself to be the most important man in the organisation. He also found it necessary to convey that he was a personal friend of the Director-general.

The head of the Banking Division told me he no longer was on speaking terms with the Comptroller and only wanted to sell his products directly through the

118

Head Office because he had no confidence in the management of and knowledge in the branch offices.

And so on, and so on. A real-life soap opera, if ever I saw one. Amidst all this I adopted a neutral attitude and avoided having to take sides. Automation had to be accessible to everyone.

As is common practice in a divide-and-rule organisation, every division had organised its own Automation. Every branch office had a unique terminal with software unique to that terminal. The terminal would record all desk transactions and put them on a cassette. The data on the cassettes would then be processed on the same terminal but with a different software programme at the back office.

All transactions of the branch offices would be collected on cassettes and sent to the Head Office where the data would be entered into a lager computer and would produce bookkeeping statistics and reports.

The banking system and the personnel system were subcontracted to a business connection. The bank transactions of all the branch offices were added manually to balance sheets and were sent to the Head Office where about a dozen 'punching ladies' would punch in the transactions and put them on digital tape that could be processed by the external banking system.

In the meantime three large computers had been purchased which were to be positioned in the Back office in three of our largest branch offices. They had not been brought into use as yet. The level of Automation was disappointing and presented quite a challenge.

I always looked forward to visiting the branch offices, because that is where I met the people on the work floor. Their accessibility and their fantastic attitude towards work made quite an impression on me and I became very fond of them.

During the bilateral meetings with the Director-general I discussed my experiences at the branch offices. Of course I did not breathe a word about the difficult internal relationships. He talked to me about company strategy and policy and I told him how Automation could help to accomplish all that. We also discussed on many occasions the threats our company had to face such as the rise of 'plastic currency'[7] and the Unification of Europe.

---

[7] Even though some countries are examining the possibilities of distributing plastic bank notes, in this book plastic currency still refers to the plastic credit and debit cards.

Slowly but surely a picture started to form in my mind with regard to the kind of Automation the company needed to reach its goals. And pressure was also mounting because not much time was left and the Dutch National Bank was not satisfied with the quality of the reports it received.

I also informed the Director-general of the low level of Automation knowledge of staff and management and I suggested improving their level through the purchase and installation of about a dozen IBM-PCs on the desks of the secretaries. He agreed to this and I also asked him if I could bring in my former secretary. She was an experienced PC user and could therefore train the other secretaries. The Director-general agreed to this as well.

My former secretary was pleased with her new position and enjoyed the fact that she would be working with me again. We were a good team and were good friends to boot. During the recruitment process one of the programmers had asked us to consider his wife for the secretarial position. It took quite a while to convince him that even though his wife probably was an excellent secretary, she would not be a good choice for the position given the confidential nature of the information involved in the job. And if that was not enough I also added that this change in their situation would not be beneficial to their relationship.

At the end of the year A Christmas dinner was always organised by the Director-general and his wife to which all Members of the Board and their partners were invited. It was common practice during those dinners that after each course people would change places. That is how my wife had the misfortune to end up sitting next to the Comptroller. And the Comptroller could not help but mentioning to my wife that he was convinced that my secretary and I were having an affair. Subsequently my wife sat next to the Director of the Banking Division who told her that I could automate anything I liked as long as I kept clear from his bank. I had quite some explaining to do once we got home. Fortunately my wife accepted my side of the story.

I learned that for this company Automation was of the utmost importance in order to survive in the future. All the opposition I was facing made me more determined and my desire to win grew stronger and stronger. The Director-general and the people on the shop floor kept me motivated and I tried not to get entangled in the internal relationships between people. I did learn that I could not afford to make mistakes because that would be the end for me. I should not provide anyone with opportunities to blackmail me.

The best situation for a company would be if everyone would pursue the same goals. Unfortunately, this is usually not the case. Of course everyone tries to do his bit for the company but on the whole everyone has some sort of a hidden agenda. So will your customer. So do not be surprised if a customer adopts an unfamiliar attitude all of a sudden. The best way to proceed then is to engage the customer in conversations that are not directly related to the market and the product. Move in the direction of topics the customer can relate to and that are on his mind. A real salesperson can find a balance between talking shop and talking about what is on the customer's mind. In that way the salesperson will also continue to have an open mind towards topics that are not directly linked to sales.

Selling through the soccer club

Fortune was smiling on me once more. Because of my new job I had more money to spend on my family and I also drove a lease car. Given the nature of the job I had to work much harder and also in the evenings and weekends. At home I worked on my Information and Automation Plan on my new laptop computer (the first, very heavy IBM laptop). After the soccer match on Saturday and the relaxing moments afterwards I was very creative on Sunday morning putting in a few hours of work while my wife and daughter had a long lie-in.

For the soccer team I had to attend training sessions twice a week and I even started to enjoy it because I could not help but notice that I was getting in much better shape (both physically and mentally). My part in the team became more and more important and as a 'mature' player I was soon made captain and leader of the team. The younger players accepted my increasing responsibility and worked hard to compensate my decreasing running capacity. More and more I became the 'smart' player.

As a team player I learned a lot about managerial skills. Our team manager was a kind man but did not always take the right decisions at the right moment. We had to play our biggest competitor for first position in our league. He thought it would be a good idea to put two of our best players on the bench. He had told me of his plan during a training session and I had not passed on the line-up on to the other players.

On the Saturday of the match I made the line line-up, included the two good players and we won the game. Everybody simply accepted my adjusted line-up including the team manager. Playing on the team was good fun and we used to sing at the top of our voices in my lease car while we were heading for our away matches. The perfect way to relax as far as I was concerned.

My wife also started to find her feet. She now helped a friend of her father's, who was a doctor at the hospital where here father had been nursed. In his spare time the friend was part of a project to help junkies stop using drugs. My wife helped him with this scheme and it seemed to motivate her. She also played tennis and seemed happy running the home.

Our marriage lacked all excitement. There had been problems at work involving my secretary since the Comptroller had suggested to my wife that I had been having an affair with my secretary. This was definitely not true, especially since it was exactly the kind of problems I did not need in a company where some people were waiting for me to make a mistake.

I thought of solving the problem by inviting my secretary for dinner. The two women would get to know each other and my wife's mind would be put at ease. Unfortunately the dinner party was a complete disaster. My wife was very jealous and made that abundantly clear. They really did not like each other. They never showed their animosity at company outings though, for then they appeared to be the best of friends. Every night when I came home from work my wife asked after my secretary.

My daughter grew up fast en enjoyed school and village life. She went to the soccer club quite a lot and decided that she wanted to play soccer herself. She started borrowing my tracksuit and insisted that I would attend every match she played and wanted me to become her personal coach. It struck me immediately that the perception of ladies´ soccer differed tremendously from men's soccer.

The soccer club was the hub of social life in the village. Many of those who loved to watch matches turned out on Saturday to watch us. It was one big happy family and my daughter and I felt we belonged there. A warm, sociable and safe surrounding for my daughter.

From all this I learned that I thoroughly enjoyed living in this open and honest culture where people did not judge or condemn each other but left each other alone. I felt like a fish in water and the whole atmosphere generated a lot of positive energy.

If you feel completely at ease, everything will work out much better. The ease that surrounds you will also appeal to others. This is very important when it comes to sales. Attract people, for you will always need people to sell your product to. The more accessible you are, the more people will surround you. And as a result you will create more sales opportunities. Nevertheless, we have the tendency to put on a bold front. Always share our success stories hardly ever the ones where you fell flat on your face. Who would you rather talk to, the person who is a big success in everything he does or the one who tells it as it happened and dares to be vulnerable...... Right. So why do we always share the success stories? How infinitely strange.

Selling through 'brain-picking'

The first draft of the Information and Automation Plan had been completed. This financial establishment was a very special company. On the one hand it was a retail chain depending strongly on tourism and could give an exact account of the days earnings. On the other hand it was a full-fledged bank that tried to sell banking products through its Head Office and branch offices. Two completely different cultures entangled in an integration process.

The organisation aimed at efficiency and effectiveness through costs cutting. My mission was therefore to lower expenditure through Automation and implementing the necessary adjustments and systems as cost effective as possible.

The whole of this was easy to measure because I had to limit the number of customer service desks at the branch offices through Automation. The level of knowledge concerning business Automation was extremely disappointing. The knowledge required for an operation on this scale was locked inside the heads of small group of managers.

My research showed that the strategic approach and policy for the future were not quite clear. This company had not yet ascertained the significance of the threat posed by the rise of 'plastic currency'. Also integration of the bank and its future had not been defined properly.

The consequences of my research regarding the Information and Automation Plan led to the compilation of the following starting points:

1. Improvement of Automation knowledge throughout the entire organisation
2. Buying and implementing standard software instead of home developed software. The buying of standard software was the equivalent of business knowledge. The purchase of hardware was to be determined through the purchase of software.
3. Buying and implementing standard hardware. The company was too small to re-invent the wheel.
4. Fit out a small Automation Department.
5. The use of standard methods and techniques with as an added extra and as a first phase a preliminary investigation aiming at determining strategy and policy. So I could map out the problem areas mentioned earlier.
6. Set up a project organisation headed by a Steering Committee, which had to be led by the Director-general in order to initiate projects and check them.

For every project a project plan had to be submitted for approval to the Steering Committee.

I had compiled a flow chart containing all defined projects and activities in order of execution. In addition to that I had drafted a plan of the functional and technical infra structure including de Front-office systems of all branch offices, which were to be connected online and real- time to the Back-office systems at the Head Office. I had made my plan as simple as possible.

In order to attune the Information and Automation Plan I had made an appointment with 'my friend' the Interim Automation Manager. In the mean time I had discovered that he was not well liked apart by his colleagues except for the Director-general. He would continue to fill the interim position until the Information and Automation Plan had been approved of. Once that had been accomplished, he would then move on to the position of Automation Project Manager for the customer service desks at the different branch offices. He had read my concept plan and during our meeting and to me it was obvious that he had made no significant contribution to the plan.

During my next bilateral meeting with the Director-general it turned out that 'my friend' the Interim Manager had already discussed the concept plan with the Director-general. The Director-general was truly impressed with the contribution of the Interim Manager to the plan and he thought it was a sound and solid plan. I was flabbergasted. The nerve of the Interim Manager. Incredible!

I wondered how this could have happened and why I had not been informed beforehand. I was furious but managed to keep my feelings in check in front of the Director-general, for it had been the Interim Manager who got me the job in the first place. After the meeting I rang the Interim Manager and told him there and then what I thought of him. I now knew that he needed me to secure his own future.

The Director-general and I discussed all the ins and outs of the Information and Automation Plan. He wanted to be informed about every single detail and through him I got to know more about the company. Those were very prolific sessions. I had not put together an income-expenditure analysis with regard to the plan because a number of subjects still needed in-depth investigation. He approved of this approach because he wanted to take decisions step-by-step based on project plans. In this way he could control expenditure and investments.

As a result of this gradual approach he was not ready as yet to appoint a Steering Committee. He preferred taking decisions concerning Automation matters in consultation with me. As a compromise I was allowed to write up a report of our meetings and distribute those reports among all other senior manager for their information. In this way other managers were involved in the Automation developments. To me commitment of the entire management team with regard to the realisation of the Automation Plans was essential.

I learned that I could rely on my intuition regarding the behaviour of certain people. The 'behaviour' of my so-called friend was above all his problem! His misuse of my goodness and plans for his own sales process ('brain-picking') I had to accept for a fact at this point in time. It was not the right moment to pick a fight.

Whenever people work together situations, as the one described above, will arise. There will always be people who steal other people's brilliant ideas. Then it requires quite a bit of ingenuity to establish what is in it for the people who do it. Sometimes it is better for you to put matters right, in other cases it is better to leave matters be because a goal can be reached that you could not have possibly reached on your own. Some people just have better access to the decision-makers. So think carefully before dropping a bombshell. Being in the right does not always mean this will be acknowledged even if you are right. Think beforehand of possible repercussions.

Selling an Information and Automation Plan

My advice to the Director-general was that I needed the commitment of the entire Management Team in order to realise the Information and Automation Plan. This entailed that I had to attune the plan with people from both within and outside the company. I had to attune the plan with the shareholders' Automation Managers, the external accountant and Internal Accountants Security auditors, the Automation Committee of the Works Council, the personal advisors to the Director-general and of course my fellow managers and senior managers. The internal attuning I had to do on my own.

Our company had three shareholders, a bank (43,5%), an insurance company (43,5%) and Dutch Rail (13%). Dutch Rail was important as a shareholder since about half of our branch offices were located at their railway stations.

I enjoyed attuning with external parties and the Director-general helped whenever he could. Our in-depth discussions of the plan were now gradually beginning to pay off. On the other hand the results of talking to those 'in the field' were disappointing. I had been hoping for input and discussion yet nothing of the sort happened. Only the external accountant was convinced that I should have used their method. I knew nothing about their method and the Director-general solved the matter by renaming the plan a Preliminary Information and Automation Plan.

The internal discussion was much more heated. First of all I had to attune the plan with the previous senior Automation Manager. He was also Chairman of the Automation Committee of the Works Council. In addition to that, I had also appointed him head of the calculus centre and manager of the 'punching department' where ten ladies were entering all bank transactions from the different branch offices into the external banking system.

By appointing him to a position in my department I could keep an eye on him, because he was well liked and very powerful in the informal organisation. He was quite frustrated about my appointment and his own demotion and I had to be very careful where he was concerned.

He immediately ascertained that the online network to all branch offices would make his 'punching department' redundant. I could not and would not deny that. I knew I could count on the support of the Director-general who had decided that there would be no forced redundancies. A recruitment freeze would be implemented, though.

The former Senior Manager of the Automation Department had planned a dinner party with the 'punching ladies' a week after that. He told me about this and I asked him if I could join to meet the ladies and present my plans to them. He was not in a position to refuse this.

I tried my best (and it was not much of an effort) to involve all the ladies in the conversation and my sense of humour did the rest. I noticed that they quite liked me and without beating about the bush I informed the ladies of my plans. They understood and I promised I would do my best to find suitable positions for them. They were impressed and I could tell by the look on the face of the previous Senior Automation Manager that he was not happy with the turn of events. I knew I had won the first battle and in the lion's den at that.

The second battle I had to face was the one with the Comptroller who was also responsible for Automation matters. He told me straight away that he hated my plan and that implementation of the plan would mean bankruptcy for the company. He had drawn up a few financial overviews and more or less forced me to make certain claims about expenses and investments. I flatly refused and referred him to the Director-general as had been agreed upon. The Comptroller was not a friendly person and it was not a pleasant meeting to say the least. There were no financial figures in the plan, which meant that the Comptroller despite the name of his position had no control over me.

The bank director, who was to retire in a couple of years, was pleased that I had initiated an extra investigation into the integration of the bank's products with regard to the future of the company. His main aim was to delay any decision until he had retired.

The Marketing and Sales Director, who was also responsible for dealing with the rising influence of 'plastic currency' and the consequences for the company, was pleased with the idea to initiate an investigation into the development of 'plastic currency'. He was of an insecure nature and wanted certainty.

The H&R manager, also responsible for Training, was pleased with the plan because he wanted a Personnel Information System and I had proposed to set up such a system as a trial case for the implementation of software packages. In addition to that he was enthusiastic about the prospect of providing computer training to staff.

The Board of Directors and the managers of the branch offices were pleased because through Automation I intended to minimise all the manual tasks. As a result of this they could increase opening hours and process more transactions.

In the meantime ten IBM personal computers had been placed in strategic positions at the Head Office (with all the secretaries) and my secretary together with a very friendly external consultant started off providing training sessions for the use of the PCs. It was a very successful project. Still, one day the

Director-general walked by and noticed that those very expensive computers were not always in use and I had quite a bit of explaining to do regarding the use of the personal computer and their importance in the future of the company.

Once more I learned that transitional processes in an organisation lead to opposition. In order to overcome the opposition you always need the support of Senior Management. You always need to state the advantages clearly to people whose daily work is about to change, but not be afraid of a confrontation. My drama lessons in high school now really paid off. Unfortunately this time I had to play all the parts myself.

Often it is not the plans that lead to opposition, but the changes itself. For about 95% people do things automatically and unplanned. For about 5% they do things consciously and planned. If and when we want to change, for instance, a mode of operation, the changes will be implemented. Human nature dictates, though, that as soon as anything does not go as planned we revert to the old familiar pattern. That is why it is so difficult to implement change. People need to behave differently. Changes demand thorough preparation. Motivation is an important element and one also needs to think about what to do if people revert to their old behaviour.

No sale and a bad loser at that

Our company had been a good customer of a certain hardware supplier. The Director-generals of both companies were close friends and our Comptroller was also a loyal customer and had obtained his own computer system from this supplier.

The hardware supplier had developed for all customer service desks at the branch offices a unique terminal. The same terminal was used at smaller branch offices in their Back-office and for the three major branch offices three large computers had been purchased. The latter three computers were not in use because nobody knew what to do with them. A strong relationship had developed over the years between my company and the hardware supplier.

Interesting detail was that for my previous employer I had worked closely together with this supplier. I knew quite a few people and also 'my friend' the Interim Manager was closely linked to the hardware supplier.

My Information and Automation Plan for my company was based on purchasing and implementing standard hard and software that had been tested in the market. When I considered the functional and technical infrastructure I could only conclude that the hardware supplier could not in any way provide the systems we needed according to the plan.

They had, for instance, no solution to the problem of dealing with 'plastic currency' they could not provide a suitable banking system and could not supply personal computers. In addition to that I considered it bad service to supply three large computers nobody could interface with the network of the branch offices.

I had already discussed the issue with the Director-general and his advice was that I had to present my plan to a number of representatives of the hardware supplier. I took his advice and I went for a visit to the 'lion's den'. I had to present my plan to all Sales Managers excluding the Senior Sales Manger. The people present all knew me and at first there was a friendly atmosphere with lots of banter and jokes.

The atmosphere changed though, during the presentation. Things got awfully quiet and all the banter and laughter subsided. My final slide conveyed in no uncertain terms that there was no longer a match between what we needed and the products they could supply. They all left the room fast and some them even forgot to shake my hand on departure. The message was clear.

The next day my secretary received a phone call from the secretary of the Senior Sales Manager of the hardware supplier. They were to set up a lunch meeting for us at very short notice. I had known the Senior Sales Manager for quite some time but we had lost touch. The hardware supplier had been a quite successful player in the market, which was largely due to the Senior Sales Manager.

We met for lunch in a very expensive restaurant. I was a bit tense and nervous because I knew that this was going to be a very difficult meeting. We started off talking about the good old days and about my previous employer. Then I decided there was no point in putting it off and I explained to him my Information and Automation Plan. I also included the part where their hardware and our demands no longer matched.

He could tell I was dead earnest about the matter and changed tack immediately. He had always thought that my new employer was not the right place for me to develop my managerial and human skills. As far as he was concerned the company was too small and he offered me a managerial position with his own company. I could not believe my ears and immediately turned down his offer. He wanted to remove me from the company I now worked for, his good customer.

When I flatly refused his offer he made a big mistake. He was furious and said to me "If I'm not mistaken your daughter crosses the street every day on more than one occasion. I would be careful if I were you." I could not believe he would actually stoop as low as to threaten me. He was painfully aware of the fact that he would lose out on millions of turnover in the future (and bonus) which obviously infuriated him. He completely lost control.

I looked him straight in the eye, got up from the table and left the restaurant without a word. I had not touched the food. I looked in control on the outside but on the inside I was incensed. I walked back to office, stopping at a burger shop for a burger and to recover from the shock. I felt truly sick. Nobody should even think about harming my daughter. I was not sure whether I still wanted to do the job if the safety of my daughter was at stake.

The next day I quietly informed the Director-general. He was genuinely shocked by the Senior Sales Manager's behaviour and immediately arranged for security for my daughter. He took the threats seriously. He was right behind me and that made me go through with it all. And some good had come out of it. Because of the behaviour of the Senior Sales Manager it was now clear to all those involved that we could no longer do business with this company. This kind of threatening behaviour cannot be tolerated under any circumstances.

What I learned was that you only have business friends if you can do business with them. Their own interests will always prevail and they will not consider your company's interests. But you cannot win them all, accept that and no matter what, always remain a Gentleman. You never know when you will run in to one another again.

A large and important customer is called a Key Account in Sales. A Key Account needs intensive supervision and attention. You need to know everything there is to know about the customer, the organisation, every product ever bought, what their purchasing strategy is like, and how they intend to expand their market share. If you do your job well, there is no way you can be surprised by a presentation of the Automation Plans of your key account. If the customer makes the effort to pay you a visit and present its plans you make sure that everyone involved is present. You do not just show up in case of problems. That is not good for profit and if you know that you have done everything within your limits and still lose, take your loss like a man. A good response might lead to advantages in the future. The response of the Senior Sales Manager signified the end of a long-term profitable relationship. And this was probably not the only one because bad news always travels fast.

Saving and selling a project

The Director-general had told me that the part of the project involving the branch offices would be supervised by 'my friend' the Interim Manager. I would, therefore, be able to concentrate on other projects derived from the Information and Automation Plan. The Interim Manager was also the Director of a small software company. I was grateful to him that he had introduced me to my current position and we had agreed that his software company would be preferred supplier for external consultants. I would be allowed to choose from three candidates, though, because I did not completely trust ´my friend´

His project concerning the branch offices was disaster prone. There was a special terminal (with unique software and hardware) developed for all the desks at the branch offices. The desk transactions were recorded on a cassette by the terminal and after closing time the data on the cassettes would be read-in at the same terminal in the back office at the branch office. This would have to be done with an altogether different programme in order to compile the day's proceeds per branch office. For the largest branch office a large, unique computer had been purchased in order to process these data and for two smaller branch offices two additional unique computers had been purchased. Those large computers had been acquired but were not used because nobody had time to invest in operating the computers. Because of the uniqueness of our terminals we were totally dependent on our hardware supplier.

Due to the growth of the company, more branch offices were being opened and the number of spare unique terminals was quickly depleted. If we wanted to order additional terminals a whole new production line had to be set up in the factory of our hardware supplier. This would lead to an unacceptable price level for the terminals and the Director-general foresaw difficulties if he had to ask shareholders for more money to fund the project. The project was running over budget anyway. The Interim Automation Manager paid me visit to discuss the matter and find a solution.

At my previous employer I had learned to work with the IBM PC and my proposition was to replace the unique terminals in the back office at the branch offices by a standard IBM PC. As a result the terminals from the back offices could be placed on the desks at the branch offices.

It was not easy, though, to create an interface between computers of two rival hardware companies. Additionally, the IBM PC would not be used as a personal computer but as a production computer. The Interim Manager located a small technical company that employed a Whiz kid programmer. We gave him the two computers and the assignment to create an interface without the use of the hardware suppliers.

I went to visit him every week to see if there was any progress and to offer help if necessary and motivate him. In the end he managed to create an interface. We were happy and proud. This would save us an awful lot of money and the Director-general would not have to ask the shareholders for additional funding. The IBM PC was now capable of replacing almost entirely the three large computers and we sold those to a dealer in second-hand computers. The only party involved that was not happy with the outcome was the supplier of the standard unique terminal.

We compiled a trial set up and invited the managers of the branch offices to come and see how the system worked. They were very pleased and wanted to implement the system at their office straight away. An additional extra was the use of standard computer software such as word processing and spreadsheets.

Then disaster struck. The Interim Manager took his wife and two children (a son of 14 years old and a daughter of 11 years old) for a skiing holiday. During the holiday something awful happened. His son and daughter ended up skiing off-piste and his daughter fell into a ravine and was killed instantly. I was shocked by the bad news and of course I forgot that until then I had called him 'my friend'. What shocked me even more was the response of some of my colleagues. Some of them had hated the Interim Manager and thought he had got his just deserts. Incredible, for among them were colleagues who went to church every Sunday. I told the Director-general about this and he took these colleagues to task immediately.

The loss of a child is something you do not wish on anyone, not even your biggest enemy. You should be able to keep business and private separately. It was the second time in my life I had to attend the funeral of a child. It was an incredibly sad occasion having to witness the bereavement on the faces of parents and son. At a later stage I talked to the Interim Manager a great deal about his loss, but the family was unsettled for years and I am not sure whether things ever went back to normal. The whole family suffered a great deal.

In order to relieve the Interim Manager temporarily from his duties so he could devote a lot of attention to his family I took over the branch office project from him. This project had turned into a never-ending story because both the products and the environment were subject to constant change and the Automation Department had to take up the latest developments.

We eventually managed to create a Local Area Network for the branch offices with IBM PCs on the customer service desks. From the Back-office there was a direct connection with the Back-office computers at the main office. A total network!

Once every four months the Director-general and I went to visit a number of branch offices around the country. I used to talk with the managers and staff about their problems and of course in particular Automation problems. Every time I returned from one of these visits I became more motivated to do my utmost for those who had to earn the money on the shop floor so that I could spend it on Automation.

What I learned is that when things are at their worst and problems seem insurmountable, you really become very creative. But also that one dramatic accident can destroy your entire life.

Large, dramatic events have a huge impact on the way we live our lives. It takes people to a different level of thinking and experiencing daily life. People often say that events like these put things into perspective. In the end, and after a while, you will be able to determine that everything bad that happens in your life will also lead to something positive. In the end the man in the story had become more accessible than before the horrible accident.

Making a new customer happy

Changing hardware supplier was not easy. We based our search on the demands and wishes regarding the technical infrastructure derived from the Information and Automation Plan. It was definitely not easy to find a new hardware supplier, who could provide a system that would serve both a financial institution and a retail chain. In addition to this I also wanted to use only standard hardware.

The bad experience I had had with the unique terminal of our previous hardware supplier had taught me that a unique terminal had not been a good solution for the company. In addition to that, it had also been a costly solution making the company dependent on the hardware supplier. No, I was convinced I had to find a hardware supplier who could supply standard hardware because my company was a mid- sized establishment and way too small to re-invent the wheel. I did not feel like an extended search for the ultimate hard ware supplier and I contacted the number one hardware supplier in The Netherlands and discussed our requirements with them.

Once again the Director-general agreed with my decision especially since our shareholders had been customers of the hardware supplier I had selected for years. His only fear was that given the size of our business we would not receive the full attention of this huge hardware supplier.

I invited the Senior Sales Manager of the hardware supplier to a presentation of my Information and Automation Plan. This was a well-known and respected person in the Automation industry. I could not have been more surprised when his entire sales team showed up for my presentation.

Presenting a plan was always an invigorating experience for me. I was pleased with the way I had presented my plan to the Senior Sales Manager and his Sales Team and afterwards I had a private meeting with the Senior Manager. I decided to lay my cards on the table. I told him everything about the problems we had had with our previous hardware supplier and the disastrous link between two computers. I also shared with him our Director-general's fears with regard to the size of our company compared to the size of the hardware supplier and its regular customers.

He listened intently to my story and subsequently told me that his company was good at selling mainframe computers but that he was delighted at the prospect of seeing their smaller computers on custom service desks at our branch offices. This would offer the opportunity for all our customers to see their computers.

After due consideration I decided that between us we had created a win-win situation. He then asked for his account manager to join the meeting and guaranteed his undivided attention to our business. On our parting he also asked me to set up a meeting with the Director-general.

I was, of course, also included in the meeting with the Senior Sales Manager and so was the Account Manager. We could look back upon a prolific meeting with the Senior Sales Manager not showing any arrogance he might have derived from being the number one hardware supplier. As a matter of fact, he gave our Director-general the idea that he welcomed him as a new customer.

The two of them smoked a cigar together and the Senior Sales Manager complimented me on my good and structural approach toward the Information and Automation Plan. He also told me that he personally wanted to remain involved in the whole procedure. The meeting ended by the Senior Sales Manager telling us that he always exchanged money at our largest branch office and therefore enjoyed the opportunity to welcome us as a new customer.

All this sounds like a good sales pitch, but he the Senior Manager was true to his word and I received all the support I needed from this hardware supplier.

What I learned was, that it is also possible to create a win-win situation with a supplier, which can subsequently form the basis for success.

What matters in Sales is, of course, finding the right balance between what you give and what you get out of it. At a first glance it seems as if buyers have a powerful position because they can choose from a multitude of suppliers. Salespeople feel they have to work from an underdog position and are willing to make concessions. But appearances can be deceptive. Continuity is also in the interest of the buyer. Not in the least because he has to carry out extensive in-depth research. If as a salesperson you are capable of helping him in this respect, that is your first move towards becoming preferred supplier. If you are also of assistance in reselling or the handling of the product that is your second step towards preferred supplier. Be aware of the specific problems your customer has to deal with and act upon that knowledge.

Believing in miracles

When I was first dating my wife I went to her house quite often to pick her up. Her sister and her husband used to live with my wife's parents because they had to get married. They had a little girl (Jane) who simply adored me. Her parents were always absent to earn money so they could furnish their home and did not spend a lot of time with Jane. Jane was always happy to see me and I used to play with her and took her for a ride in my car. On occasion we visited my parents who spoiled her rotten. Jane and I became firm friends.

During the first years of our marriage and after the birth of our daughter, Jane came to stay with us on a regular basis. I never thought she looked healthy and sometimes she looked sad. She loved staying with us, though, and never wanted to go back home.

Thirteen years later while I was preoccupied with my job as Senior Automation Manager with a mid-size company I had to pay regular visits to a small software company. This company was developing a clever interface between two computers from different software suppliers. Its office was located close to my home village and also close to the neighbouring big city.

One Sunday morning my mother phoned me. She told me that my brother in law had been admitted to hospital in the neighbouring big city. He was asthmatic and had suffered a severe attack the night before. I decided to pay him a visit at the hospital straight away. It was a Sunday and we had not made any other plans. During my visit he seemed to be improving. He had been given the correct medication and he was even cheerful. After visiting hours we walked back to our car to drive home.

All of a sudden we ran in to Jane's mother. We were quite surprised and asked her what had brought her to the hospital. She told us that Jane was in hospital and we immediately went along with her to visit Jane. Seeing Jane in her hospital bed greatly disturbed me. She was in a ward with young girls who were all terribly skinny. A terrible sight, the more so because one of these girls was Jane. She sat straight up in bed with an unopened present at the foot of the bed. The present was a gift from her father.

Jane suffered from a condition called Anorexia Nervosa. What I did not know at the time was that Jane and the others were being observed through two-sided mirrors and that hospital staff had noticed that Jane was clearly happy to see me and responded well to my presence. It was a horrendous disease that might easily have killed her. Terrible because all the children on that ward had been missing out on love, attention and affection in their lives. It turned out that Jane and I had established quite a bond from the time when she was just a baby. The

138

doctors had tried to talk to Jane's parents about it but they did not understand. They had always given Jane everything she ever wanted (in a materialistic sense anyway).

It all came together. I had to visit the small Software Company often because it gave me the opportunity to go and see Jane. I visited her at least twice a week because I had gathered that I could help her by just being there and talking to her and show her my love and affection. I just knew I had to do this for her. Nobody had asked me. Fortunately Jane's condition did improve and after a while she was allowed to go home.

All this made me think. It was all too much of a coincidence and there is no such thing as coincidence. It all fitted together quite nicely, my work, my visits to the small Software Company, and my brother in law the visit to the hospital. It was all part of some larger plan and I just had to play my part without asking too many questions.

I learned that there is no such thing as coincidence and that there is more than us mortals can see. Love and warmth are essential to our well-being. And especially that you have to follow your intuition without wanting to know why. I thanked my God every night that I was allowed to do the things I did and could learn. Miracles do happen!

Investing in another human being can really pay off. It is important that you do not only concentrate on business. Also in a networking organisation we can see this misconception. A person can be a part of a group to bring in new customers. There is nothing wrong with that. We do see that these customers are not part of a larger network. If someone recommends you to somebody else he needs to like you and trust you. Only then will he recommend you to someone else. So show your good sides and enjoy the pleasant opportunities that arise from it.

Selling a department

One chapter of the Information and Automation Plan concerned the set-up of an Automation Department. This department was to deal with the implementation and maintenance and development of standard software packages. The plan did not involve the actual setting up a programming department but to subcontract this to a supplier.

When I started the job the existing Automation Department consisted of three young computer operators, the ten 'punching ladies' and a manager. No one was employed at the level of Information Analyst or Functional and Technical Designer.

Through interviews with the Director-general it had become clear to me that the organisation was still a retail chain and by no means a banking company. The money had to be earned first before it could be spent. If, for instance, it had been a very busy period (like Easter when many tourists visit The Netherlands) I was allowed to invest money in computer hardware. The decision making process was then easier and no permission from the shareholders was required in those circumstances. The Director-general also wanted me to build-up the Automation Department step by step. He would rather have me appoint an external consultant to see how things would develop and if this turned out to be what the company needed, I would be granted permission to recruit an internal consultant.

With regard to the build-up of the Automation Department, I opted for appointing a number of experienced Automation experts who could act as coach to the younger trainees who could start their career with our company. It was not easy to recruit the right people, though, in a hectic Automation world. To those suited for the job it was not exactly a challenge to work for a mid-sized company. Next to that, it was not really considered worthwhile to implement standard software since most Automation experts wanted to develop their own software in those days. We were thus forced to recruit and re-train internal staff. Fortunately the idea of a brand new department and all our plans for change held an enormous appeal for those selected.

Since our main office was too small, I started off with two external consultants in an office situated above one of the branch offices in our capital. Together we spend our time writing and developing policy plans concerning the consequences with regard to electronic bank transactions. From our current location it was easy to interview the relevant managers and specialists. They had to make time for us. And it took an effort to convince people that we had to compile a plan first before we could start working. We were under close scrutiny and when one of those expensive external consultants took a coffee break that took a bit too long according to one of the office managers, he called me to take the consultant to task.

The level of knowledge regarding Automation maters was poor but fortunately it coincided with the PC boom and I could use that perfectly to improve the knowledge level. My secretary and an external consultant did a wonderful job in promoting Automation through the use of the personal computer.

My secretary had been busy working for me but also with providing PC training sessions. She had asked for an assistant and an assistant had been appointed. We had opted for a young external assistant. One day the young lady did not show up for work without notification. We tried to get in touch with her but failed to do so for two days.

The third day she did show up for work with a black eye and her arm in a sling. When we asked her what had happened she told us her boy friend had beaten her up and that he had locked her into a closet for two days. It goes without saying that my secretary wanted to help her and made her promise not to go back to the abusive boyfriend but to go and stay at her sister's. She talked to her at length and gave her a lot of attention. We allowed her some time off to move to her sister's place. After two days she phoned my secretary and announced that she had moved back in with the boyfriend and that we should start looking for a replacement.

I learned that I found it a wonderful challenge to deploy my knowledge and experience for the good of this company. I had to 'sell' every move I made and every penny I spent. Every thing I did for the company I did wholeheartedly, but helping people with all your heart is not always appreciated.

A salesperson usually operates separately from his managers and colleagues. This requires a great deal of discipline. His job comprises visiting clients and potential customers within a certain time span. Nobody can check whether the salesperson visits the right customers, puts out correct quotations and spent his time efficiently. His manager needs to trust him but needs to impose some form of supervision on the salesperson. There will always be doubts and that is why a salesperson needs to sell himself to his own manager. The salesperson also needs to accept that he will be checked. A salesperson has a right to supervision for it will keep him on edge.

Buying my 'own system'

Another chapter of the Information and Automation Plan was dedicated to the set-up of a project organisation to realise all defined projects. An Automation Steering Committee had been formed consisting of the Director-general and myself.

I had also created four Committees that were to deal with the technical infrastructure, Human resources, IAS (Internal Accountants Services) audit and for setting up the administrative organisation. In addition to that, I had allocated a trial project to gain experience with the selecting process of standard software and its implementation.

A manager of the user organisation usually took the position of Chairman. The Director-general was insistent though, that I should be part of all Committees and project groups to pass on my knowledge and experience, but also to guard progress.

The Committee in charge of the Automation of H&R issues comprised the H&R Manager, Training Manager, a representative of the Works Council and myself. This Committee announced the recruitment freeze and ascertained no forced redundancies would take place because of Automation.

The IAS audit Committee drafted a security plan that all projects had to adhere to. It was not easy though, to convince our IAS auditor that this plan should be drafted beforehand and not afterwards. Fortunately the IAS auditor of the external consultant agreed with me.

In a retail chain people are not too keen on procedures and instructions. Proper procedures and instructions for the sales of banking products were nevertheless essential. Since there was no discernible administrative organisation, a Committee was formed chaired by the Comptroller to set up a proper administrative organisation.

My biggest worry remained the lack of knowledge regarding Automation in the organisation. How was I to carry out projects if the users did not have a clue as to what we ware talking about. At that point in time the Dutch Government had instigated the so-called PC for private use projects. Owning and using a personal computer was the perfect way to familiarise yourself with Automation.

The H&R Committee advised the Steering Committee to set up a personal computer programme for all employees. They could choose according to their budget for a cloned PC or an IBM PC. Receiving relevant training was compulsory. It was a huge success because more than 80% of the employees registered. We organised thirteen days in which training sessions would be held throughout the country including an introduction to the Information and Automation Plan. Once the introductory session was over, the employees could take their own Personal Computer home.

This is how I managed to involve nearly all employees in the Automation Process. At the same time I could create awareness regarding the threat of 'plastic currency' and the Euro and could reinforce the importance of banking products. An important side effect of the training sessions was that we learned of the many demands and requirements from the 'front line'.

The H&R manager was very eager to have his own Personnel Information System. This was to be the trial project. At that point in time only the payroll services had been subcontracted and this company had to collect an awful lot of data manually. Given the fast changing external regulations it had become next to impossible to produce the required data manually.

Every meeting started off with H&R Manager complaining about the Director-general and the Comptroller for about half an hour. It was not always easy to sit through this and sometimes I took charge and tried to steer the conversation away from the complaining. I wanted to remain friendly with him though, because this trial project had to be a showcase project. We had to gain experience towards the selection and implementation of standard software for the company. I had been able to convince the Director-general of the use of the project and he had granted permission on the condition that the Comptroller was included in the project group. The atmosphere in the project group was chilly to say the least, but on the other hand the complaining part only took half an hour and it was worth it in the end.

For this project I had appointed a very experienced external consultant who possessed extended knowledge regarding Personnel Information Systems and the implementation of the available standard packages. At that point in time I was unaware of the fact a standard package had been selected from a company that I had worked for as a Project Leader.

The standard package had been developed by a previous employer in conjunction with the software supplier and was now sold by the software supplier. As soon as this package was added to the 'short list' I withdrew from the decision making process. I wished to avoid a conflict of interest situation at all costs.

The software package was selected and much to my joy I knew the designer of the standard package quite well. I contacted him and he advised us on the implementation free of obligations. The project simply had to be successful but I had not counted on this lucky break.

One drawback was that we discovered that there were no standard methods and techniques available to implement standard packages. Alongside the trial project we had to develop our own methods and techniques for implementation.

The implementation of the standard package also demanded a considerable amount of basic process knowledge, in addition to the ability to adjust the processes and working method instead of the standard software package. The lack of knowledge of these processes in the organisation was considerable. Many employees carried out their daily routines as instructed by their managers, but hardly anyone ever asked himself why.

I learned that the will to win can command good fortune. I thanked my God for this.

Make sure you do the things you want to do. Only too often are we too preoccupied with creating the perfect picture that meets every single requirement laid out by our surroundings. If you choose to do just the things that suit you and that you enjoy doing, it will not take up any energy, it will not wear you out and you will not even need a holiday to recharge your batteries. A side effect is that good fortune will be coming your way.

Sharing experiences with others

During a 'plastic currency' seminar I met the editor of a well-read weekly Automation trade journal. We got to talk over lunch and I told him I had written a number of well-received articles for the local soccer club magazine. He asked me whether I was willing to write something similar for his trade journal and asked me to forward him a few stories. I promised I would do so but only if the stories were to be published under an assumed name. He agreed to this.

Over the weekend I wrote down a few stories and sent them to the editor. One week later he called me because he was very enthusiastic about the stories and asked me if I could do one every week. Now this was getting a bit too much and we cut a deal that I would write a biweekly column for his trade journal. This was a well-paid job and the money could be put towards things that make life more agreeable. We could do with the money.

I compiled the stories in my head while commuting in my car. At home I would put the story on paper which would take up about half an hour. Typing up the story was not an easy thing for me to do so I asked my secretary to help out. It goes without saying I offered her part of the proceeds and she was pleased with the bit of extra cash.

My stories involved people at work. I never mentioned any names and I always made sure there was a humorous touch to the story and I set out never to hurt someone. My stories featured my ex colleagues and ex managers. I had assumed a rather simple pen name but no one discovered who was the author of the columns.

On one occasion when I paid a visit to one of my fellow Senior Manager I could not help but notice that he was reading that particular trade journal. Without prompting he told me that he always read the column of the mysterious author first. It was his favourite part of the journal. I was struggling to hide my pleasure and tried to respond in a neutral fashion. I had to acknowledge the fact that what I had experienced over the past years was not very different from the lives of other Automation experts. What I had experienced in my private and business apparently struck a cord.

When the trade journal celebrated its 25th anniversary the editors also invited me to the party. No one present knew I was the mystery author, which seemed to me a preferable situation. None the less, in one of the next editions of the trade journal they had included a number of pictures taken at the party of those present. The caption of one photo indicated that this was one of their regular columnists while the caption of the photo that included me indicated that this was the mystery author. My cover was blown.

146

That week I received many phone calls from people that I had met and fortunately they were all positive about the stories and even wanted a complete edition of all the stories to re-read them. Fortunately no one at my then employer had any idea that I had been a mystery columnist in a trade journal so I could continue doing my job without much ado.

When I asked the editor he told me that the trade journal had received many phone calls from people who wanted to know the real identity of the author of the column. He said he had decided to disclose my name because he felt I was entitled to the fame and honour that was now coming my way.

I learned from this that it is very difficult to keep a secret. This time it all turned out for the best. Recognition had not been what I was after I had just wanted to share my experiences with others.

It's all sales

Selling consists of experiences. It is the task of the salesperson to tell customers and prospective customers about examples and situations. In this way the customer will have some idea of what the market is like and that his decision to buy something from you is quite normal. Even if the salesperson will not reveal his sources, he will use them to convince a customer. Sometimes it is a good idea to reveal the source because the source may bring in new customers. A salesperson is once again obliged to do a balancing act.

Selling a new bank

Since no specific policy had been defined with regard to the banking side of the company, I had indicated in my Information and Automation Plan that a preliminary investigation should be carried out concerning the strategy and policy for the bank.

The current situation was that the bank sold its products as a general bank straight through the main offices and that hardly any use was made (only for cash withdrawals and deposits) of the branch offices for the sale of banking products.

The Dutch National Bank was dissatisfied with the reports it received and the bank was also reconciled to the idea to organise the automated administration. Then there was also the additional threat of the Unification of Europe and the single currency. The Director-general considered an expansion of the bank as the answer to all the threats and problems. There was one snag though; the current director of the bank was to retire in three years time. He would not exactly be looking forward to the upcoming changes.

A project group including the Bank Director, the Comptroller and myself was established on my advice, headed by the Director-general. Subsequently I was appointed Chairman of the work group that included the Operational Bank Director and an External Consultant who was to write the preliminary investigation report.

Now I could put to use all my experience and creativity to describe the bank of the future. In the work groups we formed enthusiastic teams and designed a retail bank (open 24 hours a day 7 days a week) for all branch offices and a Wholesale bank (open during office hours) for the main office. We determined the criteria and yardsticks to select standard software to support the Automation of the banking processes.

The most important criterion was that we had to find an affordable solution. With that at the back of our minds we compiled a 'long list' of all standard software suppliers and sent them a 'request for information'. I also called all my business friends in my network to ask them if they had heard of a good standard software package.

One of my former colleagues told me he was carrying out a selection process for a small bank and that he was to attend a presentation and demonstration by a supplier of this great software banking system. He invited me to join him anonymously and attend the presentation by a hardware supplier unknown to me.

Not even in my wildest dreams could I have imagined the possibilities with this standard banking system. The system had been set up by a group of bankers for a major American bank. This bank had changed its policy and the bankers had started their own business with the software in the United Kingdom. The only problem was that so far they only had one customer in Switzerland and that unknown hardware (Prime) and the equally unknown operating system 'Pick' operated the system.

Now the project group had to choose one supplier out of the six suppliers we had short-listed. Two companies had been short listed for company political reasons i.e. one of them was a system from the software supplier handling banking production and a system from our hardware supplier.

When comparing the systems to our selection criteria the unknown system had the highest score by far. We had every member of the project group compile their individual yardsticks but also under those circumstances the unknown system came out top of the list. By approaching the decision making process in this way, the entire senior management was involved.

We organised a workshop at the hardware supplier that was to be given by the banking people of the organisation of the software supplier. We invited all those involved like the managers, works council, external consultant, IAS auditors, the Automation directors, shareholders etc. And fortunately after the two weeks everyone was convinced we had to purchase and implement this system.

The only one who was not pleased with the new system, and rightly so, was the Comptroller. With the banking system we had chosen he could process the financial administration of a bank but not the entire company. The Steering Committee then decided that the Comptroller could select and implement his own administrative system as long as it was compatible with the hardware of the banking system.

The next step was to submit the investments for approval from the shareholders. I compiled a project plan for the implementation of the standard banking system and we started contract negotiations with the hardware and software suppliers.

I learned about myself that I thoroughly enjoyed being creative. It was like living in a dream and my God gave me a tremendous amount of energy. And on top of it all, I was convinced it was all for the good of the company.

When it comes to the selling of investment goods, the role played by the DMU (Decision-Making Unit) will increase. In addition to extended product knowledge the salesperson will need to know the ins and outs of the buyer's strategy. Who takes the decisions, who has an influence on the decisions? Not only be aware of their existence but also know who they are and what their criteria are. When it comes to major decisions, which involve more departments of the buying customer, it may be useful to deploy more people at different levels. A result of this Multi-level approach can be that people in different positions throughout the organisation are familiar with what you offer.

Selling my daughter to my wannabe son in law

There he was, my daughter's very first boyfriend. She was thirteen, played soccer on the ladies team and had met this guy on the soccer pitch. At the soccer club he was known as a talented player and one of his brothers was on my team.

The first time she brought him round to the house he never said much and just sat there smiling. As a father and man I was, of course, very well aware of the danger a 14 year-old boy could pose. I made a point of being kind to him and talked to him about soccer. He did enjoy that but his eyes kept following my daughter wherever she went, whilst talking to me.

I did not waste any time in telling my daughter that I liked the guy, because I remembered having seen a show by a famous Dutch comedian about his daughter's boyfriends. "They all came over to our house and stayed for dinner. I spent a fortune on feeding a bunch of semi strangers. But I sang the praises of every single one of them because if I liked him, according to my daughter he couldn't possibly be cool."

A week later my daughter asked whether I would be at home that Saturday night. On my affirmative response she informed me that the boyfriend would pay us a visit once more because he enjoyed talking about soccer with me so much. I could not help but tease my daughter and I asked her whether he was her boyfriend or mine. This first romance did not last long since it was only based on soccer. I met the ex boyfriend on many occasions later on in life and he never forgot to inquire after the well being of my daughter.

My own soccer career was also going well. We had contracted a new trainer and he was determined to win the championships with our team. Once more I had to live up to expectations with regard to my position on the team. My father had taught me to have one single drink a day and at the weekend one at twelve in the afternoon. My dad's favourite drink was Dutch Gin, but my favourite 'poison' had always been a Dutch brandy-and-Coke. You always have to take to heart your father's sound advice.

One Saturday afternoon before the match was due to start, the new trainer smelled alcohol on my breath. In his opinion this was unacceptable and he kept me on the bench. I hated that because I always wanted to play.

The match was a bore and after about 20 minutes my replacement got injured and was taken of the field. I had to replace him. As soon as I got hold of the ball, I scored a goal and scored two more after the break. A 3-0 victory for our team. The trainer did not say a word but the week after he asked me whether I had taken my magical drink before the match. 'Of course' I replied and continued to play in every single match thereafter.

One Sunday my wife was very quiet and withdrawn. After lunch she told she was going to lie down for a while. Very unusual behaviour for my wife and when she had not come down after one and a half-hour I decided to go up and check whether she was all right. On entering the room I found her crying and as if in a trance. She stretched her arms and said softly "Daddy, I'm coming." Much to my distress she kept repeating those words.

I tried to wake her up but when I took her hand in mine it felt cold. It was not a normal cold hand, but it seemed to me the cold of death. Her whole body felt cold. She did not respond to the sound of my voice and I did not know what to do. Calling our GP[8] was certainly an option but it would take at least half an hour for him to arrive.

I tried to warm her up and started rubbing her body with my hands. I worked arduously and concentrated because I had the notion that if I ceased rubbing her body, something terrible would happen. I kept calling her name and slowly I felt her body temperature rise. After an hour or so she came to, but could not remember what had happened.

That night we talked about her father and their relationship. I knew theirs had been a troubled relationship at the best of times. My wife did not want to hear any criticism about her father. It was not possible for her to talk about her father in a realistic sense. She also did not want to talk to me about it, she only conveyed that she missed him tremendously. I asked her to go and see our GP and ask him for advice, since she had always been able to talk to her GP. She promised she would do that.

The first lesson I learned was that it was not easy for a father to accept a prospective 'son in law'. The second lesson taught me that warmth and love can keep people from death's door.

---

[8] GP = General Practitioner or Family Doctor

Even though this story is not intended as such, it does contain a metaphor. If you wish to keep a customer you have to spend a lot of time and effort on keeping him 'warm'. Provide the customer with up-to-date information, which will invite the customer to talk to you. If you pay attention to a customer, the customer will not take his business elsewhere. No, the customer will want to do business with you and only you.

Selling plastic currency awareness

One part of the Information and Automation Plan was to carry out a preliminary investigation into the consequences of the introduction of 'plastic currency' (The bank card[9]). It was important for us to know what its impact would be for our cash points and as means of payment for our company.

The placement of cash points (24 /7 access) by banks posed a direct threat to our service concept regarding Euro Cheques and Cashier's Cheques that could be exchanged for cash money. The customer paid for the service but in return this cash service was available 24 hours a day. We provided this service for all banks. If all the banks were to supply their customers with a plastic banker's card and cash points would be located everywhere, the banks would stop issuing the cheques altogether. Especially since they were susceptible to fraud anyway. We were bound to lose customers.

All our branch offices would also accept credit card cash withdrawals. This service was a huge success and many tourists made frequent use of this service. The internal processing of the transaction, sometimes through one terminal in the back-office, would take up a lot of time much to the annoyance of the customer and our employees. One of the main desires of the management of the Branch Office Organisation was to speed up this process.

In our country banking was divided. On the one hand you had the largest bank in the Netherlands the Dutch Postbank while on the other hand there were the other banks, representing the other 50%. The Postbank and the other banks fought each other over the patronage of both the customer and the retail chains. My company, also a retail chain, saw eye to eye with all the banks, including the Postbank. Still, our position was complex since we were also trading as a bank. This made us an important player in the market.

The Sales and Marketing Director regarded 'Plastic currency' as his 'baby'. He had this idea that nobody really appreciated the importance of the recent developments towards 'plastic currency'. He was not able, though, to increase awareness of the management and his colleagues. He was relieved to find a staunch supporter in me, someone who possessed extended knowledge on topics such as banker's cards, cash points, and cash machines. The knowledge I had gained while working for my previous employer now served a purpose. We

---

[9] Also known as Debit Card

had contracted an external consultant to compile the preliminary research report.

The whole retail side of the company was an exciting experience for me. I had always been employed by banks and had been dealing with 'bank people' yet now I got acquainted with managers of credit card suppliers, oil companies, telecom operators, mail order companies and both larger and smaller retail chains.

The results and the conclusion of the preliminary research report were clear. The rise of 'plastic currency' posed a serious threat to the future survival of the company. It was of the utmost importance to keep abreast of the current developments. It was our aim to accept all bankers' cards, including credit cards and debit cards as legal tender at all our customer service desks. All this had to be processed on one cash machine linked to our service desk terminals. As a result of this, a network had to be created comprising software and hardware to deal with the authorisation of transactions from the company that had issued the card.

Additional advice entailed that about a dozen cash points would have to be placed on a trial basis in a number of branch offices. We could carry this out in our capacity of bank and could derive the return on our investment from the combined banks guest user rates. In this way we could compensate for the financial loss generated by cash payments on cheques. Until that point in time we had been on good terms with the Dutch Postbank and it was not going to be easy to explain to them why we had decided to place cash points.

Once again I was happy contributing to innovation. I learned so much, which generated extra energy. With the knowledge I had obtained earlier I felt completely at home with this company.

Not only to retain or develop your market share but also to continue involvement of the sales staff, it is in the company's best interest to keep developing new products and add them to the existing range. It keeps sales staff enthusiastic and motivated. Even though salespeople tend to stick to what they already know because change disturbs the day-to-day routine. Sometimes the interests of the sales staff and management do not run parallel. From a strategic point of view, management can decide to introduce new products and expects its sales staff to support the new additions. These new products will not be profitable from the start. Since many salespeople work with a commission system their interest lies in selling existing products that already generate turnover. The existing products will be replaced in the long run by products with a good perspective.

Selling my department within the company

My automation department was scattered over three different locations. The Computer Centre had been located at the Head Office above the Central Train Station while the development department for the new system was located in the basement of one of the branch offices. Additionally, there was also the 'new' development department, which was located in a separate building close to the Head Office, in an area populated with junks and prostitutes. In the meantime a new Head Office was to be built where all three departments would be reunited.

My new department was growing rapidly. Especially the Information Centre for the introduction and support of the Personal Computer (PC) was expanding and many employees started their career in this department. We had recently contracted a few professional automation experts and the young and inexperienced colleagues could learn from the experts on the job. All the young employees received proper training. The company's policy aimed at finding a solution to a problem by using a PC, before we would revert to the use of the central computer. Decentralisation would prevail over centralisation. The atmosphere in the department was good, and we formed a hard- working team with lots of jokes and banter. The opposition from the rest of the organisation had turned us into a close team.

My secretary (black hair) now had a female assistant (blond hair), an incredibly attractive and fun duo. When the assistant laughed everybody joined in whether they wanted to or not. Their office was located next to mine and sometimes I had to apologise to my guests whenever a wave of laughter emerged from the office next door. Usually their laughter would bring a smile on our faces.

Every other day someone making obscene phone calls would pester the secretary's office. He never said a word he would just breathe heavily into the mouthpiece. At some point my secretaries got used to him and got into the habit of teasing him and making the occasional smutty remark. All this was highly entertaining and the ladies had a good laugh. Until at one point I was engaged in a tele-conference with a hardware supplier. At the other end there was a meeting room filled with people and I had been invited to explain our problems to them. When the secretaries tried to put me through to the contact at the hardware supplier it had gone completely quiet and the secretaries were convinced that it was the heavy-breather once more. They started their usual teasing and jokes much to the amusement of those present in the meeting room. It was quite embarrassing, to say the least, and I had quite a bit of explaining to do. Fortunately they saw the joke and I could not help but notice that some of those present were interested in meeting my secretaries.

The manager of the Computer Centre and my predecessor also occupied an office in our building. He also acted as our 'newsletter' and we hardly ever caught him doing any serious work. Instead he usually positioned himself next to the coffee machine to chat incessantly with his colleagues. One afternoon he had hung his jacket on a hanger with his wallet in his inside pocket. Whilst talking to his colleagues he received a phone call from the manager of our branch office in the city centre to inform him that this junk was trying to withdraw cash with his credit card. The Computer Centre Manager sprinted to his jacket only to discover that his wallet was missing. That day he was very fortunate.

Our highly appreciated Information Centre external consultant always parked his car close to our office, but after three break-ins and three stolen car stereos he decided he had had enough. He was absolutely fed up with it and set about to purchase one of those removable built-in car stereo sets so he could take out the car stereo and take it into the office. Much to his chagrin this car stereo was stolen as well. He was so upset and disappointed that we decided to pass round the hat to buy him a new car stereo.

Our Comptroller and some of his staff were located a floor above us. Every Monday morning an infuriated Comptroller would barge into my office. He would sit down at the meeting table and start throwing some abuse at me along the lines of 'you're the guy ruining the company with all these investments and automation expenditure'. After this had happened twice and he barged into my office once more I decided not to respond. I remained seated behind my desk and continued working without acknowledging his presence or his outburst. About five minutes later I heard the door slam and the Comptroller had left. That put an end to his Monday morning visits to my office. My secretaries suggested that his wife had probably refused him sex at the weekend, which is why he was in such a foul mood. I refrained from commenting.

The Human Resources Department had organised a big party on a party boat to celebrate that a number of employees had been with the company for 25 years. All managers and employees had been invited to join a boat tour along one of the rivers in our capital city. The Director-general, who happened to be an excellent orator, was to address the employees. During his speech he all of a sudden addressed me and promoted me on the spot to senior department manager. I had not expected this to happen at all, and all those involved had kept it a secret. I was extremely proud and I even turned emotional because I finally felt appreciated for all the work I had done. There was no better way to motivate me to complete the enormous project successfully.

A large number of managers were involved in the construction, completion and furnishing of our new Head Office. I was not involved because I was preoccupied with the automation projects. That was until my hardware supplier pointed out to me that it might be a good idea to install a cable system in the new building. I immediately informed the Director-general and fortunately we were right in time to make the necessary adjustments.

The Director-general had made sure the Automation Department would be comfortably situated and we were offered the fourth floor, which also happened to be the top floor of this new building. This meant our department could grow. My office was one of the most attractive offices in the whole building, which made me feel proud, but soon after we moved in we were nicknamed the 'golden boys' after our high salaries.

I learned that the opposition from the rest of the organisation led to the construction of a closely-knit team of people who could rely on one another and wanted to win. It made us strong and determined. But also slowly but surely the appreciation for our work increased from within the organisation because of the increased awareness of the major improvements.

When you oversee everything and have explored every possibility, the time has come to stand behind our own decisions and stick to those. All this, while at the same time maintaining an open mind to changes that can happen. Too often good plans are obscured because of unsolicited input from others in the hierarchy. Your plan stops being your plan, and will therefore lose strength.

Selling the participation in the Electronic Payment Trial

Because of the risk of petrol station and retail hold ups the pressure on the banks and the Postbank increased to introduce 'plastic currency', so less cash would be available in the cash register. Paying with a bankcard would also mean that the amount was debited to the account of the customer immediately and credited to the account of the shopkeeper instantaneously (direct debit).

Two bank blocks both had their separate system to carry through transactions and refused to link up the systems. The Postbank reproached (for political reasons) the banks that their payment systems were not reliable enough. Still, another battle had yet to be fought. The battle between the retailers and the two blocks of banks, since retailers did not appreciate the fact that they were being charged for transactions by the banks and the consumers were used to transactions free of charge. So what it came down to was who was going to pick up the bill?

The different battles were fought during seminars about electronic payment in The Netherlands where usually most parties were present. The retailers, to which we also belonged, did not form a united front.

The smaller oil companies did form a united front but the larger retail chains did not co-operate. The Sales and Marketing Manager and I took part in all these seminars and tried to lobby as much as we possibly could. I increasingly enjoyed taking part in these seminars and my company gained importance.

Ultimately, succumbing to the pressure of the retailers, the banks and the Postbank decided to join forces after all and set up a trail trial for electronic payment in one specific region of the country.

It was sheer madness because the banks had decided not to link up their networks but to construct a special terminal comprising two tangible parts and two programmes. One for the Postbank and one for the combined banks. They would include one PIN pad for all bankcards with a Pin Code linked to the terminal and the terminal would not be linked to the cash register system of the retailer. This set up seemed acceptable for a trial run.

In the selected region we had two offices and it was quite a victory that both offices were equipped with one terminal each to take part in the trial run. We were now truly considered a retail chain and that had been our objective all along. The trial run was started by one of the Dutch Cabinet Ministers, which generated quite a bit of free publicity.

Together with all the other participating retail chains we had set up a periodical meeting to discuss and evaluate the trial run. The trail run ended up being a success for the consumer but the retailers wanted a more simple system, linked to their cash register system. The transactions would have to be processed faster because no one was interested in customers queuing in front of the checkouts. The Sales and Marketing Manager and I could put pressure on the banks because the speed of the transactions was of the utmost importance to us. Now the war between the retailers and the banks really took off. Of course we remained on the sideline albeit actively.

I learned to look after the interests of my company and to play 'political games' if that was required. Every battle won motivated me even more, while at the same time we felt as if we were skating on thin ice.

The required skills for a salesperson: switching between direct approach to political approach and vice versa. This also determines the quality of a salesperson. If selling was easy, anyone could do it, but at the end of the day there would not be many salespeople left because cheaper options could be applied like tele selling. A true salesperson uses his psychological knowledge to approach his customers.

Selling in between two stakeholders

In The Netherlands the installation of cash points by the banks had a side effect. A hardware supplier had become very successful supplying the so-called 'fault tolerant' systems that were to be used in the back offices of the banks. These systems were operated by a standard software package. The cash point had to be available 24 hours a day and so the banks needed to acquire a system that was available 24 hours a day.

I had known the Director-general of the hardware supplier rather well since dealing with him whilst working for my former employer. He had started off as a Sales Director and had become very successful. In my previous position my then employer had been one of the first banks to purchase their hardware and three other competing banks had adopted our choice unquestioningly.

The war between the banks and The Dutch Postbank regarding the introduction of cash and payment points in The Netherlands was fierce. It goes without saying that the Postbank had opted for a different standard software system and a different hardware supplier. The war between the banks and The Postbank and the retailers was fought at the seminars and was on occasion quite amusing.

The company that now employed me operated as a bank as well as a retail chain. In addition to that, the company had a good relationship with both the Postbank and the other banks. In our policy plan we had included that we would try to serve both bank blocks but our status would remain neutral.

Our Sales and Marketing Manager was a close friend of one of the Senior Managers of the Postbank and since I had some good contacts with the other banks we could perfectly maintain our neutral position with all stakeholders. We attended every single seminar on electronic payment on offer in the country in order not to miss out on any of the arguments between all parties involved and attune our actions accordingly. Our take on the matter meant that our role as a neutral party was becoming increasingly important.

The above mentioned hardware supplier had organised an Electronic Payment Seminar in a rather luxurious hotel close to a beautiful lake in Switzerland. They had invited all the major players in the field. I had also received an invitation. I discussed the invitation with the Director-general and the Sales and Marketing Manager, who admittedly envied me my interesting outing. Together we attuned the company's policy with the policy plan in mind and once we had established our starting points, I was at liberty to accept this honourable invitation.

It turned out to be not an altogether pleasant trip as far as I was concerned. Upon arrival in Switzerland I was picked up by a chauffeur-driven white Rolls Royce to take me to the hotel. I was not the only passenger, though. The two other passengers turned out to be two delegates from The Postbank who also needed a ride to the hotel. One of the Postbank officials was also known as the 'Bull dog'. Without beating about the bush he asked me whose side my company was actually on. Or in other words was I friend or foe.

Fortunately we had stated our position into detail in the policy plan. I took a deep breath and as quietly as I could I told him and his colleague about our ideas and policy concerning the introduction of plastic currency and our long-lasting good relationship with the Postbank. And most of all I stressed the fact that I represented a neutral retail chain that wanted to offer its services to all banks, including the Postbank. The 'Bull dog' understood and got off his high horse. Unfortunately I had not been able to enjoy the Rolls Royce ride in beautiful surroundings one bit. I had been on edge all the time.

But the real fun started during the seminar. The two Postbank delegates set themselves apart from the delegates of the other banks. And I sort of manoeuvred in between both sides. Sometimes with the Postbank delegates, sometimes with the delegates from the other banks, lobbying all the time to maintain our neutral position. This role came to be accepted by all stakeholders and I was used more and more as a go-between both parties.

At that point in time both parties were not interested in co-operating and the security risk attached to transactions over the network were used as a reason to sabotage the possible co-operation between both parties. During one of the sessions one famous metaphor was used. The Postbank 'Bull dog' accused the other banks of 'letting their transactions run naked along the corridor'. What it came down to was that the security measures taken by the other banks were not sufficient. Both parties just did not want to co-operate but at the same time they were aware of the increasing pressure from the retailers. The retailers were absolutely not keen on the idea of having two cash points for the separate systems on their shop counters.

For me this seminar was hard work and no play. I made sure I stayed fit by retiring early and not having too much to drink. I did feel a bit lonely between all the delegates. I had to look after my company's interests and when I think back, I cannot remember an awful lot about the excellent food and the boat trip on the lake. A pity I could not enjoy all that was on offer.

After lunch on the second day I went for a walk in the beautiful hotel garden. All of a sudden a Director-general of a large bank taking part in the seminar, joined me. He complimented me on the work I had done so far and was very kind to me. He then happened to mention that he had a piece of valuable advice for me.

His bank had commissioned a survey into the 'best positions for cash points' in the Netherlands and the outcome was that the best place to position a cash point was at a train station. A lot of people commuted every day and liked to make cash withdrawals en-route. My company had the exclusive rights for bank transactions regarding the train stations, including the placement of cash points. I soon realised that this was valuable information indeed and that something had to be done.

I learned to appreciate the importance of defining company policy. Moreover, believing in the policy plan and carry it out was essential. Good arguments are accepted all round and make it easier do your job and command respect. I did enjoy playing the part that had come my way. Once again my experience in amateur dramatics came in useful.

As a salesperson you represent your company whereas at the same time you represent the customer of your company. This requires tact. Only too often being tactful is seen as a weakness. As if you do not support your product or company for the full 100%. Nevertheless, a good salesperson will make it known to his customer that he is important and gives the support of your customer within the company.

Influencing sales by using lipstick

We had started negotiations with hardware suppliers to purchase the standard banking system and the supporting hardware platform. This standard software would only run on the special hardware supplied by one of the smaller hardware suppliers. We wanted to set up a comprehensive deal and for this reason the Director-general, our company legal advisor, the hardware supplier and I went to visit the standard software supplier. We all stayed at the same hotel.

Our legal advisor was in my book 'a strange character'. I trusted him about as far as I could throw him and he was well aware of that. In the past the same company had employed us. The Inland Revenue inspectors had raided the company and as it turned out someone on the inside had tipped them off. At a later stage a book was written about the raid and the legal advisor was named as the possible informer.

And when the Director-general had informed me that an ex colleague, the legal advisor, had been appointed, I felt I had to warn him and I told him about my suspicions concerning the Inland Revenue raid. In spite of my advice to the contrary the Director-general informed the legal advisor about my negative feed back. At some point the legal advisor came to take me to task about the matter. We were not on the best of terms nor would we ever be and he was just waiting for the opportunity to get his own back. Whenever we were involved in contract negotiations together he always made me feel he was on the side of the supplier and against me.

The salesperson delegated by the hardware supplier was a young man. He had already invited the Director-general and me to pay a visit to their plant in the USA but I had turned down his offer. At that point in time no formal deal had been made and I did not want to be influenced. After conferring the Director-general had decided to accept the invitation to visit the US plant and combine it with a visit to the IMF. The salesperson did not like the fact that I had turned his invitation, but I did not want to create the impression that the race was already won. Because of the compatibility of the software with his company's hardware, he was in a strong bargaining position already.

The salesperson had told me that in his spare time he was an inventor of some sort and had shown me a number of his inventions. He hoped to get rich with one of his inventions one day. He was very proud of what he had invented so far and was always carrying some or other invention around with him.

So during the negotiations with the software supplier, we had a glass of whisky in the bar of the hotel afterwards. The legal advisor and the software salesperson hit it off really well. Once again I understood the part I was expected to play and left the two 'new friends' to their own devices. I had a day with heavy negotiations ahead of me.

When I got home I dumped my dirty laundry in the laundry basked out of habit. But when I got home the next day I was greeted by an outraged wife. She showed me my shirt and demanded to know why there was what looked like red lipstick on my collar. I had a closer look and oddly enough the red stains were at the back of the collar of my shirt.

I was convinced that the legal advisor and the salesperson had played a trick on me with one of the salespersons inventions. Unfortunately it was a trick I found very hard to explain to my wife especially since I could not call upon any witnesses. I decided not to show my discomfort and did not say a word to anyone. I was warned though, and would keep my eyes wide open in the future.

I learned again that in business you always have to be aware of every move you make, who your friends are and what their interests are. Salespeople want to close a deal and will go to any length to get that deal.

The informal side of doing business is very important. Try to hold on the informal atmosphere and try to show another side of you. The only reason for this is that you want the other to like you. The rest will follow. When it comes to networking this basic principle also applies. Try to come across as interesting, be sincere and try to do something for someone else. For instance, refer someone to someone else. In doing so you are helping three people, the person you are referring to, the person you are helping and yourself. Out of gratitude they will return the favour.

Selling as Santa Claus

A friend of my wife owned a clothes shop in our village. She did not only sell designer clothes but also sweaters manufactured on knitting machines. Once a year the entrepreneurs in our village used to stage a fashion show in our town hall and among the items on show would be the home-knitted sweaters.

My wife, daughter and I were invited to take part as models and show the clothes. That night the town hall was packed with locals and it made me feel good to be a part of it. I felt at home. The locals made us feel as if we belonged there.

The husband of my wife's friend also happened to be the chairman of the Organisation of Entrepreneurs in the village. In December they usually organised a lottery. Sinterklaas[10] and later Father Christmas were to draw the lucky numbers in one of the participating shops. The prices were always items from the shop hosting the event that evening.

The villagers were looking for someone to play both 'Sinterklaas and Father Christmas and given my career in amateur dramatics I volunteered to play both parts. For the first time in my life I had to ride a horse because that is what Sinterklaas does. And I had to endure being transported in a horse driven cart as Father Christmas. I thoroughly enjoyed playing both parts and getting to meet both children and adults. For my daughter these were wonderful days, because she was one of the few children who was let into the secret of the identity of Sinterklaas and Father Christmas, which made her a local celebrity.

The highlight of the Dutch festive season in our village was the arrival of Sinterklaas all the way from Spain. The mayor would receive him on the balcony of the town hall. As it happened the mayor of our village had been appointed mayor of the larger neighbouring village a month earlier and he had decided to receive Sinterklaas in the neighbouring village and to have our Sinterklaas (that being me) met by one of the councilmen.

---

[10] The Dutch and Belgians celebrate two festive periods in the month of December. On 5 December they celebrate present night according to the old Dutch and Belgian custom. Sinterklaas (Santa Claus) comes all the way from Spain by boat to celebrate his birthday with the children. In stead of receiving them, though, he gives presents to the children. Sinterklaas rides a large white horse and like Father Christmas he distributes his presents through the chimneys. The Dutch and Belgians also celebrate Christmas. On Christmas Day and Boxing Day they spend time with their family whilst enjoying large amounts of food. In recent years more and more people have started giving presents for Christmas as well.

There was quite some rivalry going on between the two villages and when the mayor had decided to meet the Sinterklaas of the neighbouring village, some of the locals were quite annoyed. In my speech on arrival I addressed the issue of the mayor not being present to welcome Sinterklaas and even before I had finished, the local children and their parents started cheering and singing. My entire speech was printed in one of the local newspapers.

Whenever I visited the shops whether as Sinterklaas or Father Christmas I always noticed the same woman wearing a headscarf standing at the back of the shop. I could tell from the way she looked that she did not have a lot of money to spend and never bought anything. She always showed up for the lottery and would leave the shop with a sad look on her face because her number had not come up.

The situation unnerved me and I decided to do something about it. The final lottery draw of the festive season had been planned in a liquor shop owned by a good friend of mine. I told him about the woman and together we decided to display our own brand of magic. When the lottery draw was to start my friend had managed to read the number on the woman's ticket and had passed that information on to me. That night she won the star prize and left the shop with a smile on her face. Now I felt like a real Sinterklaas or was it Father Christmas.

The lesson I had to learn was that there would always and everywhere be poor people who are still grateful for the smallest of presents. I thanked my God that I had witnessed it.

This story reminds me of the possibilities you have as a salesperson to do something special for your customers. Not because of personal gain but just for the sake of being kind to someone else. For instance, referring a customer to someone else who can give proper advice on how to deal with a certain situation. In doing so you build a strong relationship that will help your customer but in the end will also work to your advantage.

What people say is not always what they do

Working for this financial establishment and the part we were playing in the Electronic Payment Movement was really up my street, especially because I got the opportunity to meet people from different sectors. In particular the problems of the retailers with regard to electronic payment served as real 'eye openers' to me.

I could not help but notice that the oil companies knew everything there was to know about customer behaviour. They had discovered that their customers did not particularly enjoy stopping for petrol. Which had led them to invent ways to make stopping at a petrol station a fun experience by establishing shops for fun shopping to make the wait more agreeable. They wanted to turn stopping for petrol into a fun break.

An additional extra was that petrol stations started to make more money out of the fun shopping than from supplying petrol. Unfortunately also the bad guys had discovered that and given the isolated location of most petrol stations they were perfectly situated for hold ups. It had become increasingly popular to protect staff against robberies and to train staff properly. They wanted less cash in their cash registers and tried to convince the banks that the introduction of electronic payment had to be accelerated.

The largest petrol supplier in the Netherlands had already introduced a plastic card and this card turned out to be very popular with its customers. In those days it was not considered ethical to do business with South Africa given its Apartheid policy. The large Oil Company was still doing business quite successfully in South Africa, though.

The media urged people to boycott the petrol stations of the large Oil Company. And when asked, most consumers said they avoided those particular petrol stations. Yet the Sales Director of the Oil Company told me that their number of customers had increased considerably since the introduction of the plastic card.

The smaller petrol stations co-operated and they all used the same cash terminal and the services provided by the same software supplier. This was a small company completely financed from their own banks (so no bank credits). This company strongly depended on its customers, the petrol stations, and to them it was of the utmost importance to keep abreast of the current developments concerning electronic payments. They wanted to obtain the sole rights to provide the electronic payment terminals.

The Director-general of this particular software company was quite an interesting character and was always present during the seminars to look after his interests. Sometimes he displayed obnoxious behaviour in the sense that like a pit bull terrier he would get his teeth into his prey and would not let go. It was amusing to see how on his arrival certain bankers would make themselves scarce just to avoid him. To the banks he was a nuisance because he did not need them. I respected him because of his never failing efforts for the good of his company and I was pleased for him when in the end he was awarded the order to supply the terminals.

I learned that most companies have their own interest at heart and that I could not always rely on market research because people do not always do what they say. I also learned that putting up a fair fight for the survival of your company commands respect and trust.

An emotional and rational thinking process guides human beings. That explains why people and situations can change unexpectedly. And their own interests, of course, play an important part. First the Anti apartheid movement is an important issue while at a later stage this can move to the background. That is why it is complicated to reach conclusions derived from market research. More often than not the outcome of such research does not match real customer behaviour.

Selling the placement of cash points within the company

The valuable advice the friendly Bank Director had given me during the seminar in Switzerland strengthened me in my own conviction that the positioning of cash points could be very profitable for our company. I, therefore, decided to put in some extra work at home and write a policy paper for the Board of Directors regarding the placement for testing purposes of five cash points in the outer wall of one of our largest branch offices.

We also traded as a bank after all and were, therefore, entitled to placing cash points. Since we would offer our services to more customers of other banks than our own bank, this would be profitable for our company because of the guest user rates the banks had agreed upon. The revenue stemming from this service could compensate for the loss we were making regarding the cashing of cheques issued by all the banks. There was one problem though. We could not offer our services to customers of the Dutch Postbank since they did were not a part of the guest user service.

It was a bit odd that the Senior Automation Manager (me) had to introduce this plan and not the Director of the Office Organisation. It turned out that he regarded the cash point as a threat to customer desk services! It was such a pity because that was not the case and I did not want to wait any longer.

It was not an easy matter to get my plan approved. The Director-general was interested, but the Sales and Marketing Director was a close friend of one of the directors of the Postbank and was afraid that the Postbank would refrain from doing business with us. One of our Comptrollers had compiled a cost-benefit analysis of a cash point and had calculated that a cash point could never be exploited profitably. I asked him where he got the number of expected transactions from and he responded 'I just know'. No market research had been carried out and there was no basis whatsoever for the figures the Comptroller had produced.

I kept pursuing the Director-general to grant his approval to my plan and he decided that our Internal Accountant Services Auditor could compile a new cost-benefit analysis based on the facts and figures I had provided. I was able to convince the Internal Accountants Services but this took quite some effort and energy. And now all of a sudden a cash point could be exploited profitably.

We invited the Director of the Dutch Postbank to discuss our plans to place cash points. Our Sales and Marketing Director was rather nervous that day. I had prepared a good presentation and managed to show that our company was in serious danger of losing revenue given the declining number of cheques that were cashed and that the placement of cash points would be the answer to the problem.

The director of the Postbank was well prepared and had established that the train stations were perfectly suited for placing profitable cash points. He suggested the possibility to place Postbank cash points in the outer walls of our branch offices at a certain rate. This would lead to a conjoined block of cash points. It was a truly great suggestion because as it turned out we had more customers than we ever had with cashing cheques.

It took a lot of trouble to convince the employees of the Office Organisation that the cash points would not be detriment to the customer desk transactions.

I had started writing a project plan for the installation of five conjoined cash point blocks. We struck a deal with our shareholder (a large bank) about the usage of their system for the settlement of cash point transactions and the Postbank would deal with the Postbank transactions. The most work turned out to be the installation of the cash points and the security procedures surrounding the filling of the actual cash machine.

Six months after the placement of the conjoined cash point block at our largest and busiest office in the centre of our Capital, the Board of Directors of a cash machine supplier from the USA came to pay us a visit. They had come all the way from the States to watch their most successful machine at work in its natural habitat. They just could not believe the actual number of 24/7 transactions.

The project was also important with regard to sustaining our neutral position in the banking industry. We once again were able to prove that we wanted to offer our services to all customers of every bank. Our cash points were a huge success and because of this, the banks decided to lower the guest user rate. That was a slight disappointment but it did not dissuade us and in the end we placed more than 60 cash points at the Central Train Stations. The Office Organisation was now very interested in placing the cash points given the revenue derived from them.

I learned again that I would put up a fight for causes I strongly believed in. I thoroughly enjoyed doing that, especially since we could pose a threat because of our success. It took up a lot of energy and as it turned out success has many fathers.

For a salesperson in particular it is of the utmost importance that he can assess the situation he is confronted with. Sometimes the chances on success are slight or even worse, you stand no chance at all. The prospect could still be a potential customer, though. You have the idea to give it a miss and look for other opportunities. Very often a salesperson discovers that his negative assessment of reality is not correct. It is therefore important to go for it. Approach the customer, engage him in conversation and listen to him. At some point the customer will offer an opportunity for doing business.

Unsatisfactory dealings with a legal advisor

The company intended to purchase the standard banking system from a supplier to implement it for our bank. Our legal advisor had established that the standard contract of the supplier did not meet the requirements of the bank at all and had suggested to the Director-general to compile a new contract. The supplier was not from the Netherlands and therefore the content of the contract had to meet the demands of the supplier's country. I was quite surprised by the Director-general's decisions.

The legal advisor and I were not on good terms. He was still nurturing hostile feelings towards me because of the negative advice I had given towards his appointment. He kept opposing my every decision whenever he could. And he managed to compile a 200-page contract sent for us to read and discuss it with him.

One day I travelled by plane with the external consultant to the Head Office of our supplier to discuss the contact. On our way from the airport our taxi was involved in an accident. Fortunately we were not injured but we were shocked and upset and the delay took more than an hour.

Upon our arrival at the supplier's Head Office our own very furious legal advisor greeted us. He was angry with us for being late and he never even bothered asking why we were late, let alone showing any concern for our well-being.

The legal advisor did not demonstrate any relevant automation knowledge whatsoever and we went to an awful lot of trouble to drive our point home. A very important issue was the availability of the programme code in the unlikely event the supplier went bankrupt. This issue happened to be one of the demands set out by our external Comptroller and prompted by the Dutch National Bank. The legal adviser turned down our suggestion point blank.

On our return the external consultant and I discussed the strange behaviour of our legal advisor, for the latter did not understand what was going on. I had to conclude that it was bad for the company if I continued to be involved in the contract negotiations. The legal advisor simply detested me, which was definitely a bad starting point for negotiations. And in addition to that, the content of the contract was a sheer disaster since it was clearly favourable towards the supplier. It contained all sorts of loose ends and details about unimportant issues.

During my bi-weekly meeting with the Director-general I gave him a matter-of-fact summary of the proceedings. I withheld my personal opinion since I knew the legal advisor and the Director-general were close friends. I then informed him that it was not good for business if I were to be involved in the contract negotiations given the troubled relationship between the legal advisor and myself. The director just frowned and asked to pass on to him my remarks regarding the contract. He would then discuss them with the legal advisor. This is exactly what happened and I never had any dealings with the legal advisor on this matter again.

From this situation I learned that when people dislike or detest you, doing business is impossible. People only buy from people they like.

The number one condition for good agreements is a good relationship. And that is exactly what sales is all about. Since the stakes can be high, we occasionally allow ourselves to overlook a bad relationship in order to enter negotiations. This often leads to disappointment on both sides. In a case like this it is better to have a colleague take over negotiations. A colleague may have a different approach, more suitable to this particular kind of negotiations.

Doing business with a Comptroller

Our Comptroller was not at all content with the options the standard banking system would offer for keeping accounts and the ledger of the company. The possibilities were limited to the use of banking administration and not at all suited for keeping accounts. At that point in time the Comptroller made do with an old system requiring many manual adjustments. I had never been able to examine the possibilities of the old system for he had never allowed my automation colleagues or me near his departments.

It would be safe to say that the Comptroller and I had a love-hate relationship. When he needed me he would be friendly and as soon as the need subsided he would call me the most horrible names. But now he was faced with a big problem. The Board of Directors had accepted the banking system, as had all users and his friends at the external accountants' and he was the only one left with a problem. I had made it abundantly clear to him that it was not possible for my department to implement the banking system and a new financial administration system at the same time. These were hard times for the Comptroller and he was very eager to select and implement a new system for his financial administration.

There was an additional problem within the company. I had discovered with the trial project for the H&R department that the organisation was desperately lacking operational procedures and that the Administrative Organisation had not been set up properly. Some people from the internal control department who were to report to the Comptroller had put a few job descriptions together. In order to implement the new banking system it was of the utmost importance that the Administrative Organisation (procedures and regulations) had been constructed properly.

My plan was to set up an Administrative Organisation as a sub division of the Automation Department. Due to the implementation of standard software I foresaw a shift in importance from the Information Analyst to the Organisation Analyst who should be capable of describing the banking processes. The standard software laid bare the necessity to adapt the process to the standard system. The programmes were available, the next step was to compile the necessary procedures and regulations. The controlled did not want to talk to me about it since he felt I should mind my own (automation) business.

I grew increasingly worried about the poor Administrative Organisation in our company and kept looking for solutions. As it happened the chairman of my soccer club, who also happened to live in the same street, specialised in Administrative Organisation or Administrative Information Science. He was a professor holding a chair at the University and worked part-time for our external accountant. He was also a published author of a number of books on the topic. At the soccer club he was always referred to as 'the professor'

I had attended one of his seminars once and his enthusiasm and his ability to turn writing simple procedures into an attractive activity struck me. I approached him in the canteen at the club and we arrived at the idea to organise a mini seminar on Administrative Organisation for the Board of Directors and Managers of my company. He would address the audience for a reasonable price. Fortunately the Director-general agreed with my proposition and the mini seminar was a huge success. And of course the professor recommended that the Administrative Organisation Department would become a sub division of the Automation Department.

I was biding my time for I knew the Comptroller was about to cut a deal with me. And indeed, his secretary approached me to set up a meeting. My part of the deal was to allow him to start the selecting and implementation process for a system for the Financial Administration. All this, of course, according to our methods and techniques. On his part he allowed the special committee for the Administrative Organisation to carry out the structuring of the Administrative Organisation and incorporate this division into the Automation Department.

I learned that sometimes you have to accept the way some people are, because you cannot change or replace them. But for the good of the company you must always try to involve them in what is going on and to remain on speaking terms, no matter how difficult that may turn out to be.

It's all sales

Also in Sales you have to deal with a variety of people. For instance your customers. It is easier to get along with the one customer than with the other. A good salesperson is able to get along with everyone. With someone you are on friendly terms with you can be informal. Yet when the relationship is a bit strained, the salesperson will have to find a way to get through to a customer and find out what he is interested in. Whenever you encounter someone whose behaviour towards you is downright unpleasant try to determine where this behaviour stems from. The salesperson mistakenly assumes that the customer's behaviour is a response to him. Why not ask why the customer behaves the way he does. Sometimes it clears the air.

Feeling responsible and selling responsibility

One of my friends from the soccer club was known as the 'player who could play against the wind (read storm) and score from a 40 meter distance with his muscular thighs' had been forced to leave the club because he had accepted a position abroad. He had invited our team to come and play his new team. We rented two mini-vans and drove 800 kilometres to play soccer.

I was the oldest player on the team and I felt responsible for my younger teammates. I intended to bring them back to our village in one piece. It was not easy, though, to manage a group of young, exuberant and drunk youngsters.

After the match our hosts had organised a party in the canteen and much to our surprise there was exactly one female present. She was the girlfriend of one of the players on the host's team.

Almost every single guy on my team fell in love with her instantaneously and was bending over backwards to attract her attention. I even had to protect her from an overwhelming amount of unwanted attention. On the way back I did most of the driving because my mates were still under the influence of alcohol. When we finally got home I was glad we had made it back home and that they lived to think back of a memorable weekend for all those involved.

My daughter was a huge Madonna fan. She tried to imitate Madonna's dance moves, owned every CD and her bedroom was covered wall to wall with Madonna posters. My daughter had got wind of Madonna touring and that she would perform in the Netherlands in a large football stadium. She desperately wanted to go to that concert. Unfortunately she was rather late with informing me about this, because the concert had already sold out. Through my secretary I managed to get hold of three black market field tickets that cost me an arm and a leg.

Once we were out there on the field in this gigantic football stadium I realised it was a rather dangerous situation amidst 5000 overexcited fans. For as soon as Madonna would appear on the stage all those fans would move forward to catch a glimpse of their idol and could crush us. I managed to secure some standing room in front of the sound system. Here we were relatively safe and could keep an eye on each other. And what a magnificent concert it was. One woman being able to entrance 50.000 people and give them a night to remember, it was incredible. I truly respected Madonna. My daughter was completely enraptured by the concert and would never ever forget this night. I was rewarded with a kiss.

My wife's birthday was approaching and she wanted to have dinner in a highly rated and expensive restaurant. For the first time in her life my daughter was expected to accompany us to an expensive restaurant. Up till that time she had been used to eating out at McDonald's and similar fast food establishments. She made quite a fuss over it and flatly refused to join us.

I tried to explain to her that it would be a special experience but she kept nagging about it. This made me angry and I made it clear to her that she had to respect her mother's wishes since it was her birthday. On arrival at the restaurant the proprietor, who was an acquaintance of mine, gave us a warm welcome. Our waitress was a young and amusing girl who paid a lot of attention to my daughter.

My daughter also discovered that guests at the table next to her were speaking in a language unknown to her. That she found intriguing and soon she was involved in a conversation with them. They winked at us and clearly enjoyed talking to my daughter.

For dessert the young waitress presented my daughter with a selection of tasty sweets, which she obviously enjoyed. After that dinner she lost interest in all McDonalds had to offer and wanted to have dinner in expensive restaurants all the time. She would check the menu for the desserts first. From an educational point of view a good development, but bad news as far as my wallet was concerned.

One night my daughter told me that 'all her school girlfriends' received a clothing allowance from their parents so she wanted an allowance as well. In my opinion a good idea. Until that point in time she had only bought expensive designer clothes, paid for by Dad and had not worried about the price of these garments. I inquired after the allowance her friends received and discussed it with my wife. We decided to give her a monthly clothing allowance. I had to instruct my wife not to provide additional means from the housekeeping budget, otherwise my daughter would not learn anything from it.

The very first month my daughter bought a beautiful coat and spent every single penny of her allowance. That hurt, and she thought this whole clothing allowance thing was not such a good idea after all. She wanted to stop it immediately and return to the way things had been. I did not budge and explained to her that she had to save up her allowance if she wanted to buy something special. After a while it all worked out fine. She stopped buying designer clothes and in every shop she tried to negotiate about the price. I will never forget the arguments we had about whether undergarments were to be paid for from her allowance. Great arguments from my daughter and I enjoyed it immensely.

I became aware of the fact that you have to be very special to entrance 50.000 people. Only a truly artist can pull off something like that. But as I got older I also felt an increasing sense of responsibility for the world around me. I just had to accept that and try to pass this feeling on to my daughter.

It is a market mechanism. When you are able to do something that many people enjoy, it means that prices increase and that you have to do something about productivity. In this case not the local pub but a football stadium. Responsibility is a strange mechanism. It encourages you to go the extra mile. However, since you want to do well, you run the risk of not being able to do everything you want to. You hold back out of fear of failure. You do not want to run that risk, which is why you do not always reach the goal you set out for. Sometimes it pays off to put your sense of responsibility on the back burner and to act freely.

Language and the sales process

We were now approaching the final negotiating stages regarding the purchase of a standard software system for our bank. This enormous contract had been compiled by our own legal advisor and contained numerous stipulations favouring the supplier and quite a few loose ends.

My aim was to implement this system for our bank. We were in need of this system to be able to survive in the future and to meet external regulations. I had no choice; I just had to accept this disastrous contract, for commissioning another contract was not an option. I had to go in there, negotiate and try to substantiate all loose ends for the sake of my company. I had to rise above the bad relationship between the legal advisor and myself. The company was ready for implementation so we had to proceed.

For the final negotiations the Director-general had invited in his office the Director-general of the supplier, our Bank Director, our Comptroller, our legal advisor and me. The meeting was to be conducted in the language spoken by our supplier and the contract had been written in that same language. I could not help but notice that the Bank Director and our Comptroller were clearly struggling with the language.

We talked through every single article in the contract and ended up discussing the chapter on investments and expenditure. The requirements stipulated in the contract required no obligation of best interest from the supplier etc. During negotiations we discussed, after having obtained permission from the Director-general from the supplier, some issues in our own language to clarify the contents and come to a better understanding. We automatically assumed that the Director-general of the supplying company could not speak Dutch and felt at liberty to discuss matters freely in our own language.

Once we got to the part about investments and expenditure I suddenly noticed from his body language that he understood every word we said. He had never told us he could understand Dutch and it suddenly dawned upon me that he had lived in the Dutch speaking part of Belgium for a while and was therefore able to understand the language.

What was I to do? To bring the matter out into the open could bring negotiations to an immediate standstill. It was a mater of trust and trust is a basic requirement for a partner relationship. That was not an option and I had to come up with a solution fast.

I signalled to the Director-general that I needed to speak to him in private. We went to the office next door and I informed him on the language skills of the

Director-general of our supplier. He understood why confronting him with our discovery was not an option and together we decided to go for a fixed-price, fixed-date deal. Thereby tying up all possible loose ends. As far as I was concerned, this was an acceptable deal.

On our return to the meeting room the Director-general proposed our deal. The guest Director-general understood our change of tactics and knew he could not do anything but accept our proposition.

I learned how to put my intuition and gut feeling to good use in negotiations and treat negotiations purposefully. Both parties needed each other and sensitivities are subordinate to that.

The question is who is being honest in this case? How appropriate is to speak in your own language if there are people present who have no knowledge of that particular language. From the Director-general of the supplier I can understand that he did not feel the need to enlighten his partners about his ability to speak Dutch. If you want to confer as delegates, it is considered good manners to talk to each other separately. What matters is that people who are negotiating a deal should be able to trust each other. If there is no trust, the co-operation will fall through.

Playing for high stakes

The standard banking system had been selected, the project plan indicating its implementation had been written and approved of, the necessary employees had been informed and allocated. All that needed to be done was to sign the contract with the supplier. However, the contract was not signed, as yet, the management was not ready to take a decision.

Every other week I had my regular bi-weekly meeting with the Director-general and every time I would ask him whether a decision had already been taken. And every time he told me I had to be patient, no decision was made as yet. The underlying problem was that the Bank Director was to retire in three years time. A successor had been appointed who was also working for our company, but the Bank Director refused to accept him as his successor. At the same time I had been the one to advise our Director-general the implementation of the banking system should take place under supervision of the newly appointed Bank Director as head of the Project Group.

The implementation of a new standard banking system implied that the existing banking processes and the existing bank organisation had to be adapted to the new banking system. That was a major change process requiring strong management. The Bank Director as head of the project group had to be able to take drastic measures when required. I had talked at length with the Director-general and I could understand perfectly well that the current Bank Director was not keen on undertaking a job as challenging as the one in hand. While at the same time the bank needed to grow and introduce new products to the market, based on that new flexible standard banking system to compensate for the results of the single currency in Europe.

At some point I had been waiting for six months and felt increasingly unhappy with this status quo. I had been appointed to carry out this important task for the benefit of the company. I intended to complete the Information and Automation Plan successfully and I was convinced that my plan would be the salvation of the company.

I decided I could not wait any longer for I was beginning to lose face within my own organisation but also with the suppliers. I raised the stakes and informed the Director-general during our bi-weekly meeting that I would hand in my resignation if no decision were taken before the end of the month.

The Director-general did not appreciate being put under pressure. I had learned, though, that he was good at taking decisions when under pressure. I, on the other hand, had no idea of what I was doing, there was not another position in sight and I had a family to take care of. I was trembling all over my body when I left the Director-general's office. I did not want to leave because I really liked the people I worked with and enjoyed my job. Would I be able to feed my family next month?

Two weeks later and before the end of the month I paid another visit to the Director-general. It goes without saying that I was quite nervous when I entered his office. Without beating about the bush he informed me that the Board of Directors had decided that I could proceed with the project. He also told me that there was not a new Bank Director available and I had to carry out the project with the current Bank Director. He subsequently handed me a hand-written piece of paper.

The piece of paper contained a contract that stated that I as project manager would be responsible for the implementation of the new standard banking system and that I would not be allowed to leave the company during the implementation project.

We looked each other straight in the eye and understood each other well. I had been playing with fire and he had let me have my way. He still had to point out that he was in charge of the company by drawing up this contract. I signed the contract without so much as blinking an eye.

I got to know myself as target oriented and that I was willing to go the extra mile to reach my goal. I was not after personal gain but I was willing to take chances that would benefit the company I worked for. My God sometimes offered unexpected advice and gave me super-natural powers.

It is of the utmost importance to determine how good you are or how good your product is. In addition to that, it is important to know as a salesperson what the alternatives for your clients are. To be aware of where your client can turn to when you are not able to supply the customer. If you made a good assessment, you can act upon that decision without even running the 50% risk.

Being successful at a New Year's reception

My department kept growing steadily, in line with the systems we implemented and the tasks that were allocated to us. Fortunately there was enough space available at our new Head Office to grow. The entire top floor was allocated to us and so far we had only taken up half of the available space.

For the newly developed Administrative Organisation Department (a sub division of the Automation Department) I had recruited a new outside manager. He was a rather 'formal' man and he emanated that he loved 'procedures' and 'regulations'. In appointing him I had made the right decision because it must have been hard for him to co-operate on the Administrative Organisation committee with the head of the Internal Accountant Services, a vassal of the Comptroller. He and I were involved together in several battles to win the war. His extended knowledge, his meticulousness and unruffled behaviour saved the day on many occasions.

One of the consequences of the implementation of the standard banking system was that two additional sub divisions had to be added to the Automation Department. One group controlling the banking system and a Computer Centre set up according to the regulations as stipulated by the Dutch National Bank and checked by the external accountant. There was one problem, though, because I had appointed my predecessor Head of the Computer Centre and I considered him unsuitable to set up and lead a new Computer Centre. The Head of the Computer Centre played an important part in the informal organisation of the company and had quite a number of 'friends' in strategic positions.

Elections for the works council had been announced since the current chairman was retiring. It meant a lot to the Director-general to find a suitable successor. All of a sudden it dawned upon me that a solution to my problem was to propose the current head of the Computer Centre for the position. He would additionally be appointed to the position of Facility Manager and would have enough time on his hands for the works council.

At first the Director-general was not really taken with the idea but realised in time that there was no other suitable candidate. He gave me permission to go ahead. When I discussed the matter with the head of the Computer Centre I could not stress enough the importance of the position of Chairman of the Works Council and how much the company would benefit if he would accept the position. My strategy worked and the idea started to grow on him. All I could do was hope that my wonderful idea would not backfire and cause harm to the automation plans.

I was allowed to recruit a new Computer Centre Manager and I succeeded in recruiting an experienced 'hardware' expert who was genuinely excited about the idea of managing a production department. With this problem solved I could concentrate fully on automation policy and initiating projects.

My management team grew steadily and in everything I did I was aware that it worked in my favour that I had written the Information and Automation Plan. It was clear to everyone, including the 'new arrivals', what was about to happen and why certain decisions were taken. I had produced three slides that were to return in every presentation and ensured that we were all heading in the same direction. The plan became more or less our 'Bible'.

In addition to the experienced managers I had also recruited young talented people not only internally but also from outside the company. Essential was that also the new colleagues enjoyed growing in their career together with the novel approach of automation. As opposed to the market figures, we employed quite a high number of women in automation and also our absentee rate was considerably lower when compared to other departments in the company.

My secretary played an important part and much of the department evolved around her. She was my right-hand woman and we worked really well as a team. She believed in my abilities and in the plan I had compiled and she was always on stand-by whenever I needed her help. Sometimes our smooth teamwork also led to problems because of the jealous tendencies of our colleagues. Many rumours circulated on the 'grapevine'.

We would not let it get to us, though, because we were just good friends and that was all there was to it. Truth always wins in cases like this. We were aware of the rumours and knew how to deal with the situation.

I had always been an early riser. I loved coming in to work early, start quietly, answer my mail and prepare for meetings. My colleagues knew that if they wanted to talk to me my door would always be open to them.

One day my secretary asked me whether I could pick her up early next morning (Friday) at the garage. Her car needed servicing and her garage was situated en route to the office. So I picked her up early that Friday morning and we drove together to the office. As soon as we entered the main building together we noticed straight away that new rumours were spreading faster than the speed of sound. When I arrived at the office of the Director-general that same morning the first thing he did was inquire after my secretary. I told him that we were just good friends and that I had picked her up on my way into the office etc. etc.

Honesty and openness worked once more. The stream of rumours had to stop. The Director-general understood that I was not pleased with his question about my secretary. He tried to make amends by asking whether she would mind taking minutes during the Automation Steering Committee meetings. This pleased me no end because first of all this meant the Director-general was about to form an Automation Steering Committee, which was what I had wanted all along and it meant recognition for my secretary.

At the beginning of every New Year the H&R department organised a New years reception to which all employees would be invited. The branch offices would rent coaches to enable staff to attend. A different group every year because of the long opening-hours of the offices. A large number of people usually turned up for the occasion and everyone tried to be there.

I had strongly advised the people in my department to attend in order to get closer to their colleagues. Within the company my department was also know as the 'golden team' because of our high salaries, so it would be worth our while to attend and 'sell our work'.

The highlight of the reception was always when the Director-general addressed his employees. He was a gifted speaker and everybody always listened intently. On some occasions it was good to have your name mentioned in his speech on others it definitely was not, but all those present would analyse his speech for many weeks to come. He had told me once that his parents had demanded from him at an early age that he would deliver the speech at Christmas Dinner. So for him addressing a crowd was a matter of habit. I was happy being surrounded by my fellow workers, to meet them, to talk to them and to listen to them. It was the perfect opportunity to approach me informally and I could do the same.

I learned that team building was one of my strong suits. Building a team consisting of people who were very different was quite a challenge. But to reach your goals together with a group of dedicated team members was a wonderful and inspiring challenge. Meeting people from the branch offices motivated me time after time. For them I wanted to work hard.

Sometimes it seems a bit like manipulation, but you will also benefit from it if you manage to make situations work to your advantage. It is important to be well connected. Contacts have their own contacts and your network will increase. Making contact is usually intuitive. The people you wish to associate with must 'feel good'. Do not just think 'what can they do for me'. If a relationship is based on only that, it will work against you.

Selling an important project

The Board of Directors had given the go-ahead and we could start implementing the Standard Banking System. The detailed project plan had been completed and the Director-general had appointed as the new Project Chairman the former Bank Director and had appointed me Project Manager.

The first step we had to take involved buying and installing the hardware. We were negotiating the purchase of a hardware system with a supplier but that proved to be a lengthy process. We had the feeling that the supplier was taking advantage of his unique relationship with the software supplier. To speed up the process help came from unexpected quarters, namely the Dutch Government. There was this rumour (probably leaked deliberately) that a new law was to be introduced that would be detrimental to investing in hardware. Our accountant had informed us that this new legislation would take effect the next Monday.

We were to purchase the new hardware that very weekend in order to make it partly tax-deductible. That Saturday the Bank Director phoned me around midnight to announce that we were to meet the hardware supplier the next day to sign the purchasing contract.

And we did meet with the hardware supplier that particular Sunday and purchased two computers. One of the computers was to be deployed as a production computer for the Banking System and the other one for the Standard Finance Information System.

I had come to an agreement with the former Bank Director. I had explained the Project Plan to him and had also shared my experiences with regard to the implementation of a banking system with him. In addition I informed him about the opposition his was likely to face. He accepted full responsibility for the implementation and asked me to assist as his right hand man.

We decided upon giving a Project Plan presentation for all managers and employees involved. In our opinion this was the best way to inform them about what was expected of them. This because of the extra efforts they had to make for the project, next to their regular assigned tasks. The Bank director allotted me one and a half year for the implementation of the project. That was the entire time span the organisation could afford. I was content with the allotted time span and I turned it all into an appealing presentation of the plan.

We organised two presentation sessions after office-hours, one for the bank employees and one for the Automation Department. I was a bit nervous because the implementation of this system would generate 20% FTE[11] through more effective and efficient execution of the banking processes and an increased level of automation.

I was truly impressed with the former Bank Director's demeanour. He approached his audience self-assuredly and as an introduction to the presentation told them that there really was no other option. This project had to succeed or otherwise the bank would go bankrupt. He also assured his audience that there would be no forced redundancies but that a freeze on recruitment of new staff had to be implemented. He ended his speech by stressing once more that in order for the bank to survive, every single employee had to contribute to and support the plans and that he would not hesitate to take action against those who would not co-operate. You could have heard a pin drop once he had finished. Everyone was duly impressed. He had made his point and it was easy for me to carry on with the presentation of the Project Plan.

All this seemed to me like a dream come true. As a Project Manager you always hope that senior management accepts responsibility for a project of such importance. Given my past experiences with senior management I was well aware of the fact that in most cases senior managers are not very willing to accept responsibility out of fear of losing their positions. Yet, with this Bank Director on my side I felt invincible for he never disappointed me and definitely lived up to my expectations. And all this right before he was about to retire.

I learned once more that for a successful completion of a project or activity it is important that the solution reduces the 'pain'. And the pain needs to be exposed in order to get everyone on your side and up in arms.

----

[11] FTE = Full Time Equivalent is a way to measure a worker's involvement in a project

If you are selling a product try to convince yourself that the people who need to work with it must be involved. It is the company that will benefit from this approach. It takes true skills to convince the users of the products of what the advantages are for them. Still, people do not respond well to changes. So if they have to adjust their working methods for long-term benefits you have to introduce intermediate stops in order to keep them satisfied. This means checking every once or a while whether everything goes according to plan. For instance, offer a reward and/or incentive. You, the salesperson is responsible for monitoring this process successfully.

Selling 'NO' to another company

I thoroughly enjoyed working for this company. I was able to set up a department with young people I loved and with older coaches who were my friends. The mix of many different people who shared the common desire to win motivated everyone. The department culture was based on sincerity, honesty and most of all on respect for each other and each other's knowledge. This working environment gave me energy. I felt responsible for all these people and their future.

During one of the weekends I read through the plans I had compiled for the company and I was genuinely amazed. Had I written this? Wow, where had all this come from? My God must have helped me a great deal. At that point in time I became very much aware that the strength, perseverance and knowledge stemmed from one and one source only. My faith and the desire to keep the company I worked for from disaster had enabled me to perform miracles. The impossible had been made possible. Every night I prayed to my God to thank him and ask for strength. Not only had he given me strength but had also kept me with my feet firmly on the ground. I was not very positive when it came to judging my own actions. I was critical and always pointing in my own direction when things went wrong. Many people mistook me for being very extraverted only a handful knew me for the introverted person I really am. I was a gifted actor indeed.

My belief in a benevolent God that I had named 'my God' (and it does not matter what you call this deity) had alienated me from the Church. I no longer believed in the Church as an institution and was convinced that no matter which denomination you adhered to, human beings were responsible for many wrongdoings. I tried to be a responsible human being when it came to helping people with an immediate result in my own surroundings. I tried to live a good life and use my energy to help those I felt deserving and people I felt related to. I felt the need to build something and work towards the future; a New World for posterity. That is how I wanted to live my life and remain as true to my own core values as I possibly could and try to help others while running the risk those others would take advantage. To me the latter was not a problem though it hurt occasionally; it was much more of a problem for those who took advantage of me.

My efforts had not gone unnoticed in the market. A head-hunter contacted me who offered me a job as Automation Director and member of the Board of Directors with one of the largest insurance companies in the Netherlands. In my opinion it was always worth your while to go and talk to a head-hunter because you never knew when you might need him. I therefore talked to him and he convinced me that I should go and meet the Director-general of the insurance company. The head-hunter would not join me for he was convinced I would be able to handle this meeting on my own.

The Director-general's secretary showed me into his office and I noticed immediately that the Director-general's desk did not feature a PC. He was a very kind but uninspiring man, a typical insurer. He talked with pride about his company and about the automation facilities. He even told me confidentially and proudly that they deployed the latest version of the operating system on their IBM mainframe computer.

I was quite surprised and was well aware that I, as far as automation was concerned, definitely came from a totally different planet. I was not very impressed with what he had just conveyed and asked him whether he possessed the relevant information required to manage the company. I explained to him that access to information outweighed the importance of owning the latest operating system. From the conversation that followed I gathered that the Director-general had become fearful of his own Automation Department. He had been through so much misery already that all he wanted now was peace and quiet.

I subsequently told him about my vision on automation with regard to a company, the usage of standard software and that all this should be used for the purpose of realising the strategies and achieve the goals as stated by the company. He listened intently and told me that he did not have the strength to guide his company through another process of change. He was not up to the challenge and he outright feared his own Automation Department. That same evening I informed the head-hunter that I was not interested in the position on offer.

What I learned from this situation was that automation experts could jeopardise progress and advancement. Where automation experts in the past advocated that the user had to change through automation they were now no longer capable of change. This was a deplorable situation since stagnation means decline. If you have construction workers build a house for you, you do not want them to tell you what the bricks are made of. You just want a house that you can live in comfortably. Automation should enable a pleasant business environment to the benefit of the customer.

It is always flattering when asked to consider a new position. Someone appreciates your expertise and has attached a value to it. From your own point of view it is often exaggerated what they say about you. What is it you actually do that is so special; it is just the way things go. When you assess yourself you have much more information about yourself and your actions than other people do. Because of this we have the tendency to be much more critical of our own behaviour. We often raise our personal bar sometimes to a, sometimes, unattainable level. This is not necessarily a bad thing, but do learn to accept a compliment.

Overcoming opposition

Sometimes the Works Council demanded I put in an appearance to answer questions about and explain the details of the Automation Plan. I could always count on the support of the Director-general and I only needed to attend during the agenda item Automation.

The chairman of the Works Council was the former head of the Automation Department and now also responsible for the General and Technical Services Department. He no longer reported to me. I had done my utmost to prevent him from being demoted in the organisation and I had recommended him for the position of Chairman of the Works Council. He still bore a grudge about his demotion, though, something, which unfortunately I had failed to recognise. He had (deliberately) failed to inform me on possible problems dealing with Automation.

The Works Council consisted mostly of managers and workers employed in the offices. Before the Director-general would call a Works Council meeting he always met with the Chairman of the Works Council beforehand to discuss the agenda and the decision-making process. The Director-general usually played the part of 'wise old man' in the company. This was, for that matter, not just play-acting it was something close to his heart. Under normal circumstances Works Council meetings did not pose a problem to him.

He now confronted me during our periodical meeting with a long list of complaints regarding office automation issues. I had to admit that the Automation Department had been working very hard to get the systems at the Head Office up-and-running, but had neglected the particular office related problems.

The managers and office workers did not appreciate what was going on at the Head Office. Not until the systems at head office were operational could we bring online the systems at the branch offices. This would have made quite a difference to them.

I discussed my approach with the Director-general before the Works Council meeting was to start and asked for permission to present my solution to their problems. He agreed with what I had suggested. As soon as I entered the meeting room all those present fell quiet and the Chairman looked at me as if to say "you're in deeeeep trouble". He obviously savoured the moment.

I decided to put on the hair shirt and immediately addressed the meeting. I apologised profusely and simply stated that we had overlooked the automation issues at the offices. I also explained to those present why and suggested to set up a professional help desk, staffed with people from the offices so we could understand and deal with their problems instantaneously. A good solution because it would enable the helpdesk workers and office workers to communicate directly.

The atmosphere changed for the better after I had launched my plan and when I asked the participants whether they wanted me to deal with their individual problems there and then they declined. I promised to get back to them at the next meeting and report on the progress. The delegates were satisfied when I left the meeting and the Director-general winked at me. The chairman, on the other hand, did not look me in the eye and forgot to thank me for attending. He had lost for I had not been humiliated.

What I learned was that some people are not capable of mastering their frustration and do not ever forget. It is not such a problem to admit your mistakes and usually by just admitting to your mistakes you can solve the problem. Honesty is the best policy.

It's all sales

One of my former employers had appointed me as a trouble-shooter in one of his supermarkets. In one of my first days on the job I told someone 'You people should learn how to work'. Afterwards it turned out that I had spoken these words to the one employee who was the hardest worker of them all. I had forgotten about this incident altogether. After five years I asked the same man about why he was so reserved in his dealings with me. He then disclosed what an effect the words I had used five years earlier had had on him. It had been on his mind for five years. By admitting that I had been wrong the problem was solved within five minutes.

Selling my Development & Maintenance Manager

The number of those employed in my department increased rapidly. I had already successfully appointed a head of the Information Centre, a head of the Computer Centre and a head of the Administrative Organisation. I was still in charge of the Development and Maintenance Department but that was no longer feasible since I had also been appointed Project Manager for the implementation of the Standard Banking System. The Director-general had given permission to recruit a Head of the Development and Maintenance Department.

I had conducted the interviews together with an H&R employee. He was also convinced this was the person we needed and he advised me to make him an offer. There was only one thing holding me back. And this one thing was this tinge of unease I felt every time I met with the candidate. I could not put my finger on it but it was definitely present. On the basis of my gut feeling we decided to submit him to a psychological test. The outcome of the test was downright positive so we decided to hire him.

The first complaints about him reached me after only two months and after he had ended his probation period. He was putting my team under unnecessary pressure and would throw abuse at them without any apparent reason. Also the ladies in my department found fault with him and called him 'that creep'. He was disrespectful to the ladies on the team. I was facing a genuine problem because he was discouraging my 'winning team.'

I decided to talk to him first and he denied every single accusation. He then told me that everyone who had the nerve to complain about him should be fired. He also included a number of names of people who should be fired anyway because he felt they did not like him. It was plain to see that he was a very domineering manager and I now understood why I had experienced this tinge of unease during the recruitment process. He did not subscribe to my style of managing at all since I believed in equality and coaching. A major problem because I had personally selected this person and I had made a big mistake.

I discussed the issue with the H&R manager and he informed me that there was no other suitable position available for this man. I gave him a bad assessment and recommended to find another position. I was very domineering myself during the interview because I had to address him in a language he understood.

Well, he obviously liked the salary the company paid him and it was not easy for someone like him to find another job. I was lucky once more because one night I received a phone call from a head-hunter who approached me for another job.

I was not interested but I gave him the name of a very suitable candidate; the Head of Development and Maintenance.

Two weeks later the head of Development and Maintenance came to see me and told me proudly that he had found a good new position through a head-hunter. He handed in his resignation and did not leave before telling me that he considered me an unsuitable automation director. I looked at him suitably surprised and congratulated him on his new position.

At that point in time we had been very busy with the development of the Private PC project. We had organised one-day training sessions for all office employees and once they had taken part in the training, they could take the computer home. We had planned twelve training days, six for me and six for the Head of Development and Maintenance. We used to drive out there by car accompanied by the departmental secretary who could offer administrative support.

One night my secretary phoned me. She was very upset and told me that her colleague had called her and told her that the Head of Development and Maintenance had assaulted her in the car. My secretary informed me that her colleague was not going to come to work the next day because she did not want to face that 'creep' ever again. And as far as my secretary was concerned, she was not going to come in for work either. I immediately contacted the H&R manager for this was an extremely delicate matter and had to be dealt with properly. The H&R Manager then contacted both parties and promised to support the secretary.

The Head of Development and Maintenance denied all the accusations and felt he had been framed. A difficult matter because it never became clear what had actually transpired. Apparently he had opened the door for her from the inside and in doing so had leant over her. She had experienced it as sexual harassment. A difficult case, according to the H&R manager and he wished me the best of luck in trying to solve the problem.

The Head of Development and Maintenance had already resigned and I phoned him to inform him that I did not ever want to see him at the office again, without accusing him of something. I then called my secretaries and told them about what I had decided. They were pleased with the outcome and showed up for work the next day. The problem had been solved as far as they were concerned and I asked them to keep quiet about the whole matter.

I learned once more that I had to rely on my intuition and gut feeling. I had to take time to rest and increase the ability to get in touch with my inner feelings. I did find it difficult to take decisions based on emotions. I had no choice, though.

It is never easy to rely on your intuition. The first question you should ask yourself is, can I trust my intuition. This is a matter of life experience and practical experience concerning your field. The problem is, though, when can I rely on my gut feeling and when should I discard it. In fact it is really simple. As soon as your gut feeling tells you to respond in a certain way, ask yourself a control question aiming at the way you would respond. Is the outcome good? Then go for it. Did you make the wrong decision? Accept it and count your losses.

Selling an up-and-running system

The list of complaints that the Works Council had given me was not an isolated incident. We had started up a professional helpdesk and also from their reports it became clear that the two unique terminals on the service desks showed signs of wear. In the mean time the two unique terminals had been linked up to the PC in the back-office with an electronic switch, but many of the complaint kept recurring. This to the immense frustration of the helpdesk staff.

One of my staff was responsible for the installation of the hardware in the offices. He used to drive throughout the whole country in his lease car, which he considered his inner sanctum. He was a kind person and very well liked by the office staff because he was always willing to help. He had even fixed their coffee machine. He was also popular with the ladies, who always welcomed him with a kiss. For some reason he commanded this kind of behaviour from the female members of staff. We called him 'the rocket' but he was without a doubt the best salesperson of the automation plans in the field. I truly respected him and always made sure to talk to him whenever he came to the office. I showed a sign of my appreciation by awarding him an annual bonus. He deserved it for he worked hard.

At some point in time he came to the office and told me that the unique hardware was so worn out that it was impossible for him to construct one functioning terminal out of the two terminals. We were also running out of spare parts. So we faced a huge problem that had to be solved within a year.

We decided to initiate a trial project for the conversion of the programme of the unique terminal to a standard IBM PC. Unfortunately it was not possible to use the standard keyboard, printer and screen of a regular IBM PC. We had to come up with a solution. Still, IBM used retail purchasers and after a month the Project Leader came to see me and informed me that they had come up with a solution. He then asked me to contact IBM.

In those days an attractive woman had been appointed our Account Manager and was therefore responsible for our company and I immediately contacted her to set up a meeting. I was very pleased with her because on arrival she told me that our company had been classified as a bank, but in order to solve our problem we had to consult the retail sector. In addition she told me that requests from female staff would get priority status. This to promote female emancipation within IBM.

My account manager enjoyed using her special status and got down to business straight away. She came up with the perfect solution for the keyboard, the printer as well as the screen. To show her my appreciation I offered her an expensive lunch.

We copied the applications from the unique terminal onto our IBM PCs and added some additional applications so the offices would have some extra options to work with. The PCs could intercommunicate in a Local Area Network. As soon as we had finished the conversion and the system had been tested, the first person we showed it to was 'the rocket' and the helpdesk staff. They were overjoyed and 'the rocket' even rewarded me with a kiss. He also told all office staff about the fantastic, brand new service desk terminals.

We subsequently invited the Board of Directors of the offices, the office managers and the Works Council to come and see the new system. We demonstrated the new system to high acclaim. All the managers were eager to take the system to their own branch office and start working with it. The pressure on management to invest in new hardware increased and the number of complaints the helpdesk had to deal with, decreased. Automation had regained its high standing with the office staff.

I learned that sometimes you can positively capitalise on certain changes at a supplier to create a win-win situation. And selling a running system is much easier than selling a design for a system.

It should go without saying that people do what they say. Although this may not be the case in real life, it should be considered as a starting point. And if people do not do what they say it is acceptable to confront them. The problem is, though, that first a make-believe world appears in which many agreements will not be lived up to. It should not really matter whether you sell a service (on many occasions intangible) or a tangible product. Starting point remains whether you have managed to determine what the customer is in need of. Whether you know what he thinks is important, so that you can meet his demands with products and/or services. If that matches, a deal will be made.

Selling to a teenager

When my daughter was still in Secondary School they had advised us that the best option for her would be to attend a school for Intermediate General Education. My daughter was not at all pleased with this outcome for she would rather have attended a school for Higher General Education. This was not feasible though, because of our relocation and a bad teacher. I reassured her by guaranteeing that she could study as long as she wanted and that her time would come.

She did well in school and this level of schooling did not pose any problems at all. Motivation was not an issue and in fact I even had to slow her down on occasion and urge her to take it easy for a while.

But she was growing up and reached puberty, an age where she became difficult to deal with. The type of school my daughter attended was characterised by the fact that the girls were preoccupied with boys. Something the father in me really worried about. I considered her too young for dating and being a man myself I was only too well aware of what boys were after. I spent much time talking with my daughter about life in general, what really mattered, her education and also about boys. My daughter was doing battle with herself, her mother and me.

At night dinner sometimes turned into a battle zone because my daughter had turned arguing with her parents into a fine art. No matter what we said she would always oppose us. She wanted to go to the Disco because 'all her friends were allowed to go'. I was opposed to this because I considered her too young. I used to pick her up by car after every party she went to. At weekends I lost quite a bit of sleep. I just had to accept that my daughter was growing into adulthood and was more often fighting with herself than with us. Yet, every now and again she would just sit next to me and put her head on my shoulder. Nothing needed to be said, everything was all right.

I understood why the fights were important to my daughter. At this time in her life she had to experience the hard way that there was something in between 'black and white' namely the golden mean. Fortunately, she was an extraverted girl and wore her heart on her sleeve. She trusted me and I tried to understand her and treat her as an adult. She did not hide anything from us and that is why things worked out well. Yet, sometimes she thought that the only one who truly understood her was our dog Bobo. Her suffering did hurt me but there was no way to avoid it. As a parent you never know whether you are doing the right thing.

One day on her return from a tennis lesson, two men in suits accosted my wife. They approached her and asked whether she was my wife. As she acknowledged that fact the two gentlemen said they were told to inform me that I was doing a good job. There was nothing to worry about, because I could count on their support. When my wife told me what had happened I did not know what to make of it. What a strange turn of events. At the time I was involved in a mega process of change with supporters and opposition, both from within and outside the company. Who was I to trust? Who was to gain from what I was doing? I decided to leave it be for the time being and refrain from informing the Director-general. If someone had something he wished to share with me, they had to approach me directly and not through my wife.

I learned was that it was difficult having to deal with an adolescent. It made me feel insecure because I wanted to be a good father and wanted to get a hold of the situation. It took up a lot of energy but it was worth it because I wanted to be there for my daughter.

It's all sales

Sometimes it is not easy to convince a customer that what you have to offer can be of use to him. If the customer cannot see the benefits, you have to let go. It is of the utmost importance to determine what is important to the customer. Always ask for the customer's opinion, let him tell you what he thinks is important. Sometimes what the customer considers important is not directly linked to your product. Sometimes you have to dig a bit deeper. There is, however, always a link to be found with your product. For instance, when you offer a product to a retailer who needs to sell it to his customer. To a retailer product properties are not that important but the turnover rate, profit margin and display material are. In the end it is not the product or service that you are selling but what it can do for the customer.

Selling to the Dutch National Bank

Implementing a total Standard Banking System was a process unique to the Netherlands. Ours was the first bank to meet the challenge and in addition to that, we were also the third customer of our hardware supplier. There were not even any standard methods available in the market for the implementation of standard software. We had to devise our own implementation method. I wanted to finish this project successfully though, because it was the only way to save the bank.

There was another financial institution very interested in finding out what we were up to, namely the Dutch National Bank. They sent a young financial auditor to our company to discuss my plans concerning the bank. He had been assigned to assess the risks of the implementation of the Standard System. It was very important to convince him because the National bank could stop the whole project. I had to convince him and took his visit quite seriously.

During his visit he was rather formal. I took charge of the meeting immediately and presented him the preliminary report and the project plan for the implementation. I made it clear that we had no other alternative but to implement the standard software because the banking knowledge, the level and availability of staff were insufficient to develop our own banking system. And even if we could the development costs would exceed what the bank could afford.

He listened intently, but I could tell from the look in his eyes that I had not totally convinced him. He was after all the independent financial auditor. He consulted his list with questions and asked me 'Do you have the data model for this system?' On which databases do these applications run? Which programming language is used? These were exactly the same questions many fellow automation experts would come up with if they were reluctant to implement standard software. I realised that this was the moment to come up with the right answers. I was on edge. This was when it mattered.

I did not shirk and kept looking him in the eye. I asked him politely whether I could ask him some questions before I answered his. He agreed to this and I asked him "Sir, do you use Microsoft Words?" He nodded in agreement. "Are you satisfied with the programme?" Once again he nodded. "Do you use all Words applications? Do you know Word's data model? Do you know its programming language and do you know which database is used?" He nodded and suddenly it started to dawn upon him

I continued by telling him that we intended to use the Standard Banking System in the same way as other standard software and that we considered it to be a black box. I also explained that all security measures and check-up procedures would be installed and that our Internal Audit Department played an important part in the whole project.

I saw that I had convinced him, but as a true internal auditor he could not tell me this to my face. He wished me the best of luck with the project and wanted to meet with me once every fortnight to keep abreast of things.

I learned that my strong belief in the necessity and the successful outcome of the project, including the high pressure and stress, gave me extra strength and as a result of that I had this angel sitting on my shoulder.

As a salesperson you cannot and may not have any doubts regarding the product that you are selling. A good salesperson knows his product and is familiar with all possible objections that can be raised by a potential customer. Because the salesperson knows exactly what he should say about his product and how to answer every possible question, he feels in control and invincible. Who can possibly get the better of you …

Keeping the suppliers happy

The software company owned by my predecessor, the Interim Automation Manager, ran into trouble. He tried to get youngsters straight from school and train them as automation experts. As it turned out, it was very difficult to find positions in the market for these young people who did not possess sufficient knowledge. He tried to find positions for them himself first and he also tried to interest me, but I refused to cooperate because I had too many people to train myself.

In the meantime he had appointed two Sales Managers but that did not work out. As a result his company was taken over by a much larger software company. His company provided me with products I only used for the non-banking systems. Moreover, everybody was aware that the company employed the son of the Director-general. The Interim Automation Manager had not been well liked and also those opposing the Director-general lost no time in telling me about the problems at the software company.

I told them that I had no problems with the company and that as far as I was concerned I was still free to choose any external consultant I thought suited for the matter in hand. I had also met the Director-general's son and he had struck me as an intelligent person who would find his own way in automation, which, as it turned out, he did. The opposition did not abate yet, since I was now able to work with a larger software company it was easier and the number of consultants to choose from had increased considerably.

My company had also been the first customer of another software company. This company though, had been very successful in the market. We had outsourced the old banking system to them. The Director-general and the Director of the software company were close friends. The Director of this particular software company also served as personal advisor to our Director-general. Whenever they had been out to lunch together I would be called into his office to defend my plans. The problem was that the Director of the software company had his own best interests at heart and hardly ever tried to think along with plans that would benefit my company. In fact, his advice always served his own purposes. I was well aware of the fact that he was bound to lose out on business since we intended to implement our new Banking System ourselves. I knew his company employed a number of good and knowledgeable consultants.

In order to put a stop to the arguing, since arguing and fighting did not serve the best interest of my company, I suggested to the Director-general to grant his friend's company the status of preferred supplier. This would put a stop to wasting time in consulting other suppliers. Every other year we would assess whether our preferred suppliers were still up to the mark. The Director-general agreed.

In the Standard Banking System you could incorporate your own bank by means of filling in standard tables (the setting of parameters). Yet, in order to fill in the numerous tables, lots of primary banking knowledge was required and it took up an awful lot of time.

It became clear that the whole project met with delays because the knowledge of banking processes was limited to a small number of bank managers who worked very hard in production. It also turned out that a number of bank employees were not able to reproduce the required knowledge. And at the same time the day-to-day running of the bank had to go on and the work on the automation project meant extra work. The day-to-day job was often used as an excuse for the lack of knowledge

As Project Manager I discussed the problem with the Bank Director and Chairman of the Project Group. He totally understood and we decided to appoint five external consultants with specific banking knowledge to help out the bank managers. They would be appointed by the bank and would subsequently report to the Bank Director. This was an excellent solution because the bank managers felt they would get some help and none of them could come up with an excuse not to get involved with the project. They could also expand their knowledge given the expertise of the experienced external consultants.

So in the end the Director of the software company was pleased and much to my pleasure the external consultants were very impressed with the extended applications the Standard Banking System offered so we had five more 'salespeople' for the Standard Banking System.

I learned that sometimes it is not possible to get straight to the point in order to reach your goals. Compromising for the good of the company cannot be avoided, but can sometimes lead to a win-win situation after all. I remained convinced, though, that it is essential to keep business and private separately.

In everything you do it is important to formulate your goals. You may change your mind along the way and it goes without saying that you have to adapt your approach accordingly. Still, compromising with regard to your plans is something you need to consider carefully. Of course there are always hierarchical issues involved, but your plan is based on your approach. Adapting it too much can lead to a plan that is no longer your own. We already pointed out earlier that you can only realise a plan if you are convinced of its feasibility and success.

Selling your ailments is never easy

My wife's eldest brother (my brother-in-law) had always been an important person in her life. Since her father's death he had become her best friend. He had always looked after her in one way or the other. When her elder sister had to move in with her parents and she had to move out, she used to live with her brother, his wife and their little boy. Both of them had never worn their hearts on their sleeves but it was clear without saying that they loved each other.

My brother-in-law was employed as an electronic welder, was good at what he did and made a lot of money. He had married a much younger woman as the result of an unexpected pregnancy. They had a son. My wife and I truly loved the boy and spoiled him rotten. Sometimes we also looked after him. My brother-in-law's wife worked in a bar before and during her marriage. That is where they had actually met, because he really liked to have a pint. They were saving up to make their dream come true; to own their own bar/café.

One day he told us that they had acquired a pub in a neighbouring village. It was an old pub with a small number of regulars. His wife was to run the pub and he would continue to work as a welder. They had also included a number of slot machines and soon the local youth had discovered the pub and had turned it into their regular meeting place. The pub became that popular that my brother in law quit his job and also worked full-time in the pub. Eventually it all became too much for them and they lost control over their own lives. Their marriage was in a crisis and their son was still roaming the streets late at night because nobody seemed to care about him. Still, they made money, lots of money.

After two years they sold the pub and acquired a restaurant close to the Dutch border. That was the next step in their dream plan. In addition they had bought an expensive bungalow and lived among the rich in their village. They continued to work hard because they were used to it and their only day off was the Monday when the restaurant was closed. Sometimes we used to pay them a visit in their restaurant and occasionally I took business relations to the restaurant. My brother-in-law appreciated it when I did that and would serve his finest dishes. My brother- in-law and I liked and respected each other.

Yet all of a sudden his behaviour changed. He started phoning my wife every Monday and talk to her about his problems with his wife and son. He and his wife had grown apart and his son displayed no respect whatsoever for his father. He was usually slightly drunk when he called and used to cough a lot during these phone calls. My wife was very worried about him. She gave up her tennis lessons and started neglecting her social life in our village. She was not doing well and I worried a great deal about her.

One Monday evening when I returned home from work my wife looked as if she was in a trance. She was aggressive and very angry with me. She was ranting and raving and I could not get her to calm down. Fortunately my daughter was not at home. I did not know what to do and wanted to calm her down before my daughter would return home. I got in touch with our doctor and he arrived shortly. I took him to the bedroom and he gave her something to calm her down. As soon as he was downstairs I asked him what was wrong with my wife. He just looked at me and left. Later I realised that my wife had consumed far too much alcohol. She had been drunk.

The next morning my wife told me that her brother was seriously ill and had to be admitted to hospital. He suffered (just like his father had) from lung cancer and needed an operation for they wanted to remove one lung. He would have to continue living (restricted) with one healthy lung. I now understood my wife's erratic behaviour of the previous day and I forgave her. Her brother needed her now.

I learned that having a dream does not always end as a dream. Working hard at the expense of your family life is not worth it and does not solve problems.

Working hard is just one ingredient of leading a successful life. Working should be approached as 'smart working' though. A salesperson needs to use his time and energy effectively. Ideals are necessary to feed your ambitions for otherwise you have no goal in life. So plan and have goals also to enrich your life, you will be appreciated for it.

Selling every decision made for the benefit of a project

The day-to-day organisation of the implementation of the Standard Banking System comprised the Banking director and myself. Every Monday we called a project group meeting. Most of the decisions that needed to be made were prepared prior to those meetings.

We both knew that as a result of the implementation of the Standard Banking System the banking processes had to be adapted. Even the products would have to be adapted if required. To adapt the new system would only involve additional spending. When we found the Standard Banking System we were convinced we had discovered the Rolls Royce while the bank would at first only make use of it as a Citroen 2V. We were very well aware that we had to grow in order to save the company from the detrimental effects of the Unification of Europe.

Even though all the managers, as future end-users of the system, were aware of this, they still felt the need to adjust the system and not the processes. They also feared the consequences regarding staffing issues since the high level of automation required less FTEs. Still, the remaining FTEs could be put to good use for the 'New Bank and its new products'. The 'lack of time' issue we had already overcome by appointing external consultants with extended banking knowledge. The additional spending as a result of the external consultant had not been incorporated in our budget. This also led to mounting pressure for us to stick to our planning.

The Bank Director did a wonderful job. For every suggestion to adjust the standard system he would compile a short description of the reason for possible adjustment, costs and alternatives. Subsequently the item would be put on the agenda for next Monday's meeting. Yet, prior to the meeting the Bank Director would pay a visit to the person who had submitted the idea for an adjustment. The Banking Director's standard question would be "are you sure that with this adjustment there will be a return on investment?" Usually the submitter would not have a suitable answer to this question. So the Bank Director would respond "Well, in that case we should adjust the working procedure". After that the proposal would be dealt with as a formality.

Since no standard methods and techniques were available for the implementation of the standard software this was something we had to invent ourselves. The above-mentioned single-minded approach and the will of the management to take decisions were of major importance to the success of this project.

It was also very important that we kept everything as simple as possible. We had more or less locked the supplier's technical consultants into a room. They did manage, however, to stack a bottle of whisky in the windowsill outside.

Communication with the end-user was always directed through an information analyst assigned to my department. No 'fancy' elements were added to the system, which meant we could control the planning. The four external consultants worked hard and long hours and since I understood that their intake of Whisky was what kept their motor running, I allowed it.

It was fun to ascertain that as the project continued, more and more people became enthusiastic about the system and its possibilities. The Bank Director could not help but notice that the system offered many possibilities for products that he had always wanted to add to the existing range. I even had to slow him down on occasion and make him stick to the planning. In phase two of the plan we would start developing new products.

Even now I learned that the involvement of senior management in projects like this one is of the utmost importance. The Bank Director made sure to convey his decisions to his staff directly and was always willing to listen to their arguments. That is how he kept them motivated.

It is of the utmost importance that when structural changes are to be implemented that those who have to work with the results are involved. It will simplify implementation. Yet, if management does not support these decisions, the decisions will be overruled on a regular basis, which will lead to lack of clarity and the power of decision-making will subsequently weaken. In Sales it is important that company management supports the working procedures and market approach.

Selling as a personal coach

My department was slowly but surely developing towards a professional department supporting Organisation and Automation. Several sub divisions had been set up supervised by a manager. Also a meeting structure had been put together comprising two different types of meeting. One of the meetings aimed specifically at project organisation and had been set up as an internal Steering Committee to help me prepare for the overall Steering Committee meetings. The other meeting aimed at the regular hierarchical departmental structure and set out to deal with internal affairs such as HR, budgets, administration and internal design. We had developed into a Matrix organisation.

Either my secretary or her assistant would take minutes of every single meeting. They would compile concept minutes first, so I could add or alter things if so desired. I always wrote my own report of the bi weekly meeting with the Director-general.

The meetings of the Steering Committee could be quite tedious at times. On many occasions the Comptroller would try to be as obdurate as he possibly could, to show off the power he assumed he had. The Director-general tried to correct his behaviour whenever he could, but it did not benefit the atmosphere in the team. I did consider these meetings important because they were intended to involve senior management in the Automation Process.

My secretary truly resented the Comptroller and lost no time in hiding that fact from him. And remarkably enough he would adapt his behaviour for her. She could give him this inimitable condescending look that made him avert his eyes. She was marvellous in her dealings with him.

After one of the Steering Committee meetings in which she had been even more annoyed by the Comptroller's behaviour than usual, she came to me with two blank pages from her writing pad. She said "I haven't written anything down, it's that time of the month again would you mind doing the minutes today?" While at the same time flashing me that special smile of hers. I winked at her and typed up the minutes for her. She was worth it.

All this was possible because of the departmental culture. It was an open culture in which equality, openness and honesty were very important. We had taken on many young employees who were coached by more experienced colleagues and yes I was happy being a manager and a 'father figure' to them.

Personally I was responsible for the H&R aspects with regard to staff. I supervised those who worked for me and tried to determine if there were personal issues or problems at work. Both parts were interrelated and I spent quite some time, for instance during dinner parties, as a personal coach to help my staff as a personal coach and give them advice. I always made sure to be present at their weddings, funerals and other personal events. I would take every invitation into consideration and we would devise the entertainment together.

For motivational and team building purposes all sorts of (sports) events were organised. Everyone in the department wanted to win and complete every single project successfully. We needed this feeling of solidarity to overcome opposition from within the company.

I learned that it is important to gather a winning team around you and enable young people to learn and grow. The return on this investment will be solidarity and dedication.

It's all sales

In Sales you can only be successful if you are capable of cooperating with colleagues, your employer, those at home and others around you. There should be a balance. When you are able to maintain contacts properly you can when one of them is on a lower level compensate by asking a bit extra from another. This will result in a basis that will give you a feeling best described as 'a flow'. Things will then go automatically. You can devote your undivided attention to the matter in hand.

Cooperate in order to sell a Switch

According to the retailers, the trial run of the Electronic Payment System was not followed up by a finite solution. Together with a major retail chain we decided to set up a joined infrastructure for Electronic Payment in the Netherlands. In order to achieve this, a Switch computer had to be acquired an installed. This computer would enable the switch of payment transactions between the retailers (cash registers) and the card issuing companies. This switch would accept, authorise and pass on details of both the 'direct debit card' as well as the 'credit card' transactions. This switch was also an important part of the technical infrastructure of my Information and Automation Plan.

As it turned out, also two oil companies were showing an interest in our concept. They wished to take part and subsequently a project was initiated for the realisation of this project. To represent our company the Sales and Marketing Director and I had been appointed members of the Steering Committee. The Automation Department of major retail chain provided the Project Manager. I was also asked to take up the position of conjoined Project Manager, given my experience in banking.

One night after a meeting of the Steering Committee, the Automation Manager of the retail company, the Sales and Marketing director and I were walking behind the Central Station to a restaurant. All of a sudden I remembered the dream I had had years ago. A very special moment because this was a déjà vu since I already had this dream before. However, in my dream the story did not have a happy ending.

The Automation Department of the large retail chain was a company trading independently, providing automation services to all shops that were part of the concern. In order to achieve this they had equipped a large development and calculus centre. The Switch computer would be a part of that calculus centre.

The security measures at the above-mentioned computer centre were not at a level acceptable to the Dutch National Bank. Security needed extended improvements. The project went off well. Additionally we had initiated an internal project to realise the connection through the Switch computer and on the one hand our back-office systems and on the other hand the office systems.

After only six months the project all of a sudden came to a halt. Senior management of the large Dutch banks had discussed the project with the Senior Management of the retail concern. What it came down to was that the banks had decided that the current Switch of bank transactions should not be carried out by retail companies but by banks, including the Dutch Postbank. They promised the management of retail companies that within the next six months

214

they would come up with a feasible alternative for Electronic Payment in the Netherlands.

This was an unfortunate result for my company for now I was left without a good solution for the Switch of 'credit card' transactions and our own banking transactions. The banks only wanted to Switch 'direct debit card' transactions.

Everyone within the company was very disappointed with this outcome. It took some effort to motivate staff and I promised them I would not rest before I had come up with a feasible alternative for our dream; Switch all 'plastic currency' transactions to the card issuing companies through one service desk terminal. Also, to Switch all banking transactions to our head office. This network was to be accessible 24 hours a day.

I learned that the power of banks is extensive because many companies depend on them. Yet, I also learned to believe that dreams come true and that our path in life is already predestined. Only God knows the path I am to follow.

It's all sales

Whenever you have to cooperate with many people, you will have to make concessions. The question remains, how far are you willing to go. That is why it is of the utmost importance to determine your personal limits beforehand. What is the best alternative if you cannot reach a decision together? This helps you to set the boundaries. Especially when the balance of power is important you have to know your own boundaries. And of course, when you cooperate with others, trust is essential.

Saving a supplier

One day the Director-general of the supplier of the Standard Banking System contacted me. He wanted to set up a meeting with the Director-general and me. When I talked to him on the phone he sounded dejected, and I already suspected the message he had to convey meant bad news. I had already heard some rumours from staff temporarily assigned to my company. The supplier had not been able to find additional customers and therefore some of the staff had already been fired. Some of their colleagues had not been paid part of their salary. I was prepared and had decided which of the assigned staff I wanted to take on permanently. And since we had an 'escrow'[12] agreement, the programme codes for the Standard Banking System would revert to our company.

This Director-general was a strange character. I had never seen him smile and I did not trust him. Their software was marvellous, though. Almost everyone involved in the project was wildly enthusiastic about the many options the banking system offered and we were very pleased with that.

He came to visit and told me that most banks had not yet decided whether they wanted to purchase their standard software. They were all waiting until we had implemented the software successfully. He had had to lower the price of the software significantly yet the companies were still waiting for what would happen at our company. He asked us for financial support and he proposed that we would divert from the payment schedule as stated in the sales contract. The Director-general informed him that we would take his into consideration and he left our building.

These were bad tidings for us for the Dutch National Bank had already warned us through the external accountant of the risks involved when dealing with a small supplier. To stop the project right there and then was not an option. We had to proceed. Fortunately we had compiled a comprehensive contract (escrow). The software was already in our possession. Now we had to arrange for the relevant know-how to be available to our company. This could be achieved by hiring a number of specialists from the supplier's company who had already been assigned to our company. In the end we proposed to the Director-general of the supplier that we would pay the salaries of those assigned

---

[12] Something, in this case the programming codes, to be held in custody until all (legal) obligations are met.

to our company and hire them. As soon as the supplier had sorted out his financial problems he could re-hire them.

The Director-general and I discussed our proposal with the supplier. We also offered to pay one instalment ahead of the payment schedule. This meant his company would survive for the moment and he was offered an opportunity to bring in new customers. This solution meant that we decreased the risks for our company, the supplier's company was saved for the time being and we did not have to inform the external accountant. He was not pleased with our proposal but he was well aware that there was no other option. It goes without saying that he still did not smile.

In the meantime we also tried to get our 'preferred supplier' (a large software company which had provided us with many enthusiastic consultants for the implementation of the Standard Software) to take over the company of the supplying company. Unfortunately the 'preferred supplier; already had a standard banking system that they were trying to sell (unsuccessfully for that matter). They were not interested which proved to be a lack of vision afterwards.

I learned once more that it is difficult to trust a supplier. Usually they are focussed solely on their own interests and rarely take the customer's interest into consideration.

Trusting a supplier does not come naturally. A supplier is also entitled to customer assessment. This in order to keep each other focussed. In Sales it is essential for a supplier that you try to think ahead along with the development of the product or service you offer to your customer. Helping your customer sell the product to another customer increases turnover and goodwill. This is one of the most important sales arguments.

Losing out because of age

Her brother's illness changed my wife's life completely. All she did was clean the house the whole daylong. She had given up on playing tennis and no longer visited friends nor did they visit her. She had become totally self-absorbed. Our neighbour was the only person she still talked to and I was seriously worried about her.

Usually on the Monday after she had spoken to her brother on the phone she would drink too much alcohol. At first I understood why she did it and used to have a few drinks myself. After a couple of weeks she started talking to me about her life every Monday night once our daughter had turned in for the night. On occasion she would get very angry with me and she would start screaming and swearing. I honestly did not understand what was going on and why she behaved like that. I was blamed for everything. Sometimes when she was drunk she only wanted to dance to the Tina Turner song 'Private Dancer.

She did go and see our doctor every week and sometimes she would call him and he would come to the house. Usually they would go upstairs to the bedroom. After a while he would leave the house without saying a word to me. I was completely ignorant of what was going on. Nobody explained anything to me. I was forced to rely on our doctor. I also offered to find her professional help but she refused that out right.

She then decided she wanted to get her driving licence for that would make her less dependent on me and she could go and visit her brother whenever she wanted. I agreed to this because I hoped this would solve her problems.

My daughter had graduated successfully from the school for Intermediate General Education and had applied to the school for Higher General Education and got accepted. This school suited her much better. No more boyfriends and she soon settled down and studied very hard. She did not know what was going on between her mother and me. As a present for her sixteenth birthday I bought her a ladies moped and now she no longer had to cycle all the way to school. She was happy and proud.

For me it got increasingly difficult to continue to play soccer and train at my current level. My body could no longer recuperate after every match. My age started to work against me. I decided to give up on playing field soccer. I did not feel like joining a veteran team. For me that was not an option.

I wanted to quit while ahead because right now we were doing well in our league. We were ranked first with one point to spare and the runner up was another local team. In our final match of the league we would play each other and it would be decided who had won the league championship. Unfortunately I had managed to injure both ankles during a training session. I therefore could not play in the penultimate match, which my team fortunately won. Our trainer, however, was eager to have me play in the final match. This was a psychological matter to him.

And of course I wanted to play as well and therefore decided to give my doctor a call. I showed him my ankles and told him about the soccer match. He looked at me and said he was aware of the importance of the upcoming match for the youngsters on the team. He sounded genuinely appreciative. He would inject my ankles with a painkiller thereby enabling me to play next Saturday. Much to my relief I was able to play.

That Saturday I played the best match ever in my long soccer career. The audience consisted of many supporters, friends, family and acquaintances. Our physician was also present standing next to my wife. A fierce battle ensued on the soccer pitch and we had to fight for ball possession on every inch of the field. A match never to forget and the going really got tough. And to round off my career, I scored the winning goal and we were champions.

I was carried off the pitch on the shoulders of my teammates. That night we celebrated big time and there was an unlimited supply of alcohol. Fortunately, I had this internal sensor, which would let me know when I had had enough, and I never got drunk anymore. That night I had to promise the team I would become their coach next season.

I learned that alcohol enhances the current sentiment. If you are on a high, your spirits will be lifted. When you are sad, you will end up feeling sadder. Yet, alcohol also loosens tongues if you are not a real talker. It did me the world of good to feel that there were people around me who cared about me, especially now that the situation at home was not very pleasant.

Also in Sales there will be important moments and you realise you are not in good shape. An analysis is important. Ask yourself what is going on? Where does this feeling stem from? Can I postpone it or do I have to deal with this situation now. Looking at yourself critically can help you to improve or create awareness of your limitations. It is always best to postpone an important meeting and work out your problems rather than to let them be disturbed by problems. Alcohol is a bad advisor when it comes to solving problems. It does, however, create an opening to talk freely about what is on your mind. Best is always to be capable to address every issue in your life.

A soccer match with a female salesperson

Our most important hardware supplier had decided to appoint a young, dynamic, and female manager to manage my account. She was highly intelligent and attractive to boot. The hardware supplier had set up a special programme to promote women and their projects. Therefore, the projects she had to carry out for my company received priority status. We benefited from this policy and were pleased and satisfied with this hardware supplier.

One day this female Account Manager rang the office and asked whether I was interested in watching a soccer match of my favourite team. She invited my 'second in command' and myself to join her at the football match. I appreciated the invitation and accepted it. As it turned out, though, my second in command had already bought tickets for him and his son. He therefore had to decline the invitation. My secretary really wanted to go. She loved soccer. So I called the Account Manager to inform her that I would be happy to accept on behalf of my secretary and myself. I was dumbfounded when told me that the invitation only included managers and not secretaries.

It goes without saying that my secretary was disappointed but she did not mind me going. The policy of the hardware supplier to support women in its organisation but not allow secretaries to attend their business outings was lost on us. To make it up to my secretary I bought two tickets for a different soccer match so she could take her boyfriend on an outing.

The whole outing was quite something else because I joined the others in a hotel in my business suit. All those invited were dressed similarly and we were invited to dinner. After dinner we were driven in coaches to the stadium where we did not have business seats but were seated among the regular supporters.

I felt ill at ease in my suit for I had much rather worn casual clothes and be a regular supporter among the other supporters. I had no choice though, and tried to enjoy the match. My Account Manager was seated next to me and as soon as the match started she felt the need to convey to me that she did not like soccer at all but just had to come along since I represented an important customer. The match started while at the same time the Account Manager started talking, waffling, chatting, there was no stopping her. I tried to dissuade her by giving short answers and showing that I was not interested in what she had to say but that I wanted to watch the match.

After the match, which 'my team' lost, we had to walk back to the coaches for about five minutes unfortunately lose. It was raining cats and dogs and no umbrellas were provided. Soaking wet we made it back to the coaches and in our dripping suits we were driven back to the hotel. I was soaked to the skin, but I felt I had to endure the hardship for my team and for the sake of maintaining a good relationship with a major supplier.

I learned that I had to keep business and private separately. It could not be avoided altogether, but I would limit it to a minimum.

Whenever you are faced with the possibility to take customers on a business event, you need to be aware of the fact that a customer has certain expectations. In order to meet these expectations you have take stock of the customer's expectations to make the outing a success. If you organise an event the way it is described above you will reach exactly the opposite of what you intended. It is fairly easy to leave a bad impression and you have to put in a lot of effort to make a good impression. In the story above it would have been better to give a presentation beforehand and hand out hats, and a scarf of the favourite team and turn it into a party they will never forget. And.... When you invite customers, make sure you invite the right people. That secretary you will run into again and you will probably need her services as well.

Selling a user group

The financial problems the supplier of the Standard Banking System was facing more or less forced me to initiate a user club although we had not even taken the system into production yet. Throughout Europe there were two other users of the system and in a telephone interview I invited them to visit our company and discuss the possible founding of a user group.

In anticipation of the meeting I had compiled an agenda and drawn up a set of inceptive rules and regulations for a user group. The first meeting was an outright disaster. One of the participants in the meeting took to the floor immediately and started talking about his problems with the software and the lack of support he encountered. He did not stick to the agenda and kept talking about his own software problems.

After the lunch break I decided to cut him short and practically forced him to stick to the agenda. I urged him to discuss his software problems during the AOB part of the meeting[13]. He was not pleased with being cut short but at least he behaved better.

We did get round to discussing the financial problems the supplier was facing and the consequences for the users. As it turned out neither of the two other users had an escrow agreement with the supplier and 'Mr software problems' did not even have a maintenance agreement. If the supplier would have to file for bankruptcy, my company would get the software programme codes. As soon as "Mr software problems' became aware of this, his behaviour changed noticeably.

Software programme codes turned out to be the magic words and everyone present became convinced that a user group was not only useful but even essential. Also, we thought the supplier should be pleased with a user club and we decided to invite the Director of supplying company to the next meeting. We then discussed the rules and regulations and determined that all the participants should preside over the user group in turns. Given the urgency of the matter in hand we decided to meet again in two months' time.

I contacted the Director of the software supplying company and informed him about the user group. Quite unexpected he ventilated his anger about this user group. He considered this club to be a threat and regarded it as a tool we could

---

[13] AOB is short for Any Other Business. This is the part of the meeting where every participant is asked whether there are any additional issues he or she wishes to share with the group.

use against him to adapt the system free of charge. He refused to attend the next meeting. I was very surprised and I felt I had to remind him that he depended heavily both financially and commercially on my company. I had to take him down a peg or two. He did not give in, though, and he did not attend the user group meeting.

After about six months the supplier sold the Standard Banking System to a hardware supplier that also wanted to enter the software market. A market trend in those days. It concerned a large hardware supplying company that also took over the staff, including the people that had been assigned to my company. The board of directors of this hardware supplier liked the idea of a user group and was eager to take part in the meetings.

I learned that asserting power sometimes can be a tool to reach your goal. I did not resort to using it easily, yet as a last resort it is sometimes inevitable.

Sometimes it helps to speak plainly to a customer whenever he tries to take advantage of his position. Sometimes it manifests itself in rude and disrespectful behaviour. Listen to what the customer has to say and try to summarise his statements into a proposition you can work with. It can also help if you try to 'mirror' the other's behaviour. This will make clear to the other what it feels like to be treated in this way. The result is that the customer will respect you. Your 'mirror behaviour' could serve as an eye opener.

The market and McDonald's

We are all familiar with the immense success of McDonald's restaurants all over the world. A global success story that demands respect.

One night I was watching a documentary about the success of McDonald's. The documentary included interviews with analysts, who tried to determine what had turned McDonald's into a success story. One of the analysts concluded that Mr McDonald, the company's founder, must have been a visionary and must have possessed remarkable strategic insight. All this had led to the opening of restaurants even in Russia. Everybody accepted this analysis as the only possible explanation.

With all my experience in devising company strategy relating to what people actually know and are capable of I could not believe that. Was it not simply the case that Old McDonald had managed to produce a very tasty hamburger? Subsequently started a restaurant and since his customers obviously enjoyed the food he served, was able to open more restaurants. Once the enterprise became a success he probably hired a number of expensive consultants, who devised a company strategy and had it implemented. But I could be wrong could I not?

I do understand that everybody loves a success story. We thrive on stories like this and they motivate us. We do not want to hear or read about failures. However, in real life more businesses go bankrupt than turn into a success.

I learned that success stories are important when it comes to motivating staff. We want to feel a sense of pride to work for 'our' company.

It remains an interesting juxtaposition; everybody is always willing to share success stories but remains silent when it comes to sharing negative experiences. It seems as if by appearing successful you gain prestige. Have you ever wondered, though, whom you would rather meet? Someone who is always successful and will not stop talking about it? Or someone who does share his personal success stories but is also willing to talk about the failures? Most would opt for the latter. Is it not strange that we always talk about the good things that we have achieved? What would happen if we would allow ourselves to appear more vulnerable?

Selling a start date

The initial planning of the start date of the Standard Banking System, one and a half years after the start of the project, was under pressure. We had planned a possible extension of two months, to have the final date to take place in the New Year's weekend. This new date had a number of added advantages because we did not have to calculate interest conversion and we would have an extra day (New Year's Day) for the conversion of the data from the old to the new system. One major problem did loom over us because after conversion it was not possible to revert to the old system. We only had one chance and it had to work.

The internal and external accountants were also involved in the project and they had compiled an overview of the comparison of the old and the new system. This overview would enable them to check the finances and could authorise a successful conversion. This was an impossible check system and we called it a 'fake' check. However, they did not know that.

All leave had been suspended and no one was allowed to take days off during the Christmas and New Year period. The whole team was exhausted from the test runs and solving the final problems. Everyone was at the end of his or her tether from working nights and weekends. It was time the project came to a close.

The day before Christmas the Director-general requested all 'key players' to meet in the main conference room. The Bank Director and I presented a detailed planning of the final days before we would bring the new system into production on New Year's Day.

After the presentation the Director-general did something, which impressed me immensely. He asked all those present out right whether we should bring the system into production or not. You could have heard a pin drop. But then after the initial moment of silence everyone in the room said 'Yes'. Well, except for the newly appointed Bank director, that is. He had not been involved in the project for long and ended up saying 'No'. Everyone was surprised and much to my relief the Director-general completely ignored his advice and fortunately the new Bank director's advice dissuaded nobody. I think this 'NO' was the beginning of the end as far as his career opportunities with our firm were concerned.

On New Year's Eve I arrived at 11 p.m. at the office. I knew the Director-general was to put in an appearance as well and I wanted to be there and accompany him on his tour of the department. When I arrived the whole team was still working hard. Some of them had been working non-stop for 48 hours.

Our external consultants had also been on their feet for most of the time and were drowsy and inebriated because of their Whisky intake. In addition to that, they did not exactly smell of roses and were unshaven. I knew the Whisky was what kept their engine going and had therefore allowed it in spite of the criticism. The problem was that I did not know whether the Director-general was aware of the Whisky intake and whether he would accept it. The time of the conversion of the old system to the new system had been set for 2 a.m. Our external auditor would monitor the checking procedure in the conference room, with the Director-general and me in attendance.

At twelve sharp we looked out over the city and witnessed the enormous fireworks display that burst out celebrating the New Year. One of the foreign external consultants could not help but notice that he was very impressed with the way the locals celebrated the bringing into production of our new system. His remark made us laugh and tension subsided a bit.

I was quite nervous when I visited the Director-general in his office. I paid him a visit to keep him up-to-date on the status of the project. He was pleased to hear that everything was going according to plan and he showed me a number of bottles of Champagne he had brought to drink to the health of the diligent workers. Next, he wanted to visit those hard workers on the floor. This worried me because when we were walking through my department we ran in to a drunken external consultant. He was completely immersed in his own thoughts and could barely avoid walking into us. The Director-general could not help but say, "well, perhaps the Champagne wasn't such a good idea after all". That was the only thing he ever said about it. Marvellous.

At 2 p.m. exactly the external auditor arrived to check whether the conversion had been successful. Of course it was a success and he signed the required official document. Fortunately the conversion was a genuine success. Only response time was insufficient but that was something we could tackle easily by means of increasing the memory capacity of the computer.

One month later the old Bank director threw a big party for all those involved. In his speech he referred to himself the as 'father' of the project and to me as the 'mother' of the project. He was infinitely proud of the success of the project, but assigning me a female part? I was well pleased though, because the whole project had been a truly remarkable assignment.

I learned that it is very important to create a broad basis when it comes to making decisions and to include people personally. Nobody could cop out. And everybody believed in a successful outcome.

In this situation it is essential that all key players are involved in the project and in particular the decision-makers. Far-reaching changes can only be implemented successfully when supported by everyone. In Sales this principle is also valid. Always convince yourself whether the person you are talking to is also the person who takes the decisions. Decisions are only taken when those responsible agree. Therefore, let no one else ever deliver your sales pitch. Only you are capable of getting across the importance of the matter to a customer and in the right surroundings.

Devoting attention to a clever colleague

This young man was employed by my company and held a position in one of the offices. His district manager had approached me to see if I would be willing to offer him a position in the Automation Department. This man had been a Marine in the Dutch Army. When I met him I liked him on first sight. He struck me as a clever person with a winner's mentality, eager to learn and work hard and he was very taken with my Information and Automation Plan. I took him on and as most youngsters he started off at the Information Centre.

He was a fast learner and I soon discovered that his strong presence had a good influence on his colleagues and that only after a short period of time he was acting as a sounding board to the rest of the team. The Information Centre Manager was an older employee with comprehensive technical knowledge but was hardly equipped with any social skills. The two of them teaming up brought out the best of both of them.

HR aspects regarding the department were my own personal responsibility. Since this smart fellow was also an early starter we could discuss any staffing issues privately and he gave me valuable advice on people and matters I needed to devote some attention to. Because of our informal sessions I was able to prevent unnecessary escalations. He always asked me a lot of questions because he was eager to learn. Occasionally we used to have dinner together and talked about our personal lives. He appeared to be looking for happiness, love and something to motivate him.

Gradually I got to know him better and I learned that his father had died when he was eighteen years old. He had two sisters and a brother all living in Canada. His mother had assigned him the task of man of the house, so he did not exactly have a carefree youth and he had felt responsible for the whole family. An additional stint in the Marines had turned him into a real tough guy. He was used to being the strongest and having to solve other people's problems. There was no warmth in his grey eyes and the only thing he seemed to care about was his car.

One day he suddenly resigned. His best friend had set up a company and he had invested his savings in it and together they would manage the start-up. I was, of course, very disappointed but could do nothing but accept the inevitable. This, as it turned out, was his dream and I had to respect that. We did agree though, to have dinner together on a regular basis to keep in touch.

During one of our dinners he told me had started an illicit affair with the mother of his friend and fellow-manager. To make things worse, her daughter was also employed by their company. I warned him about the probable repercussions but he said he was happy with the way things were.

After about a year he told me the company was experiencing difficulties. He had had to file for bankruptcy and that had led to many problems for the family. He was seriously disappointed in his mistress, his friend's mother, who had taken sides with her son. He was blamed for everything and felt very hurt and unhappy. The only thing I could do at that point in time was to offer him a job whenever he needed one.

On a Friday morning two weeks later I phoned him to ask him how he was doing. He answered that he was just fine. I was not convinced because he sounded rather listless and depressed. I was worried about him. I tried to get in touch with him in the following weeks but to no avail. Only three weeks later he contacted me. He told me that when I had called him on that Friday morning he had decided to take his own life that day.

He had packed all his belongings, taken pills in combination with a large amount of whisky and had hoped to end his life there and then. Because of my phone call the spell had been broken. But things did not go as planned. Without being aware of what he was doing he had managed to get into his car and had driven it into a lamppost. The police had taken him to hospital where had had his stomach pumped. As soon as he woke up he saw this psychiatrist sitting at his bedside. He did not respect the psychiatrist one bit and had told him all sorts of non sense stories. But eventually they had released him and he was back home again.

It got very quiet at the other end of the line because he clearly expected something from me. I was completely dumbfounded while my brains were feverishly trying to come up with something to say, because I sensed that the way I responded was very important to him. I told him that obviously his time had not come yet. His life was not over yet. I then suggested we would have dinner together the following Tuesday. He accepted my invitation. During his phone call my secretary had been present to go through that day's mail and she had heard every word of the conversation. It had left her stunned into silence and she understood that I was shocked and upset. She left my office quietly.

The night preceding the dinner I could not sleep. I just knew that the conversation we were about to have was very important to him. This was a matter of life and death. I prayed to my God and asked him for help. I spend some time meditating and in prayer and finally I fell asleep. My God taught me to have faith.

That Tuesday night he sat down facing me and looked at me with this tough look in his grey eyes. His eyes were listless and without any other trace of emotion. I told him once more that apparently his time to die had not come yet.

After that I talked to him about his mother and his other siblings, all family members who loved him. I did notice that as soon as I mentioned his brother the look in his eyes changed and a certain degree of warmth appeared.

Much to my relief that turned out to be the starting point and I advised him to go and visit his brother in Canada to come to terms with all that had happened. He quite took to the idea and when we left I knew he was going to get in touch with his brother. When I got home I could not remember what we had had for dinner for I was completely exhausted. I was drained of all energy but I did not forget to thank my God for guiding me.

He left to visit his brother in Canada and we talked on the phone every week. Each time we talked he sounded better and slowly but surely I heard the strength returning to his voice. He and his brother got on well together and became firm friends.

I learned that friendships in life are essential. Being there when your friends need you is of the utmost importance. Yet this was the second time in my life I had been involved in a choice between life and death.

This story is all about feeling and drawing conclusions from intonation, two very important elements in Sales. If selling was easy anyone could do it. You have to be Jack-of –all-trades in order to do it well. For you have to know everything there is to know about your customer, know everything about the product, be able to negotiate, be a good listener, explain the matter in hand in concise terms, observe, watch and relate to people. The latter especially requires sensitivity. Intercept unspoken signals. The danger lies in the fact that you might interpret these signals as an undisputed truth. If you intercept certain signals and want to act upon them, try to ask yourself a check question. This will help you to determine whether you should act upon your intuitive conclusions.

Selling another partnership

It goes without saying that I was rather disappointed when the cooperation with the major retailer in order to work on a combined Switch computer for Electronic Payment fell through. I obviously discussed the introduction of 'plastic currency' in the Netherlands with our suppliers since it concerned a major development in those days.

One of the suppliers was the major and at that point in time the only Telecom Operator in the Netherlands. I was surprised to find that this key player had not been involved in the 'plastic currency' discussion. This company should be interested since it would only lead to an increase in telephone units.

Their new Account Manager listened carefully when I raised the matter and continued to ask in-depth questions. I told him all I could think of about the Switch computer, 24 hours a day access and the possibility of working together to realise this. This Switch computer would process from all terminals 'plastic currency' transaction, validate and authorise them for the card issuing company (the actual switching). It was a productive meeting but I never really expected anything to come out of it because the Telecom Operator was not known for its innovative policies.

Much to my surprise the Account Manager suggested a new meeting and came to see me, accompanied by a clever colleague involved in special projects. They wanted to discuss joining forces on a plan to install a Switch computer, which would first 'switch' the credit card transactions and subsequently our banking transactions. And as soon as the combined banks would offer a solution for the direct debit transactions they could take part as well. The Telecom Operator intended to 'switch' the credit card transactions through phone booths. This seemed a win-win situation for both companies since it enabled me to complete the network system for our company.

We set up a small team to realise the Switch plan. Apart from me the team consisted of the clever Telecom fellow and his older colleague and another clever fellow from my own company and an external consultant. It was a great team and the sense of humour and strength of will of the team members eventually led to success. We were a team of friends and every success we celebrated in the same restaurant 'The Danne'. For communication purposes we used a system introduced by the Telecom Operator called Memocon. This system was the forerunner of e-mail and an important means of communication for the team.

First of all we drew up a partnership agreement and a project plan. The agreement was simple and most of all clear. We had passed on the functional concept of the plan to the legal advisors and they had done a marvellous job in providing a legal basis for the plan.

We were not out of the woods yet because more was needed to obtain permission for the necessary investments. It was time for a 'road show' in which I had to give presentations on the topic of 'plastic currency' to many managers employed at different levels at the Telecom Operator. All this because of the notion that when strangers are around, people take in the message more easily.

In order to get the partnership agreement signed, one of the Telecom Operator's directors came to visit the Director-general of our company. The clever Telecom fellow and I were present and between us we had prepared this meeting quite well.

The Telecom director and our Director-general got on well from the start and talked informally about their interests. At some point our Director-general talked about his 78 rpm record collection. The Telecom director responded by telling him that he had inherited a number of these records from an aunt and would bring them along next time. I never knew whether the Telecom director really inherited the records or whether he had to go out and buy them at a jumble sale.

I learned that the faith my company had in the solution to the problem of the acceptance of 'plastic currency' gave me extra strength and also opened doors for me. Moreover, large companies sometimes need smaller companies to bring about changes.

A salesperson who does not believe in the company he works for and the products/services he sells has no chance of succeeding. When the salesperson believes in what he sells and displays enthusiasm he is already halfway there. The story above goes to show that you do not have to be a key player to make a difference.

My secretary and right-hand woman

She was a young and attractive woman and my secretary and right-hand woman at the same time. We had in a manner of speaking undertaken a business match. I had met her at my previous employer and had asked her if she wanted to come and join this company and work for me once more. Her parents used to work for my previous employer and her father had been dismissed summarily and had turned into an alcoholic spending his days at home. Her parents had been divorced. She never told me why her father had been fired but she was pleased that I never held it against her but judged her on her own merits. She was loyal to me and went to great lengths to protect my interests and me. We became good friends and had in common that we wanted to win for this company.

We cooperated as equals and she took female emancipation seriously. Sometimes she refused an assignment because I had inadvertently used the word 'must'. She would then look at me with her big brown eyes and from her body language it became clear that she did not accept being treated this way. Well, I had found a way to circumvent the 'giving orders' issue. I would compile a 'to do list' for her to deal with any way she wanted to. A great way to cooperate while avoiding any possible communication pitfalls.

When I met her she had been living together with her boyfriend, a professional soldier. But she was outspoken on the fact that she did not want to have any children with him without saying why. Later on they split up and during that difficult period in her life I used to talk a lot with her. Since she had also confided in me that after me she never intended to work as a secretary for anyone else ever again, I advised her to take up studying again, for especially in automation there were ample opportunities to cut out a career for herself. She did not feel like going back to school and she did not want to be alone. So, the hunting season was open.

She ran into her new boyfriend on the work floor. He was a young promising office manager and she had met him at a company indoor soccer game. After only a year they got married.

One Saturday when I was playing a soccer match in their village she came to watch and after the match I was invited to their home. On my arrival I could not believe my eyes. My strong emancipated secretary was completely subordinate in her marriage. She waited on her husband hand and foot and looked up to him as her hero and commander. After another year she gave birth to a beautiful baby girl. Three days after her confinement she was already at the office with the little girl for me to cuddle. I sensed something was amiss but I never raised the subject.

She told me that she did not want to return to work as my secretary because she did not want to work for more than three days a week and she felt that I needed and deserved a full-time secretary. She asked me whether there was another position available that would suit her and her needs. Of course I helped her and found her a position with the automation control department where she was to become a programme version Comptroller control. And so her career in automation took off after all.

After a year she told me that her marriage had failed and that she wanted to file for divorce. Once again I offered my sympathy and advice once I was convinced there was no saving her marriage. I helped her with the divorce proceedings. One day she told my new secretary that it was such a comfort that she could always count on me for help. I was pleased to hear that and also relieved because you can never be sure whether you are doing the right thing in situations like this.

I was not the only one who had offered to help her, though. My clever HR assistant also offered to help her and he did such a good job that after a while they became involved. They got married and the groom's brother joined them from Canada. It made me feel good to see these that two young people had found happiness with each other and I knew I had to thank my God once more. I had always been against relationships on the work floor but for their sake I was willing to make an exception.

I learned how important loyalty is and that it takes no effort at all to help people. I loved these two people and they had become a part of my life.

In Sales it is essential that you support the company you represent. It is not uncommon for sales teams to generate a negative atmosphere. In most cases it is caused by a lack of understanding between management and the sales team. Example: according to management the sales team needs to visit more prospects. The sales team always comes up with excuses. Too much traffic on the road, these conversations always take up more time than management thinks. What it comes down to is for a management team to understand what it is like to be a salesperson and for a sales team to continue to scrutinise working methods and techniques.

Outplaying all parties involved

Together with the major Telecom Operator we had initiated a project to process credit card transactions from our service desks and from their phone booths and offer them for verification and authorisation to the credit card companies. This we referred to as 'switching'. My company was market leader in the Netherlands for withdrawing cash with a credit card, a service we offered for every type of credit card. This was a manual procedure for which authorisation had to be requested by means of a phone call and therefore rather time consuming. The automation of this process through a 'Switch' computer would mean a tremendous improvement for our sales offices.

There was one problem, though, because the 'Switch' computer had to be linked up to the computers of at least four of the major credit card issuing companies. The necessary interface was not standardised which led to an additional problem; who was going to pay for the development of the interface.

We simply had to devise a clever approach to convince the credit card companies that it was in their best interest to pay for the development of the interface. We knew that the four major credit card companies were highly competitive and whenever one of them made a decision the others would follow suit. They were always worried that they were to lose some of their market share.

Our company was in close contact with the largest credit card company. A good and solid relationship maintained by both parties. We set up a lunch meeting with the management of both companies including the Automation Managers (i.e. me). Over lunch we discussed the whole matter of 'switching' credit card transactions amicably.

I then mentioned casually to the Automation Manager of the credit card company that his major competitor had already decided to interface their system with ours. The atmosphere was no longer amicable and we got down to business straight away and decided to split the development costs two ways.

Now we had to convince the other three players. We set up a meeting with the management of the second largest credit card company in the Netherlands. We informed them that the largest credit card company had already decided to interface their system with ours and that they were going to pick up the bill for the development costs. They decided immediately that they would pay for the development costs as well. The same happened when we approached the other two credit card companies. We wanted to shout it out loud but we could not, it was better to keep quiet about the whole matter.

I learned that cooperating with a key player in the market (the large Telecom Operator) and exploit the current market situation is essential to cut a good deal.

It's all sales

> Depending on the market situation it is a good strategy to sell Top down or Bottom up. As becomes clear from the story above, the decision was made to sell Top down and use the fact that once you have the market leader on board it has to be a good deal. This is not always feasible. Sometimes you still have to prove to the market leader that your concept is successful by proving its merits with smaller companies.

Making a deal during the holidays

We had been in the habit of going on holiday to central France for quite a number of years. We would rent a small farmhouse close to Chablis. Since my wife simply adored basking in the sun and the fact that France boasts an agreeable climate was what brought us there in the first place. There were hardly any tourists to be found and the peace and quiet made it the perfect place for us to relax. There was no television and we spend a lot of time outside in the orchard behind the house. Whenever my wife was sunbathing I enjoyed reading an up market detective novel somewhere in the shade.

Upon ten minutes of our arrival I would transform into a completely different person. I was no longer organised, never checked my watch and did not even think about my cell phone or e-mail. It was so quiet that if there was a hedgehog rummaging around the house it sounded as if the house was attacked by an elephant. I always felt at ease there since I also had the idea that this was the place were my ancestors came from. I felt at home and spent a lot of time thinking about my paternal granddad, my namesake. We rented the farm from a well-to-do and 'warm' family. Both inside and outside the farmhouse I could always feel the love and warmth that surrounded that family.

I have to say, though, that for my teenage daughter the place did not hold much excitement. Not much was going on for teenagers and usually we invited one of her friends to come along and tried to make things fun for them. She did want to come along and hardly ever complained about the lack of excitement. This time she would leave us halfway through our holiday to join the parents of her friend who were also enjoying a holiday in France. I was to spend a week alone with my wife, which suited me just fine because I wanted to talk to her. She was quite depressed and was not happy with the way her life had turned out. I wanted to help her because our relationship was no longer a happy one.

Right before the holiday she had contacted our doctor once more. On his arrival they had gone up to her bedroom straight away. As he tried to leave the house unattended I lay in waiting for him outside the front door. I asked him how my wife was doing and how I could help her. He answered that the problems my wife was facing did not have anything to do with me but with her unhappy youth. The way I was trying to help her was all I could do and I should continue with what I was doing. He never told me anything substantial though, and his answer was vague to say the least.

During the first week of our holiday we had been taking the girls out and had a good time. After the first week we took the girls to the friend's parents. That night, when we arrived back at the cottage after a long drive, I decided to get some sleep. After about an hour I woke up and found my wife drunk in the kitchen.

As soon as she became aware of my presence she started screaming and shouting. She blamed me for many things and most of the time I had no idea what she was going on about. At some point she approached me and in her anger spat me in my face and tried to hit on my head. Unfortunately this made me lose my temper and I hit her back. This shocked her immensely. She gave me a condescending look and left for the bedroom.

That night I tried to catch some sleep in the spare room but it did not work. I hated myself for hitting her. I had never hit a woman before in my life and I had never been so angry. I prayed to my God but there was no answer (yet). I decided to go outside and sit in the orchard for a while.

It was a beautiful night; the sky bright and filled with stars. I walked into the orchard and started to cry. I thought about my Granddad and fell on my knees and started to pray once more to my God. I asked him for forgiveness and asked him for advice on how to help my wife. I just sat there praying quietly and all of a sudden I became aware of an intense quietness around me. I felt the quietness taking hold of me. I suddenly realised that my wife was using me to come to terms with the problems stemming from her youth.

I only served as a sounding board, for she had never been able to say what was on her mind to those involved. She had to get it out of her system one way or the other because it had been eating away at her for many years. The alcohol made her loosen up and enabled her to get it out in the open. I decided to help her since I felt she deserved it, being the mother of my child.

The next day my wife apologised for her behaviour of the previous night. She added immediately that this was going to be the only time she would ever apologise. I accepted her apologies and offered her my help in dealing with her problems. I added that I would not make any decisions concerning our relationship until she had come to terms with her problems. It was as if she could not take it all in.

The rest of the holiday was an unpleasant affair. We were both hurt and decided to cut our holiday short. We went home.

I once more experienced that my God was there for me when I needed him. The problems had to be major though, before he would answer. I would try to support my wife while she tried to come to terms with her problems. And I always stick to my promises.

Whether you believe in (a) God or not it is always commendable to talk to yourself (a God). Sharing thoughts offers new possibilities and develops a new strength. It sounds funny because nothing tangible happens; yet you feel different. Engaging in an intensive conversation with yourself feeds your inner strength, and gives you the feeling that whatever may happen, you do not have to face it alone. Sharing makes worrying less worrying.

The Standard System in production

The Standard Banking System was up and running. The implementation had taken more than twenty months of hard work including 60-hours working weeks. Once the project was finished everyone was dead tired and needed to unwind. All those involved in the project took some time off to spend some time at home.

We had redesigned the banking processes and had defined new and different transactions within the banking processes. We did not know, though, how many transactions we would have to process on a daily basis and how many request transactions we would have to deal with.

We had enabled the users, through a functional control application to define their own inquiry requests. After a few days it turned out the system's performance was lacking and the only solution possible was to purchase additional hardware (internal memory). Unfortunately this meant exceeding the budget. At some point we also had to limit the freedom of defining inquiry requests when one of the users had requested the complete content of the database.

What we also noticed that the users were slowly discovering the advantages of an 'online' and 'real time' system. Every day we spent a lot of time printing day processing data since we were told that was necessary. After a couple of months these reports were no longer collected from the computer centre and we discovered that those who needed the data collected them online. All the heated arguments in the project group on the subject were forgotten all of a sudden. And when I ran into a group of users of the system and asked them for their opinion on the system they all were positive. They were happy with the new system and that made me feel proud. They were positive about the system and they were still only using the basic applications. In time the system would be used to its full potential.

In my department we had defined a small control group and appointed two technical Comptrollers who were very knowledgeable with regard to the Standard Banking System. In this way they could communicate at the same level with the help-desk and the supplier's developers of the system. This worked out well and for as long as we used the system (ten years) it never went down because of a software failure.

We had also initiated a functional control group for the users at the bank. This group was also successful in dealing with small changes in the parameters carried out by the group. All those involved in the project were motivated and were convinced of the importance of the system for our company. In the case of problems everyone was willing to take action whether it was their responsibility or not. Problems were dealt with instantaneously. After about six months the system was stable and was used to half of its capacity. An improvement!

One of the main advantages of this 'real time' and 'online' system was that we could introduce a 'bridging loan' as a product. Since 'bridging loans' were short-term loans it required a system such as ours. Everyone was now convinced that we could have a return on investment from the Standard Banking System.

I learned that it is rather difficult to change people's working methods. Or in other words changing people is never easy. Yet, a successful implementation of a system depends largely on the possibilities to change people and will almost always have to be reinforced by management.

You cannot change people. You can change their behaviour, though within limits. The main problem for companies is to implement changes. Why would that be? Organisational experts advise on extended involvement op people and point out the advantages of changes. Why then are so many changes unsuccessful. 95% of the things we do we do on autopilot. Only 5% we do consciously and planned. Our internal system is not made to initiate changes. We plan on doing it but as soon as we have to overcome an obstacle we automatically resort to our old behaviour. More is therefore needed to bring about changes.

Unmistakable body language

For the 'Switching' of credit card transactions we had in collaboration with the major Telecom operator opted for the same standard software as the Dutch Postbank. The Postbank used the software to 'Switch' their cash point transactions. It was an international standard software package and was sold in the Netherlands through a retail concern. This company maintained high standards and in particular high technical standards. It could take on projects and complete them against a set price and a set delivery date. Our 'Switch' would be operated through our partner, the Telecom Operator, in their calculus centre.

The senior account manager of this software company was Irish but could speak Dutch rather well. He was appointed to draw up the agreement with our company. He was good at his job and we agreed on a good deal at a set price and a set delivery date.

Doing business with him was quite something else though, because whenever we came up with a proposal he did not like he would turn bright red. Without saying one single word it was abundantly clear that he did not agree. Easy for us to determine what the internal difficulties were. I have to admit that we sometimes made use of this to tease him a bit.

We were assigned another Account Manager as soon as the project really started. She was Scottish and had a great sense of humour. I thoroughly enjoyed dealing with this software company. They were also honest enough to tell us when they already had developed a part of the interface software. We would be offered the software as a deposit for an interface that still had to be developed and all this to be included in the set price for the entire system. It was a perfect project to work on and because of the unparalleled cooperation it was a huge success.

Cash withdrawals and deposits were added manually to a debit list issued daily at our banking offices. The transactions were sent to the head office via post to be processed through the banking system.

Now for the first time in the Netherlands our banking offices were linked up to the head office online through the 'Switch'. Cash withdrawals and deposits were processed instantly. We had turned into a bank with 24/7 access to up-to-date bank balance information. Those working in the offices were very pleased with this latest development.

We had also selected a Pin pad for all our service desks. The pads were installed on the service desks outside the security glass cubicles. This Pin-pad could read-in the data for all credit card transactions and subsequently all cash withdrawals could be made immediately and online and authorized by the credit card companies. This was definitely an improvement as well and saved a lot of time.

Finally our dream had come true. We now had online access to all offices and were capable of accepting 'plastic currency' from other companies such as the direct debit card issued by the combined banks. We had provided a system that met all banking security demands. And of course our new systems led to increasing efficiency and effectiveness at our branch offices and the head office. We could now invest in developing and implementing new products.

For our partner, the Telecom Operator, this had been a unique project. It was the first project that had been completed successfully and they could accept all credit cards in their phone booths. They threw a big party afterwards and gave me an awful lot of credit for the part I had played in the successful outcome of the project. An additional bonus was that the Telecom Operator had submitted our project for an award issued by a trade journal. The award would go to the most innovative project of the year. We were elected into the top ten but never made it to the best three.

I learned that working together with a large partner company opened all kinds of doors for me that would otherwise have remained closed. My enthusiasm towards helping the offices and to win, or in other words live up to my promises, had led once more to success. I was not able to enjoy the success, though.

Body language is an important part of our communication system. It confirms what we think and do. When we are able to use body language to our advantage we can make people perceive things that are not there. You can be put on the wrong track. In Sales this can be useful sometimes. A surprised look on your face in the case of a small order, a matter-of-course look on your face when you mention the price or showing involvement by sitting on the edge of your seat.

Making a deal in fifteen minutes

The main Telecom Operator and partner in our 'Switch' project had created its niche in the market through their telephone services and the sales of telephone units. Their policy included the development of services at both ends of the telephone line in order to secure their telephone lines and telephone units. That was one of the main reasons they had decided to embark on the 'Switch' project with us. A clever strategy.

Yet, now that the 'Switch' had become operational many other players in the market responded. The four major banks in the market became aware of what was happening and they assumed that the Telecom Operator wanted to compete with them in terms of 'plastic currency'. This had to be prevented at all costs. These banks were extremely powerful since they had all granted loans to the Telecom Operator.

As a result of these developments I received a phone call from the secretary of the Director-general of the Telecom Operator. He wanted to talk to me and had only fifteen minutes at his disposal. Now this man was a living legend and a true 'Captain of Industry'. Together with his right-hand man he was set to change and privatise the company. Not an easy task.

I could not predict what he wanted to discuss with me but I sensed it had to be important. Our cooperation was at risk! What was I to say to him in fifteen minutes? Giving a presentation was not feasible given the time restrictions. People on the team came up with well intended advice but somehow none of it felt right. I decided to rely on my intuition and would let things take their course. I knew I had to unwind and relax in order to be on edge when necessary.

The Director-general and I had decided that I would take the chauffeur-driven company car. On the day of the meeting I sat in the back of the car, relaxed and I let myself be driven to my appointment. I could now fully concentrate on our meeting. I was ready and able. But I did not have plan, though.

His secretary showed me into his office and as soon as she had left he attacked straight away. He barked at me that members of the board of his bank had phoned him and accused him and my company of wanting to take over payment transfer from the Dutch banks. He blamed me for seriously endangering the status of his company with the project.

So, that was what it was all about. I managed to stay calm and keep my wits about me. I gave him a friendly look and started off by complimenting him on the fact that his company had managed to have at least one telephone installed in every home. A phenomenal accomplishment that resulted in the sale of many telephone units and therefore much profit.

I continued by telling him that the aim of the combined project was to generate additional telephone units and therefore more profit for the Telecom Operator. He got off his high horse and asked me in a more friendly tone of voice to continue. I then told him concisely about the recent 'plastic currency' developments in the Netherlands, the part the major banks and retail played and what we had achieved with our project. I stressed that all this was not intended to compete with the banks but to offer complementing services.

The Telecom Operator had never been taken seriously by the major authoritarian banks. It had always been a source of unease but because of the project he was now able to do business with the banks on an equal level. He now showed an interest and decided right there and than that he wanted to play an important part in payment transfer in the Netherlands. He was infinitely kind to me now and expressed his gratitude before I left his office. I was exhausted and it took me about an hour to recover in the back seat of the company car. I was impressed though. This was a man who was quick to understand and could take important decisions in the time span of just fifteen minutes.

I learned that it was important to get to know my partner company, its products and services and to understand their core activities. I told him what he wanted to hear and had provided him with a more powerful position in the Netherlands.

It's all sales

Selling sometimes seems to be a matter of spending a lot of time discussing the product and then ask for an order. Nothing is more from the truth than this supposition. If selling was easy, anyone could do it. Moreover, other sales tactics like telesales or handing out flyers could then replace salespeople. A salesperson asks the right questions and listens to the customer. He paints a mental picture of the customer and by doing so gets to know the customer. A good salesperson knows all there is to know about a customer including where the money comes from. Only from tuning into that the salesperson will develop a natural relationship with the customer. As soon as this relationship is established the actual selling will become a matter of course.

Selling my daughter to her school

When it came to schoolwork my daughter was very motivated but it never came to her easily and she had to spend a lot of time on doing her homework. She was determined to attain her higher secondary education diploma[14] and she deserved it, for she was very dedicated. I wanted to show her that I respected and appreciated the effort she was making, which is why I decided to become chairman of the parents' council of her school. The parents' council was initiated to advise school management on important matters and also to organise school festivities. The school principle was also a member of the parents' council. However, the parents' council consisted of two men and thirteen loving mothers! This obviously was not a man's world.

There were many lessons for me to learn because as a manager I was used to taking part in six to eight meetings a day. The meetings I attended on a daily basis were structured meetings and involved taking many decisions. And it goes without saying I was always well prepared for these meetings otherwise we would run behind schedule too much.

Now, these parents' council meetings were quite something else. The mums loved their children and thoroughly enjoyed making a contribution to the school in their spare time. The meetings represented for them an evening out, chatting to the other mums about their kids and other irrelevant matters. The meeting was a social outing. The principal and I understood what these meetings were all about. My only purpose was to end the meeting at 10 p.m. so we could go home at a reasonable hour. This should be feasible since there were not too many items on the agenda anyway. So, we would start our monthly meeting at 8 p.m. and I would let the ladies chat away happily until 9.30 p.m. And once they had finished (as far as they ever did of course) I would be able to discuss the items on the agenda in half an hour's time.

After graduation my daughter wanted to attend two years of pre University education at the same school. In order to do so she needed to attain high grades

---

[14] The education system in the Netherlands differs from that in, for instance, the US or the UK. After primary/elementary school a child can attend either vocational education or general secondary education depending on a general test and school advice. General secondary education is available at two levels; higher general secondary education and pre University education. In order to attend University a student needs to have a pre University school diploma. In the Netherlands it is possible for pupils who have attained a higher general secondary education diploma to attend two years of pre University education and then sit the pre University school exam.

for her Higher General Secondary exam. Even though she passed the exam she did not attain the required grades and was really disappointed about it. She wanted to stay at that school and sit the pre university exam. It goes without saying that I did mention to the principle before and after meetings that my daughter was very eager to sit the pre university exam.

As part of the graduation festivities a parents' evening was organised to which all pupils and parents were invited. The diplomas were handed out to the students by the principle and he addressed every individual student personally. The pupils were also asked about their future plans after graduation. When the principle addressed my daughter he was rather positive about her achievements and he asked her to stay at the school and study for the pre university diploma. I was very proud of my daughter and I could tell by just looking at her that she was incredibly happy.

I learned once more that you will always benefit from making an effort on behalf of others and that it will open the door to success.

Also in Sales it is essential to maintain a good relationship with your customer. Just being pleasant to each other is not enough. You actually have to show that you appreciate each other. You can achieve this by offering help to your customer if he is experiencing difficulties. Offer help and the customer will buy from you.

Negotiating for a standard discount

An international company employed this director; the market leader in selling cash machines in the Netherlands. The combined banks had carried out market research and had concluded that people would rather do business with a human being than withdrawing cash from an impersonal cash point.

Also, providing people with a Personal Identification Code (Pin) might prove to be too demanding. The banks did proceed to place cash points and in order to hold the lid on costs joined forces, and in doing so having to place less cash points. The customers from the different banks could withdraw cash from all the bank cash points (the so called guest use). The Dutch Postbank and its customers was an exception. The Postbank had pursued its own strategy which included placing cash point but not for guest use.

And then a miracle happened. The consumers embraced cash points immediately. They loved withdrawing cash anonymously 24 hours a day, seven days a week. Sometimes people were even standing in line to withdraw cash from a machine whereas a bank service desk 100 metres down the road would be without custom. The banks were embarrassed when faced with the long lines of customers waiting patiently until it was their turn to withdraw cash from the cash points. The only solution was to place more cash points, which they did immediately.

My company had already decided to place cash points in our offices at the train stations and we had to come to an agreement regarding the delivery of the cash machines with the supplier. We had been doing business successfully with this supplier for many years so we knew each other well.

I had been in touch with the Sales Director of the company and had requested a quotation for the lay out of the decision-making process within the company. I knew the Sales Director well and we got along well because in spite of his sales successes he was still a reliable and likeable person. Over the years we had become business friends.

In my company it was customary for the financial Comptroller to take part in the final negotiations for a deal. The Comptroller, certainly not one of my friends, thought himself a first rate negotiator and he was always very proud of himself when he could announce at board meetings that he had managed to agree on a discount of 5%.

My friend the Sales Director asked me whether our Comptroller would be involved in the negotiations and when I answered affirmatively he started laughing. I asked him why and he then revealed to me that they were aware that our Comptroller always tried to get a 5% discount. And since they were aware of this they had already factored in 5%. For the Sales Director it was now a matter of trying not to agree to the 5% discount but for instance to 3% or even less.

It was difficult for me to keep a straight face during negotiations. I had the tendency to help the supplier a bit, which of course I did not. Our Comptroller was very proud of his efforts when he could announce that he had been able to agree on a discount. Of 2%!

I learned that you cannot always rely on market research. What people say is not always what people do and especially when a product or service offers convenience, people are more than willing to make use of it. And negotiating is a game, a game I enjoyed hugely.

Market research is indispensable in order to initiate and execute plans. It offers a sense of direction to the way you think and act. As soon as conclusions need to be drawn or decisions have to be made based on market research, it becomes essential to try out your ideas in real life. How does your idea work out when put into practice? Only relying on theoretical research is risky.

Carrying out price negotiations with someone else than your regular contact can be tricky. Make sure your regular contact is present. What to discuss with the financial controller? The price is determined by the need and the right solution. It is a matter of providing insight into your overview of the costs.

Selling for my 'technical data base'

The Head of the Information Centre in my department was responsible for the implementation of all software on the PCs. He was a technical 'whiz kid' and knew everything there is to know about networks and security. He coached his staff and was always willing and able to share his technical knowledge with others. He was my technical database and I respected and appreciated him as such. I could always depend on his sound technical advice.

When it comes to 'Plastic Currency' and Electronic Payment it was essential for my company to be able to enter the discussion regarding safety and risks at the same level as the banks and credit card suppliers. The main topic of discussion was the security of the PIN code and network transactions. You had to be a 'trusted party' in the world of 'Plastic Currency' otherwise they would refrain from doing business with you. My 'technical data-base' was absolutely brilliant and it was also due to his skills that our company became a 'trusted party'. He needed a little guidance on occasion though, because if you secure everything 100% you cannot function properly anymore. Also in this, compromising is vital.

He may have been a walking technical database it was never easy to talk to him about other matters, though. In formal meetings I always had to be mindful of his body language to determine whether he agreed or disagreed with a proposal or whether he wanted to add something. I had acquired the habit of asking for everyone's opinion with every item on the agenda. So I could not overlook him. But most of the time I had to go through his proposals before the meetings in order to make sure I understood what he meant and to take the right decisions. No, it was not easy to understand him.

He was definitely not a strong communicator, which manifested itself at some point in a funny way. In one of his more sociable moods he had confided in my secretary and had told her that his sister always selected his clothes and organised and colour coded them so he could not make mistakes wearing clashing colour combinations. My secretary had therefore concluded that he had to be colour-blind and we agreed with her that had to be the case. We forgot to notice though, that he was the first person in the department to have a colour computer screen on his desk. So we went on believing this for ten years until I happened to mention it once during a drinks session in a bar. He told me that he was not at all colour-blind but that sometimes he got a bit confused and would put on clothes in clashing colours. That was all there was to it. We teased my secretary with her wrong conclusion and of course she refused to believe he was not colour-blind.

The youngsters in my department really loved him. He was always available when it came to technical issues. When it came to a social counselling we had to leave that to others. He had on one occasion advised me to appoint a friend of his as Head of the Development Department. Not a very sound piece of advice as it turned out later on.

This taught me that I had to appreciate him for his technical gifts. And that in his case it is worth it to adapt the organisation of the department accordingly. It is impossible to change him.

It's all sales

If we think that all people think alike we are very much mistaken. In general people have four ways of thinking: Visual (in images), auditive (in sounds), kinaesthetic (with feelings) and auditive digital (in detail). Every person thinks along the four ways of thinking but generally one predominates. A set of personal qualities is attributed to every single one of them. In this story we are dealing with an audile digital person. Personal qualities are: wanting to know everything into detail and not having a lot of social skills. Do not try to change the behaviour of people with this line of thinking because it will not work. Create a working atmosphere that suits his capabilities.

Buying second hand software

In most cases it turned out that a hardware supplier selling software was not a successful market approach. Selling software is a whole different ballgame than selling hardware. The supplier of our Standard Banking System was also a hardware supplier and since success had failed to materialise the company had decided to sell the Standard Banking System.

The new owner had bought the Standard Banking System for a mere sum of money. His company had already won its spurs in South East Asia with the sales of a standard financial system and Europeans managed the company. The Director-general of this company did not have a banking background although he was kind and a charismatic leader. He was almost always flying from one place to the other, needed only four hours of sleep and drank litres of coffee per day. Because of his strength and expertise he knew everything there was to know about Marketing and Sales.

What nobody expected happened. In only a short period of time he managed to sell the Standard Banking System to 400 banks in 86 countries. An amazing accomplishment. He considered the user group a fantastic means of communicating his plans and strategy and answer customer questions. He turned the user group meetings into festive get-togethers and made them into an advantage for his company. We were business friends and he appreciated my help as a reference and called me the best salesperson for his company.

Of course I attended the user group meetings, always accompanied by a colleague. At first these meetings were not very exciting because of the detailed discussions of technical software problems. But later on more bankers started attending the meetings making them more interesting. For me these meetings were always a success because almost all the delegates knew and respected me.

In general most people regarded these meetings as fun outings. The opposite is true because during one of the meetings a fellow Automation Director employed by another bank told me that his bank was taken over by another bank and that he could no longer use the Standard Banking System.

I asked him what they intended to do with the hardware they were using and he answered that they were going to put the hardware up for sale as well. The bank used two excellent UNIX operated hardware systems, which would enable the Standard Banking System to run extremely smoothly. I was interested and asked him whether my company could acquire the hardware. He thought it was a good idea.

Back at the office I informed the Director-general and the Comptroller. They also thought it was a profitable idea and gave me permission to start the negotiations.

Together with the Head of the Calculus Centre we paid the bank a visit and managed to cut a deal. I was very pleased that we were now able to do business with a major hardware supplier and in doing so diminishing the risks for our company since we no longer had to depend on the small hardware supplier.

Our regular hardware supplier was not at all pleased with our decision. I offered them to undercut the price the bank asked for the acquisition of their hardware but they could not. They were also convinced that we could make a profitable deal.

I learned that when you go on a business trip many colleagues envy you and consider it a paid-for holiday. With the deal I had been able to make I proved that my trips were not just fun and games and most people were now aware of the added value of these meetings.

It's all sales

Both in business and private situations you will come across people who have a certain image of you. Sometimes you are sensitive to that and it is always the case that you enjoy it when people think well of you. You cannot, however, control the way people think about you. It is not something you should worry about. There will always be people saying unkind things about you or have an urge to tell lies about you and for no apparent reason. You cannot control this so let it go.

A deal that cannot be made

My brother in law was seriously ill. He had been examined at the hospital and had been diagnosed with lung cancer. He could survive if he were to have surgery to remove one of his lungs. He really did not have a choice and had been admitted to hospital straight away. The hospital was a two-hour drive for us so we could visit him only once a week, mostly weekends. He was always pleased to see us and in particular his 'kid' sister. It was not an effort for us and he was worth it.

His son, our nephew, did not visit him often and when we asked him about it he had this sad look in his eyes. His wife played the part of a loving wife but I could tell that her attitude annoyed him no end. My brother in law had never been much of a talker but his body language said it all.

On a Friday he was discharged from the hospital and we went to visit him at his home accompanied by my mother in law the following Sunday. Upon our arrival I already spotted the wheelchair ready and waiting in the hall.

His wife lost no time in telling us that she had acquired the wheelchair so she could take him on little outings to the village. While she was talking about her wheelchair plans I glanced at my brother in law and I could tell by the look on his face that he did not particularly like the idea of being pushed through the village in a wheelchair by his wife.

We sat around his bed and the women were engaged in a lively conversation. There he was this strong and tough guy. Not much of him left. I looked around and at some point I felt him looking at me intently. I looked him in the eye and sensed gratitude but also emotion.

He never said anything but on our departure I took my time in saying goodbye and did so with all the warmth and love I had in my heart for him. He took my hand in his one final time and squeezed it tight and gave me this warm and grateful look. I felt this was not just a goodbye but that I was taking my leave of him and I would not see him alive again.

Back in the car my mother in law and my wife were happy with the fact that they had seen him. They had high hopes concerning his chances of survival with only one lung and that he would have many years left to him. My gut feeling told me the exact opposite but I kept my mouth shut. This was not the time or place to tell my wife and mother in law how I had perceived my brother in law's state of mind. It would probably lead to my wife drinking and smoking even more than she already did.

Two days later we were informed that he had passed away. He had no desire to live on as an invalid, confined to a wheelchair with a wife and son he could no longer emotionally relate to. My wife was very upset when she heard the news. She did not say a word though and refused to talk to me about it. It was as if she would not accept it and was in denial.

My sister in law had organised my brother in law's final farewell. He was to be cremated and her sisters would sing in church. I could not help but think that all this was not what my brother in law wanted. He had wanted to be buried without much church ceremony. From the proceedings it became clear to me how lonely he must have been. There was nothing I could do about it because my mother in law had agreed with my sister in law's arrangements. Who was I when it came to family matters?

The death of my brother in law was a tragedy for my wife. She drank more and because of the alcohol screamed and raged at me. Fortunately her outbursts took place at night so my daughter did not notice. I had given up drinking alcohol altogether and hoped that in doing so I would set an example to my wife. It did not work out that way for she still blamed me for everything that had gone wrong in her life. Most of the time I could accept her outbursts because I understood why she was she was flying of the handle. It was not always easy to stay quiet though.

One particular night she was so angry with me that she came up to me, spat me in the face and hit me. She was about to attack me further but in doing so made me so angry that I hit her back. This shocked her and beside herself with rage she went to bed.

The whole turn of events upset me. This was the second time I had hit her. I hated myself for not being able to control myself. I always treated women with respect. How could I? The whole matter left me devastated and I realised that my wife had to hate me and had no love left for me.

I learned that when you no longer want to live because you think there is nobody left who cares about you, you can pull out. The mind is stronger than the weakened body. Hitting my wife hurt me tremendously.

This story goes to prove that you can control your own feelings and physical condition. As a salesperson you are expected to have a positive frame of mind. Sometimes there are reasons to feel miserable, for instance if something in your private life is amiss. Will you let your negative feelings get the better of you? There is no point in trying to push your negative feelings aside because no matter which way you turn it will always have an effect on you. You can, however, try to work with the feelings you are experiencing. Ask yourself the question "do the feelings I currently have help me to achieve my goals?" If the answer is a heartfelt "no" you will notice that the negative feelings will disappear. A positive frame of mind will help you to get results.

The story continues……

At this stage Dick is still employed by the mid size financial institution and manages to introduce many new plans and products and is rewarded and valued for his efforts. He loves his job, is dedicated to the company and works tirelessly towards a solution for the problems resulting from the introduction of the single currency (Euro). He continues his own learning process while at the same time coaching and motivating others. But as the time of the introduction draws nearer the stakes get higher. Dick is convinced that introducing new banking products will secure the future of the company but unfortunately people from both inside and outside the company frustrate his plans. When the dice are finally cast he needs to determine where his loyalties lie: with his colleagues or the advancement of his own career.

Added to the problems at work is the loneliness he experiences at home. The tension and cold atmosphere drain him of all energy. He avoids being home unless his daughter is there because she is the light of his life. He feels that therapy might help his wife coming to terms with her past but since she refuses he cannot do anything but protect his daughter. His wife does not try to find solutions but finds unacceptable ways of not having to face up to her problems. Therefore also on a personal level Dick has to face the facts. What is best for both of them? Staying together or going their separate ways. Given the promises he made not an easy decision. At the same time he has to take the well being of his daughter into consideration and in spite of the rough patches he goes through he is able to watch her grow into adulthood and be there for her as a father, a councillor and a friend.

Both on a professional as well as a personal level 'his God' helps him to consider all options and take well founded decisions. All the same Dick feels he needs to change in order to find happiness within himself. He starts to attend haptonomy sessions and although at first these sessions add to his confusion in the end he benefits from them. He also attends a mediation course and discovers that the concept of mediation appeals to him. On completion of the course he decides to offer his services as a mediator together with a small group fellow mediators.

No matter how many transitions Dick has to go through in life he always remains eager to help others either financially or by giving advice. Certainly when it comes to financial help he takes risks but he feels it is the right thing to do.

Throughout his life Dick has had to sell his ideas, position, ambitions, decisions and feelings to others yet by the end of the book he is ready to sell a new start to himself.

Index

Business

Market

Family matters